Like The Thistle Seed

Like The Thistle Seed

The Scots Abroad

Malcolm Archibald

Acknowledgements

I would like to thank the following people for their help and information. Professor Charles McKean, University of Dundee; Professor Murdo Macdonald, University of Dundee, Mrs D. Joyner, Groenvlei, Natal, South Africa, Mrs Johanna Lerm, Durban, South Africa, Mrs Gail Smith, Morehill, Natal, May Kidd, Hole Farm, Kirkbuddo, Scotland; Mrs Brookes, Kloof, South Africa, Mrs Mauris Spence, Pinetown, Natal. I would also like to thank my wife for assisting my research and enduring the many hours when I was labouring over an often-reluctant computer.

Like his national emblem, the thistle, the Scotsman was dry, prickly, impervious to weather, hard to destroy, and scattered like the thistle seed.
Sanche De Gramont

Introduction

Scotland is a small country on the western fringe of Europe. She has a seventy-mile land frontier with England while the rest of her thrusts into the sea, as if attempting to escape the confines of her own geography. Two thirds of her land is rock, bog or rough grazing. The remainder grows some of the finest crops on earth. At one time, with one-eighth the population of her southern neighbour, she had twice as many universities and one of the most literate populations in the world, yet her people were frequently regarded as barbarous. She had a fearsome military reputation yet as an independent nation had no standing army and no history of national aggression. The national dress and international perception of Scotland is based on a caricature of the Gaelic culture that was once banned and frequently feared by the Lowland population. Scotland, then, is a land of contrasts.

Is it any wonder that such a nation should produce so many wanderers, men and women who helped create the new countries of the world, as their ancestors had blossomed in Europe? And is it any wonder that these same people should compose some of the most heart-wrenching laments for the land they left behind, even as they encouraged others to board the emigrant ships? Is it any wonder that this complicated nation should also produce a fine a collection of odd balls and eccentrics as any on Earth?

As the prickly, ubiquitous thistle is the symbol of Scotland, then the people may be likened to the thistle seed, which spreads so well over the land. Typical of the thistle seed were the hundreds of thousands of un-named emigrants who sailed from Scotland to become the backbone of the new countries. Gold diggers and bankers, farmers and factory workers, lawmakers and lawbreakers, the Scots slid from their homeland like snow off a dyke. While most settled into ordinary, respectable jobs, others rose high in their chosen profession, helped guide their adopted country to its destiny or slotted into a nether world of non-conformity.

There is no part of the world where Scots have not made some impact. Scots have wandered in the most inaccessible parts of Asia, struck out for North and South Pole, crossed Australia and Canada and loomed large in the field of African exploration. For much of the 19th century, Western Canada was a Scottish enclave, South Australia was seen as the most Scottish part of Australia, Scots settled Otago in New Zealand, and numerous remote islands were strongly Scottish. There were innumerable Scottish colonial governors and governor-generals, while Scottish engineers built bridges, harbours and roads that connected the world. It was a Scotsman that helped draft the United States Declaration of Independence and Scots who helped tame the West, when they were not making it even wilder.·

Tens of thousands of Scots took to the sea with thousands becoming shipmasters and many founding shipping lines whose vessels crossed the globe. Fighting Scots admirals founded navies in South America, reformed the Russian fleet and gave the United States a fine nautical tradition. Highly educated, the Scots exported their thirst for knowledge, taught in Europe, and founded innumerable universities while Scottish missionaries spread the Word across half the world. Militarily, the Scots had a reputation for courage and loyalty that was rarely matched and never exceeded. As well as fighting for Scotland and Britain, Scottish soldiers participated in some of Europe's bloodiest wars, often on both sides, and helped forge the independence of the United States and many South American nations. Sometimes they were defeated but they were never disgraced.

Malcolm Archibald

Other Scots gave different gifts to their new land. It was a Scot who introduced camels to Australia, a Scot who brought Aberdeen Angus cattle to America. There were Scots born American Chess Champions and a Scots born Canadian Speed Skating champion. A Scotsman created the English John Bull, and Scots cast the first dollar sign and designed the flag of Hawaii. Other Scots were more notorious than famous. The treasure of Captain Kidd has never been located, while James McPherson the bushranger hunted the back roads of New South Wales and Alexander McClung was one of the most dreadful of the killing gentlemen of the United States.

Scattered like thistle seed they may have been, but the Scots seemed seldom to forget their roots. Caledonian Societies, St Andrews Day Parades and Burns Clubs flourish across the globe. There is even a Tartan Day in New York. The descendants of Scots retain and enhance their Scottish culture, generation by generation. Often the Scots abroad seem more Scottish than those at home do, and Old Scotland could learn much from their passion and knowledge of a country that their ancestors were often only too anxious to leave.

This book will list some of the Scots who became known in their new country. There were too many prominent Scots for any book to include them all. As the selection in here is a personal choice, many Scots will disagree with those personalities included, while offering excellent reasons for including others. Such disagreement is expected: diversity of thought was always a Scottish characteristic.

However, this book is intended to give a fair cross section of those Scottish professionals and workers who forged new nations, while not forgetting the eccentrics and outlaws that also claimed Scotland as their birthplace. It does not attempt to list the thousands of prominent people who can claim Scottish blood in a distant ancestor. To do so would include United States Presidents such as Ronald Regan, whose ancestors included the Scottish Revolutionary David Downie who was transported for sedition. Other United States presidents with Scottish ancestors include Nixon, McKinley, Roosevelt and Grant, while U.S. soldiers, seamen, academics and businessmen and women would total many thousand, and that is only in one country. The Scottish contribution is immense and undervalued.

The names in this book are listed alphabetically, and where the names and initials are the same, chronologically.

Adams, Captain Alexander (1780 – 1870)

Admiral of Hawaii

Born in Angus, Alexander Adams went to sea on a Geordie brig at the age of 12 and served in the Royal Navy from 1807 until 1810. He was working on the Boston vessel *Albatross* when he arrived in Oahu, Hawaii in 1811, at a time when the islands were independent of any other power. Settling in Hawaii, he married three times and fathered fifteen children. King Kamehameha seemed to take a liking to the wandering Scot and presented him with land.

The King put Adams in command of the Hawaiian fleet of nine square- rigged and fifteen small vessels, although he apparently needed only the 260-ton brig *Kaahumanu* to remove an unwanted Russian presence from Kauai in 1816. Adams has also been credited with the design of the Hawaiian flag. Employed as the first ever Honolulu harbour pilot from 1817 to 1844, Adams saw many changes in the islands; he was present when the first American missionaries arrived in 1820 and persuaded the king to allow them to remain. He is also rumoured to have brought the mango to Hawaii from India and was thought of as a very colourful man.

Alexander, Sir William (c1567 – 1640)

Colonist, poet, courtier

Born in Menstrie Castle near Stirling, Alexander was educated at Glasgow and Leiden in the Netherlands. He used this education to become tutor to the Earl of Argyll on his travels through Europe. His writing career began in 1604 when he composed a hundred sonnets on love. Three years later he wrote *Monarchick Tragedies*, which criticised power and pride and in 1614 he completed his long, complicated poem *Doomsday*.

In 1613 William Stirling became an usher of the court of Prince Charles, later King Charles I. Knighted in 1614, that same year Alexander was also appointed Master of Requests. In 1621 he used his influence with the king to obtain an area of land in North America that he named Nova Scotia. This grant was far more extensive than present day province of the same name, extending from New Brunswick to Cape Breton Island. It was the intention of King Charles to populate these lands with Scottish 'younger brothers and mean gentlemen, who otherwise must be troublesome.'

Unfortunately there were few takers when Alexander attempted to find Scottish colonists, for at that time most footloose Scots preferred to head for Ulster or northern Europe. As inducement and to finance his idea, Stirling created the Order of Knight Baronets of Nova Scotia in 1624, with the knights accepting their lands at the Esplanade of Edinburgh Castle. Each new landowner had to part with one thousand merks. To swell the trickle of colonists, in 1625 Stirling wrote *An Encouragement to Colonies*, but still obtained little results.

There were a few Scottish settlers in Nova Scotia by 1629 and a small settlement at Charlesfort until 1632, when King Charles handed the land to the French.

Alexander, however, had other strings to his idealistic bow. As the sole printer to King James VI, he printed the Psalms; he became Secretary of State for Scotland, Earl of Dovan and Earl of Stirling, but still managed to die in poverty. His legacy remains in the name Nova Scotia in Eastern Canada.

Allan, Sir Hugh (1810 – 1872)
Canadian Shipowner and railwayman

Born in Saltcoats in Ayrshire, Allan was the son of a ship owner. He immigrated to Canada in 1826, where he worked with the shipbuilding firm of John Millar and Company, later becoming a partner. In 1839, together with a Mr Edmonstone, he formed a shipping company that later became the Allan Line. By the end of 1852 the government had awarded the company the contract for a line of screw steamers on the St Lawrence, which also became known as the Montreal Ocean Steamship Company.

The line grew from four to eight vessels, with a weekly service. During the Crimean War of 1864 to 1856 and the Ashanti War of 1874, the British government leased Allan Line vessels as troop transports.

As well as shipping, Allan was heavily involved in railways, being one of the original proponents of the Canadian Pacific Railways. He was also involved in the Montreal financial sector. He funded the election campaign of **John Macdonald**, the Scot who became premier of Canada. Possibly Allan was returning a favour, for Macdonald had granted him the charter to build the Canadian Pacific Railway. Unfortunately when this arrangement leaked out, Macdonald's government fell.

In 1844 Allan married Matilda and their union produced nine daughters and four sons. Despite his transport links, it is the Allan Memorial Institute of Psychiatry in McGill University that is perhaps Allan's best memorial today.

Anderson, John (1820 – 1897)
New Zealand engineer, politician and shipping magnate

Scots born, Anderson served an apprenticeship as a blacksmith before working in both Edinburgh and Liverpool. Married with one son, he immigrated to Christchurch in New Zealand in 1850. Eventually, now with two growing sons, Anderson established his own foundry. He sent his sons to Scotland to be trained as engineers and set to work to supply the burgeoning colonial economy with iron goods. Anderson made everything from boilers to ploughs, bridges to dredgers and even railways. He also built viaducts and bridges so that his firm became one of New Zealand's major engineering works.

It was not surprising that Anderson should become the first mayor of Christchurch in 1868, a position that only enhanced his popularity. Not content to remain in a single track, Anderson also founded the New Zealand Shipping Line and was one of the first directors of the Christchurch Press.

Anderson, John Henry (1814 – 1874)
Professional magician who burned down Covent Garden Theatre

Born in Craigmyle, John Anderson made his mark in London. Known as 'Professor Anderson, Wizard of the North', he was a professional magician who pioneered advertising to spread his fame. Anderson was perhaps the first magician to send out hand bills and display his name on posters, but he is probably best remembered for his exploits in clearing the Covent Garden Theatre of a drunken crowd in 1856. When he lowered the gaslights he miscalculated his distances, set fire to the ceiling and burned the theatre to the ground. Just like that.

Arbuthnot, John (1667 – 1735)
Creator of John Bull
Not many people in England would realise that their very own John Bull was actually created by a Scot. Born in Kincardineshire, John Arbuthnot was a mathematician, a political satirist and physician to Queen Anne. Most of the caricatures he created have faded with time, but when his collection *The History of John Bull* was published in 1727, England had a new image. Set against the unreliable foreign characters such as Lewis Baboon of France and the Dutch Nicholas Frog, John Bull is 'an honest plain-dealing fellow, choleric, bold, and of a very unconstant temper', which is how the English perhaps preferred to view themselves.

Baikie, William Balfour (1824 – 1864)
African explorer, linguist and settler
Born in Kirkwall, Orkney, Baikie studied medicine at Edinburgh University. In 1848 he became a surgeon with the Royal Navy, and six years later was included in an expedition up the River Niger. Command of the expedition was given to John Beecroft, British consul in the Bight of Benin. Beecroft's orders were to sail *Pleiad,* a 260-ton schooner rigged steamer, up the Niger, open trade negotiations and locate the missing German explorer Heinrich Barth. When Beecroft died, Baikie took command, pushing the boat 250 miles further up the river than any previous expedition had reached. Most of Baikie's success was due to his twice-daily issue of quinine to the explorers. Where most exploration trips lost heavily through malaria, Baikie did not lose a single European. What was nearly as unusual, the expedition also made a profit. Baikie, however, did not find Barth.

Baikie was back on the Niger in 1857. He built roads, gathered the first written vocabulary of native words and translated sections of the Bible into Hausa, the local language. As if that was not enough, Baikie also founded a settlement at the confluence of the Benue, becoming the first Briton to live for an extended period in the interior of West Africa. Rather than bringing Britain to Africa, Baikie adopted local dress and customs, wearing a long cotton shirt, living in a mud hut and eating fish and palm oil. He also took a local wife and produced a clutch of half-Scottish children.

Baikie tried to end the slave trade and believed the Britain should send gunboats up the Niger to protect the natives. He set up a market to buy slaves, whom he then freed, becoming so much part of Africa that he was known as King of Lokoja. Recalled home by the government, Baikie died of dysentery on the journey. Not as famous as many other explorers, and without the drama of mind-opening discoveries, he proved that Europeans could live in Africa and proved that malaria could be prevented.

Balfour, Arthur James (1848 – 1930)
Supporter of a Jewish national state
From East Lothian, Balfour was a professional politician. Secretary for Scotland as well as chief secretary for Ireland, he is remembered as 'Bloody Balfour' for the vigour with which he put down Irish rebellion. It is doubly ironic therefore, that this man was instrumental in creating an independent homeland for the scattered Jewish people. His famous Balfour Declaration of November 1917 was a major factor in the creation of the Jewish State, which came into being in May 1948.

Balfour, James (1831 –1869)
Marine engineer and lighthouse builder
Born in Edinburgh, Balfour was one of the famous Stevenson family of marine engineers. After a career as a lighthouse builder in the United Kingdom, in 1863 he was given a three-year contract to the Otago Provincial Government in New Zealand. Four years later Balfour was appointed as the colony's Marine Engineer. His lighthouses

made navigation safer around Farewell Spit and Cape Campbell, while he also surveyed the coastline of Taranki and designed the harbour at Timaru.

Balfour's career was cut short when he fell into the sea and drowned while landing at Oamaru. While his lighthouses are his best memorials, there is also a town, Balfour, on the Waimea Plains, named in his honour.

Balfour, Robert (1550 – 1625)
Mathematician

At a time when great religious struggles were taking place in Scotland, Robert Balfour was quietly unravelling complex mathematical theories on the continent. He was educated at St Andrews and then travelled to Europe, where he spent the remainder of his life. Balfour completed his education in Paris and was appointed principal of Guienne College in Bordeaux. At that time Guienne was famous for its arts and theology. Balfour was hot tempered and aggressive, both in his personal life and in his approach to his work. However, he was an excellent scholar. As well as a mathematician with a European reputation, Balfour translated Aristotle's writings from Greek into Latin. Contemporaries knew him as the 'Phoenix of his Age, a scholar worthy to be compared with the ancients.'

Barr Smith, Robert (1824 –1915)
Australian pastoralist

Born in Renfrewshire, Barr Smith completed his education at Glasgow University. Immigrating to South Australia in 1854, he accepted employment with the Scottish businessman Thomas Elder, where he rose to become a partner in the firm of Elder, Smith and Company. Around this time, Barr Smith married Elder's sister, Joanna. As their land holdings increased, the company of Elder, Smith became one of the largest wool brokers in the world and helped raise Australia's profile as a wool producing country.

Barr Smith was also involved in finance, mining and shipping. He was one of the founders of the Bank of Adelaide and established the Barr Smith Library in Adelaide University, while donating large amounts of money to the church.

Begbie, Sir Matthew Bailie (1819 –1894)
Frontier judge

Born in Edinburgh, Begbie graduated from Cambridge University in 1841, and practiced law in England for fourteen years. It was in 1858 that Begbie was sent over to British Columbia to impose law and order on a Crown Colony bustling with a gold rush. As a judge, Begbie had the final say in ensuring that this outpost of Empire did not descend to the gun law that controlled parts of the American West. In 1866, when British Columbia united with Vancouver Island, Begbie was advanced to Chief Justice of the mainland portion; four years later he became responsible as Chief Justice for all British Columbia. He was knighted in 1875.

Bell, Alexander Graham (1847 – 1922)
Inventor

Born in Edinburgh and educated in Edinburgh and London, Bell's first job was as an assistant elocution teacher. With his father and grandfather interested in eugenics, it was expected that he follow the same line of work. Immigrating to Canada in 1870, he moved to the United States the following year. Two years later he was Professor of Vocal Physiology at Boston, working with deaf-mutes and using his father's 'visible speech' system. This work led him to experiment with devices for transporting sounds and on the 5th June 1875 he sent the first telephone transmission to his assistant.

One year later he patented the telephone, following this success by forming the Bell Telephone Company in 1877. Three years later he founded the Volta Laboratory, where he invented the photophone and the gramophone. Later in life he became interested in aeronautics and invented the tetrahedral kite. On a more human level, Bell is remembered for his work with Helen Keller, who he taught to hear. He died and was buried in Nova Scotia.

Bell, John of Antermony (1691 – 1780)
Traveller and physician who rediscovered the source of rhubarb

Born in Antermony near Kirkintilloch in Stirlingshire, Bell graduated in medicine at Aberdeen. In 1714 he travelled to the newly founded St Petersburg as assistant to Dr Areskine, the Tsar's physician. After being appointed the physician to Valensky, the Russian ambassador to Persia between 1715 and 1718, he embarked on an even longer journey in 1719 when he travelled from Russia to the court of Kang Hi, Emperor of China. Bell travelled by sleigh, camel and horseback from Siberia into China. Bell recorded his experiences in *Travels from St Petersburg in Russia to Diverse Parts of Asia*, which was published in 1763. As there had never been a European woman inside China, the females of his company were sent back to Russia at the Chinese border.

Bell marvelled at the Great Wall, described chopsticks as 'a couple of ivory pins' and wrote about elephants, greenhouses, porcelain factories and the horrors of foot binding. Bell was full of praise for Chinese civilisation and mentioned their friendliness to strangers and 'decent treatment of women.' On this trip he became possibly the first Scotsman to visit Peking.

Probably more important, Bell dug up some rhubarb plants and carried them carefully to St Petersburg. At that time rhubarb was seen as a vital medicine to cure constipation but although people knew that it came from the East, nobody seemed sure of its exact source.

After further travels in Persia and a spell as a merchant in Constantinople, Bell returned to Scotland to write about his adventures. In 1746 he married Marie Peters, a Russian woman, whom he seems to have taken back to his estate as Antermony.

Bennett, James Gordon (1795 –1872)
American journalist

Born in Keith, Moray, James Bennett emigrated to the United States via Nova Scotia. Settling in New York City, he began a career as a newspaperman, working his way up until in 1826 he was appointed Associate Editor of the *New York Enquirer and Courier*, where he fought for the right of the press to report trials without seeking permission from the courts.

In 1835 he founded the *New York Herald*, one of the most innovative newspapers of its time. Published daily, which was unknown, and selling for a cent a copy, which was cheap, the *Herald*'s aim was to be self-supporting, rather than rely on a political party or business for funding. Naturally, it aimed for a large circulation and also led the way in steam technology. Bennett's editorials were uncompromising, and he was abused, horsewhipped and boycotted but still succeeded in producing one of the most popular newspapers of the era. Bennett is also remembered as the father of the James Gordon Bennett who sent Stanley to search for Livingstone. Incidentally the expression 'Gordon Bennett!' refers to the son, not the father.

Bennie, John (1796 – 1869)
Missionary, the 'father of Xhosa Literature'
Bennie was born in Glasgow in October 1796. In 1816 he joined the Glasgow Missionary Society and three years later was sent to the Cape Colony. Bennie was posted to the mission station at Chumie, smack in the middle of the Neutral Zone near the Great Fish River. On one side were the expanding white colonists, on the others the Xhosa, vanguard of the Bantu who were pressing south.

Learning Dutch, then Xhosa, Bennie started a school for the local peoples. Bennie was to produce an English-Xhosa dictionary and was the first European to put Xhosa into writing. Marrying a Dutch woman, Margaretha Magdalena Mare, he was ordained in 1831. By that time he was working on the Ncera River but left the station during the Frontier Wars of 1834-35, when the Xhosa burned down the buildings. In 1843 he visited the newly established Trekker's Republic of Potchefstroom-Winburg, the first minister to do so. His subsequent book contains the first mention of African-built stone structures in the area.

Bennie has been termed "the father of Xhosa literature" Teacher, linguist and missionary, Bennie represents all that is best in the Scottish missionary tradition.

Berry, Alexander (1781 –1873)
Australian merchant and settler
The son of a tenant farmer, Fife born Berry studied medicine at St Andrews and Edinburgh and became a medical officer in the East India Company. He worked with the Company until 1808, and then immigrated to Australia. By 1819 Berry was settled in Sydney and working as a trader to raise money to buy Shoalfield, an estate with nearly 400 convict and ex-convict tenants. He became wealthy from growing tobacco, maize, barley, potatoes and wheat.

By becoming an Australian landowner, Berry had succeeded in rising through the class barrier, which was a thing virtually impossible in Scotland at that time. However, there was a shadow on his success. Berry started as a kindly landlord but became harsh later. Known as the Laird of Shoalhaven, he was over 100 when he died, owning 40,000 acres. As well as his commercial concerns, Berry studied the geology and anthropology of the colony and served in the Legislative Council from 1828 until 1851.

Binny, Archibald (c1762 – 1838)
First man to cast the American dollar
Born in Edinburgh, Archibald Binny immigrated to Pennsylvania in 1795, where he met townsman **James Ronaldson**. The following year they started the firm of Binny and Ronaldson, America's first type foundry. The firm published America's first specimen books in 1806 and reputedly cast the first ever dollar sign.

Bishop, Isabella (1832 –1904)
Traveller, writer
With an Edinburgh background, Isabella Bishop, born Bird, was the daughter of a minister and became one of the greatest women travellers of her time. Of stocky build, Bishop suffered from a painful spinal

condition that necessitated her spending much of her time lying with a scented handkerchief to her forehead. However, the first hint of adventure seemed to dissipate her condition and Bishop became an indefatigable traveller.

When she was 22 a doctor recommended she take a long sea voyage for the sake of her health. Bishop sailed to North America. That was the first long trip of a lifetime spent travelling, often in arduous conditions and in some of the least known regions of the world. In between short stays in Edinburgh, Bishop travelled to the United States and Canada, Australia and Japan, India, Tibet and Persia, Korea, Hawaii and Armenia. It is unlikely that half a dozen of her contemporaries had visited all these places. Of her writings, *Lady's Life in the Rocky Mountains*, written in 1879, is perhaps the best.

In the early 1880s she married the Reverend John Bishop, but when he died in 1886 she immediately resumed her travels, taking to horse to tackle the Sahara Atlas Mountains. Six years later the Royal Geographical Society made her their first female Fellow. Bishop continued to travel all her life and when she died in Edinburgh at the age of 70, she was set for another major expedition to China. It is only a pity that she is not better known.

Black, Niel (1804 – 1880)
Australian pioneer pastoralist and politician

Son of a tenant farmer from Cowal, Black was fluent in Gaelic and English. He became a proficient farmer and as a representative of the company of Niel Black and Co, he sailed to South Australia in search of land. After visiting various localities he decided that the 'Scotch settlement' of Port Phillip district was most suitable. Obtaining a 44,000-acre run, he named it Glenmoriston and set about creating a profitable enterprise. As the years passed, Black bought up a neighbouring run, and then extended his holdings in the Western District. In 1857, on a trip to Scotland, he married the much younger Grace Greenshields. The marriage produced three sons.

During the 1860s Black obtained a freehold title for most of his land. By that time he was one of the finest stockbreeders in Australia. He bred pedigree Cotswold and Merino sheep, while his shorthorn stud at Mount Noorat was thought to be the best south of the equator. In 1859 Black became a member for Western Province in the Victorian Legislative Council, a position he held for the remainder of his life.

So famous did Black become that in 1867 Prince Albert visited the lavishly decorated Glenmoriston. Unfortunately, in 1869 Black lost Glenmoriston to another partner. Instead he obtained a run in the Southern District, which he believed to be inferior. A hard working, Presbyterian, Black was capable of intense generosity and gave quietly to what he believed were deserving causes. In his prime, Black was one of the best and best-known farmers in Australia.

Black, Samuel (c1785 – 1841)
Fur trader, warrior, and kidnapper
Born illegitimately in Aberdeen, Black lacked formal education but taught himself Latin, Greek and geology. In 1802 he immigrated to Canada, becoming a clerk in the XY Fur Company. By 1804 he was with the North West Company, and became involved in the struggle against the Hudson Bay Company around Red River. It was Black who waged a virtual guerrilla war against the HBC by staging false Indian attacks, stampeding their horses, setting the night-time forest ablaze and robbing their trappers of sleep. He also staged the kidnap of a leading HBC factor, an exploit, which earned him, the appreciation of his colleagues and a finger ring inscribed 'to the most worthy of the worthy Northwesters.'

When the two companies merged in 1821, Black was specifically excluded from a position with the HBC, until Governor Simpson, knowing the strength of the Black legend, insisted on his recruitment. Black became attached to a mixed race woman named Angelique Cameron, who helped nurse the plant collector **David Douglas** when he was sick and who gave Black four children.

In 1824 Black spent much time in exploring the Finlay River, and in 1837 became chief factor, but was murdered four years later.

Blackwell, Alexander (c1706 – c1747)
Adventurer
Born in Aberdeen, Blackwell was reputedly a son of the principal of Marischal College. After his education, Blackwell moved to London but his attempt to become a printer failed when his English rivals combined against him. Thrown into a debtor's prison for bankruptcy in 1734, Blackwell was saved by his wife. She drew and engraved an amazingly detailed *Herbal*, to which Blackwell added the description. By clearing his debts, the sales of this publication bought Blackwell out of prison.

By 1742 Blackwell was in Sweden, where he revealed medical knowledge by curing the sick king. Appointed the Royal Physical, Blackwell also managed a model farm, at a time when agriculture was becoming something of a royal passion throughout Europe. Unfortunately, Blackwell seemed to have made enemies as easily as friends for in 1747 he was arrested on a false charge of treason and executed. It is said that when the headsman came with his axe, Blackwell apologised for laying his head on the wrong side of the block. He excused himself by saying that it was the first time that he had been beheaded.

Bogle, George (1746 – 1781)
Asian diplomat and traveller
Born near Bothwell in Lanarkshire, Bogle graduated from Edinburgh University and joined the East India Company. In 1774 Warren Hastings sent him as envoy to the Tashi Lama of Tibet, who had written to Hastings on behalf of Bhutan, a neighbouring Himalayan kingdom that had clashed with the Company.

The first known Briton to cross the upper range of the Tsanpu, Bogle was a successful diplomat. He also became friendly with the Lama, although he spent only six months in his country. 'Farewell, ye honest and simple people,' he wrote as he left Tibet, 'may ye continue to live in peace and contentment.' However, despite his personal feelings, his detailed account of the trade possibilities between India and Tibet was extremely professional. On his return to India, Bogle and the Lama continued to correspond.

Bogle was described as a 'gentleman of distinguished ability and remarkable equanimity of temper.' He died in Calcutta in 1781.

Bridges, Sir William Throsby (1861 – 1915)
Australian soldier

Born in Greenock, William Bridges was educated at Ryde, London and Ontario. In 1879 he joined his family in New South Wales, where he worked with the Department of Roads and Bridges. In 1886 he joined the New South Wales Permanent Artillery, and fought in the Boer War, where he caught typhoid. His progress in the military ranks saw him as Chief of the General Staff. In May 1914 he became Inspector General and in August that year was ordered to create an Australian Imperial Force of 20,000 men for the First World War. General Bridges led the Australian force to Egypt and Gallipoli. Regarded as cold, he was respected for his courage and was touring the front lines when a sniper shot him. The king knighted him on 17 May, the day before he died.

Brisbane, Sir Thomas Macdougall (1773 – 1860)
Soldier, Governor of New South Wales and astronomer

Born at Brisbane House, Largs in Ayrshire, Brisbane entered the army at 16 years old. He saw active service in Flanders, the Caribbean, North America and Spain, gradually rising in rank until he became a major general in 1813.

In 1821 Brisbane was appointed Governor of New South Wales with orders to enforce discipline after the relaxed regime of Lachlan Macquarie. He started off by reopening the penal colony of Norfolk Island, Britain's own Devil's Island, and then granted freedom to the press. Firm with convicts who were still serving their allotted time, he allowed civil liberties to Emancipists, men and women who had survived their sentence. Despite the objections of Protestant landlords who were afraid of those Emancipists who were Catholic, Brisbane also granted religious tolerance.

Brisbane introduced vines, tobacco plants and sugar cane to the colony, while also helping horse breeding. However, he took vigorous action against the bushrangers, mainly ex or escaped convicts, who preyed on settlements and travellers. In 1825 Brisbane founded the mounted police, sometimes known as dragoons, or 'goons' to track bushrangers down. He gave orders, largely ignored, that the native peoples were not to be molested and tried to enforce prohibition on the rum-thirsty settlers of Newcastle and the Hunter River.

A keen astronomer, in 1822 he set up and paid for an Observatory near Government House in Parramatta. Naming it the 'Greenwich of the Southern Hemisphere' he catalogued 7385 stars. The Royal Society awarded him the Copley medal for his work, terming Brisbane 'the founder of Australian science.' Brisbane was also the founder and first President of the Philosophical Society of New South Wales, and he encouraged exploration. A party of explorers that he sent out discovered the Brisbane River.

Brisbane also believed in free immigration, so that Australia would not only be a penal colony. However, higher authority did not always agree with him, even falsely accusing him of immoral pursuits with female convicts. Perhaps closer to the truth was the charge of neglecting his duties to study astronomy.

Brisbane's best memorial is the town of Brisbane in Queensland, which he started as a remote penal settlement for hardened offenders. To his peers Brisbane was a "mild and pleasant man", while his Christianity was as sincere as his astronomical research.

Brog, Colonel Sir William (d 1636)
Soldier in Dutch service

Brog was the colonel of the first Scottish regiment to participate in Dutch service in their long war for freedom against the Spanish. He recruited his men in a number of ways. The Crown sent some, such as the outlaw Grahams of the western border, but others were volunteers, fighting for the Protestant cause or for money. There were also a few pardoned criminals.

Brog had a long career in the Dutch wars. He was a sergeant major in 1588, being promoted to captain two years later. By 1600 he was a lieutenant colonel, and a full colonel from 1606 until his death. An engraving of him in the British Museum shows a serious looking man with a long, neatly squared beard and what may be a scar across the bridge of his nose.

Broom, Robert (1866 – 1951)
South African Palaeontologist

Born in Paisley, Broom studied medicine at Glasgow University. He worked as a midwife in Australia but despite his fascination for the unique fauna of Australia h immigrated to South Africa in 1897. Between 1903 and 1910 he was Professor of Zoology and Geology at Victoria College, Stellenbosch, but lost his position when he argued in favour of the theory of evolution.

Broom became an expert in the animals of the Karoo district and in 1920 became a fellow of the Royal Society. In 1934 Broom accepted the position of palaeontologist at the Transvaal Museum in Pretoria and argued that *Australopithecus africanus* was one of humanity's direct ancestors. In 1947 he discovered the remains of an *Australopithecus* skeleton which had walked in an erect position. Broom calculated that the skeleton was between one and two million years old.

Broom's publications include *Finding the Missing Link* and *The Coming of Man.* He was sometimes considered an eccentric, wearing a formal suit to hunt fossils but also capable of stripping stark naked on a whim. His energy was terrific and, having just completed his writings on the australopithecines, his dying words were, 'that's finished and so am I.'

Brown, Robert (1773 –1858)
Botanist

Born in Montrose, Brown studied medicine in Edinburgh University but did not graduate. At the age of 22 he was commissioned as

Assistant Surgeon in the Fifeshire Regiment of Fencibles, but disliked the military and resigned as soon as he could.

Always interested in natural history, Brown spent over three years as naturalist on board *Investigator* cruising the coasts and islands of Australia. Of the more that 3000 specimens he collected, around 1800 had never before been catalogued. Brown became the world's leading expert on Australian flora. It took him four years to fully describe his finds, but when his *Prodromus Florae Hollandiae* was published in 1810, it was described as 'the greatest botanical work that has ever appeared. Despite its academic success, Brown's book was a commercial failure, perhaps because he wrote in Latin

Brown, William (1738-1789)
Founder of Quebec's first printing business

Born near Kirkcudbright, Brown was sent to America as an assigned servant, at the age of fifteen. One of the fortunate bonded men, Brown found a good master, a printer in Philadelphia who taught him the trade. In 1760 he moved south to Barbados, where his health marred an attempt to establish a printing business. However, he was more successful when he moved north and in 1763 Brown established Canada's first printing business in Quebec.

Brown, William (1752 –1792)
Surgeon general of the Continental Army

Born in Haddington, East Lothian, Brown studied as a doctor and immigrated to the American colonies. When the Revolution started, Brown joined the Continental Army, rising to become Surgeon General. In this position he wrote the first ever Pharmacopoeia to be published in North America.

Bruce, James, of Kinnaird (1730 – 1794)
'The Abysinnian'

Born in Kinnaird House, Stirlingshire, Bruce studied law at Edinburgh University but decided to enter business with his father-in-law. When his wife died within nine months of their marriage, Bruce changed the direction of his life, travelling to Spain and learned Arabic. With the death of his father, Bruce inherited the family estate, but instead of living as a landed gentleman, worked for the War Office.

Bruce acted as consul general in Algiers between 1763 to 1765, simultaneously examining and recording Roman ruins in North Africa. As his knowledge increased, Bruce decided to discover the source of the Nile.

In 1768, disguised as a doctor named El Hakim Yagoube, Bruce travelled to Abyssinia by way of the Nile, the Red Sea and Massowah. Accepted by the Emperor of Abyssinia, he became Lord of Gish, campaigning against local rebels and soaking up Abyssinian culture and traditions. It took him two years to reach the source of the Abbai, the headstream of the Blue Nile. After following the Blue Nile to its junction with the White Nile, he struggled back to Cairo. It was the French, rather than the British, who were impressed by his achievements when he returned to Europe.

In 1790 Bruce, often known as 'the Abyssinian' published *Travels to Discover the Sources of the Nile*, but critics scoffed at his description of details of Abyssinian life, such as slicing steaks from a living cow. Mainly it was the educated elite who refused to believe in the barbarity of Abyssinian society, preferring the fables of *Prestor John* and the myth of the noble savage. Bruce's accounts were later found to be entirely accurate.

Bruce, Sir Michael, 11th Baronet of Stenhouse and Airth (1895 – 1962)

Soldier and adventurer

In his autobiography *Tramp Royal*, Bruce states "beside our allegiance to God and the King, we young Bruces were taught another loyalty: to Scotland." He followed this plain fact with a life of almost constant adventure. As a boy Bruce was better at horse riding than arithmetic, he flew in one of the first aircraft to be seen in Britain and when he was just seventeen, Baden-Powell endorsed his application for the South African Police. After spending his teenage years quelling brothel riots and hunting murderers and lions through the Rhodesian bush, Bruce volunteered for military service in the First World War.

Bruce experienced a varied war that started with a skirmish with rebel Boers in South Africa and continued with service with the Royal Artillery at Gallipoli, where he was twice wounded. He faced rioting mobs in Egypt before fighting at Delville Wood in France, where he was again wounded and shell shock. After a traumatic time in hospital, Bruce was released, but a train struck him. Back in action, he was blown up by a shell in the Somme, returned to London and helped uncover a German spy ring. His return to the Line saw him participate in one of the last British cavalry charges where, nearly inevitably, he was wounded.

After time spent on an African farm, Bruce worked as a stunt extra in the film industry, joined in a riot against ex-patriot Germans in Rio de Janeiro and worked as a cattle hand in the Pampas. After a hectic time in a salt works, Bruce worked his passage around the Horn on a windjammer, crossed the Andes on foot, fought through a South American revolution and hunted gold in the Amazon. He also survived a stampede of wild South American cattle before marrying Doreen Greenwell in an England that must have seemed very quiet.

Financially ruined by an embezzler, Bruce took up a variety of positions, but when his wife deserted him he returned to work as a film extra. Married again, in 1938 he became involved in smuggling Austrian Jews clear of the Nazis, was captured and tortured before the British Ambassador ensured his release. He skippered a boat to help in the Dunkirk evacuation, lost his second wife to a German bomb, joined the RAF, where he used a case of sherry to help sink a U-boat, trained men for D-Day and took part in the crossing of the Rhine. Wounded once more, Bruce ended the war with few prospects and no money, but was soon recruited as a historical expert for a film company. He married for the third time and at last retired from adventures.

Bruce, Peter Henry (1692 – 1757)
Scottish soldier in Russian Army

Possibly born in Prussia of a professional Scottish soldier, Bruce joined the Prussian army as a young man. After fighting through Marlborough's Blenheim campaign, his kinsman, General James Bruce of the Russian army, invited him to join the Csar's service. In 1710 he joined others of the Bruce clan at Warsaw, in time to take part in the Pruth campaign.

Bruce was then sent on a mission to Constantinople, from where he travelled to Moscow and the house of yet another Bruce relative. In 1716 Bruce trained a platoon of grenadiers who were sent to the King of Prussia as a gift, but by 1719 he was tired of Russian life, but was refused a transfer back to Prussia. Promoted within the artillery service, in 1721 Bruce fell heir to a Scottish estate, but still could not get the Csar's permission to leave the country. Instead he tutored Prince Peter Aleksovich and took part in campaigns in Persia and around the Caspian Sea.

Eventually Bruce left Russia, but after 13 years' service, he had to leave behind all his possessions and wages. At last arriving in Scotland, Bruce joined the British army and in 1745 helped defend Berwick upon Tweed against a perceived Jacobite threat.

Bruce, William Spiers (1867 – 1921)
Oceanographist

Bruce attended Edinburgh University, where he studied medicine and history. In 1892 he launched a new assault on the exploration of the Antarctic, travelling south on the whaling ship *Balaena* during the Dundee Antarctic Expedition.

In 1902 and 1903 he organised, equipped and led a Scottish Antarctic expedition. His ship was *Scotia,* an ex-Norwegian whaler commanded by Captain Thomas Robertson of Newport, Fife, and she carried naturalists, geologists and oceanographers. Bruce spent 1903 probing the Weddell Sea, and in the summer of 1904 discovered Coats Land.

Bruce also made seven trips to investigate the Arctic Ocean, notably when he sailed to Spitsbergen on *Princess Alice,* owned by the Prince of Monaco.

Buchanan, Jack (1890 – 1957)
Actor and film director
Born in Helensburgh in Argyll, Buchanan worked mainly in Hollywood and on Broadway, appearing in silent films as well as in musical comedies. Most noted as a sophisticated actor, he was perhaps one of the best of the early song and dance practitioners. Later in his career, Buchanan also worked as a producer and director.

Buick, David Dunbar (1854 – 1926)
Automobile manufacturer
Born in Arbroath, the son of Alexander Buick and Jane Roger, Buick was only two when his parents immigrated to America. They settled in Detroit, where Buick attended elementary school. Although there is relatively little information about his early life, he is known to have started delivered papers before gaining an apprenticeship at the James Flower and Brothers Machine Shop; the same firm that employed Henry Ford. After a few years he changed to a career in plumbing supplies with the Alexander Manufacturing Company.

Buick was said to be impulsive, quick tempered and neat. He was also intensely interested in engineering, patenting a lawn sprinkler and creating a new method of attaching porcelain on to iron that became standard practice. Altogether Buick's outstanding engineering brain saw him take out thirteen patents. However, he did not neglect his private life for in 1878 he married Catherine Schwink, with whom he had four children

In May 1893 Buick entered a partnership with William Sherwood to form the Buick and Sherwood Plumbing & Supply Company. Although the company was successful, Buick seems to have left the financial running of his business to others while he was happiest with ideas and engineering projects. Working with two others, Buick's L-head design of motor engine proved a commercial failure. In 1900 Buick and Sherwood explored the latest fashion for gas engines. The following year Buick formed the Buick Auto-Vim and Power Company in Detroit, which was soon in debt. However, in 1903 the first ever Buick automobile appeared. His offer to sell the machine, plus its patterns for $1800 was rejected. Instead he sold the automobile for $225.

An expert at mechanics, Buick was less clever in business. After joining the Briscoe Brothers Company, he lost control of the Buick part of the company. In 1903 Flint Wagon Works bought over the Buick name, then General Motors stepped in. By 1904 Buick was working on a 2-cylinder Model B. The following year he was heading the 'experimental room' of General Motors. With his financial affairs in a mess, the company kept Buick on a tight rein. He resigned in 1908, but soon squandered his $100,000 golden handshake on speculative ventures in oil and property.

For a while Buick taught mechanics for the WMCA, but he died in poverty, ironically unable to afford a motorcar.

Burden, Henry (1791-1871)
Inventor of the self-acting horseshoe maker
Born in Dunblane, Perthshire, Burden grew up on a farm, where he soon demonstrated a talent for innovation. He made a variety of farm machinery and tools, and then embarked on a study of engineering and drawing at Edinburgh University.

In 1819 during the depression that followed the Napoleonic Wars, Burden immigrated to the United States. Finding work at a factory that made agricultural machinery, he invented an improved plough and patented a flax and hemp machine. In 1821 he married Helen McOuat, and the following year took over the failing Troy Iron and Nail Factory at Woodside, New York. By a series of innovations, including diverting a river, building dams to create a reservoir of latent power and making one of the largest water wheels in America, Burden turned the Troy works into the most important ironworks in the continent. On a roll, Burden next patented a machine that made flat rails for railroads, but on a visit across the Atlantic he realised that the British version was better. On his return to the United States he immediately reconfigured his machinery to follow the British design and became the major supplier to the United States railroads.

Perhaps it was Burden's self acting horseshoe maker that was his greatest success. By creating 60 quality horseshoes a minute, in 1862 it earned him the right to supply the entire United States Army. In an episode that could have come from any fictional spy adventure, the Confederate States attempted, unsuccessfully, to steal the pattern. The horseshoe maker made Burden a millionaire.

In one of his few failures, Burden could not build a successful steamboat, but he did draw up a prospectus for an Atlantic Ferry that would have out-greated the Great Eastern, if it had ever been built. However, perhaps the most remarkable thing about this remarkable man was his attitude to his staff. In a period when ironmasters habitually worked their men to an early grave, Burden's 1400 employees seemed to both respect and like their employer. Surely that is the mark of a really successful businessman.

Burnes, Colonel Sir Alexander (1805 – 1841)
Adventurer and diploma

Born in Montrose, Burnes could claim kinship with Robert Burns the poet. He entered the military arm of the Honourable East India Company in 1821, when he was sixteen years old. At that time few officers bothered to learn the languages of the Indian peoples, but Burnes' linguistic skills helped him gain promotion.

In 1832 he made the trip that made him famous. Wearing Afghan dress, he rode through the frontier city of Peshawar and right across Afghanistan. Burnes visited Kabul, crossed the mountains of the Hindu Kush and reached Balkh. From there he visited the fabled but virtually unknown cities of Bokhara, Astrabad and Tehran. Continuing his travels, he rode through Isfahan and Shiraz to Bushire, from where he returned to India. This epic journey made 'Bokhara Burnes' the leading British authority on the central Asian area.

However, Burnes had enjoyed certain advantages, for while his disguise ensured that bandits and badmashes would almost certainly ignore him, he carried gold ducats in his turban to use for bribes, and passports tied around his right arm to introduce himself into the highest company. In one sense he was a 19th century James Bond, in another a Columbus, marking out new lands for exploitation. It was unfortunate that his fame eclipsed that of James Gerard, the Aberdonian who travelled part of the distance with him and did much valuable survey work.

Burnes' report to the Company in London was augmented by his *Travels into Bokhara*, one of the travel books that so delighted the 19th century reading public. Burnes was immediately elected as a member of the Royal Asiatic Society, awarded the Royal Geographical Gold Medal and even gossiped with William IV at Brighton Pavilion. His geographical accounts were usually accurate and always fascinating, but his reports on disturbing Russian movement in the area highlighted the possible Russian threat to British India. In many ways it was Burnes who started the Great Game of spying, sabre rattling and political intrigue that was Britain's Central Asian policy for the remainder of the century.

In character Burnes was vainglorious, arrogant and smug. Physically he was five feet nine, slender, almost fragile but handsome. Turning down the post of ambassador to Persia, in 1836 he was sent back into Afghanistan as a politician resident. He started his expedition by boat, in an attempt to persuade interested observers that he was on a mission to boost trade. He moved slowly up the Indus as a Persian army threatened Afghanistan, and entered Kabul to talk with Dost Mohammed.

In 1839 a British army captured Ghazni and occupied Kabul. Burnes settled into Kabul life in style. At first the Afghans watched in wonder, but when they rose, under Dost Mohammed and Akbar Khan, Burnes was one of the first casualties. An Afghan mob murdered him.

Burns, James (1846 – 1923)
Australian shipowner
Born near Edinburgh, Burns came from a well-established family. Immigrating to Brisbane at the age of 16, he moved into retailing.

When gold was discovered in Queensland he avoided the labour of digging, but made a fortune from selling to the miners.

Moving to Sydney in 1877, Burns went into partnership with fellow Scot Robert Philp, and founded the Queensland Steam Shipping Company. The firm of Burns, Philp was also heavily involved in coastal and deep sea shipping.

Burns, however, was not only a businessman. He also commanded the New South Wales Lancers from 1897, and then transferred to the Australian Light Horse. His political interests saw him as a member of the New South Wales Legislative Council, while he retained enough philanthropic interest to establish the Burnside Homes for Scottish Orphans on his own land near Parramatta in New South Wales.

Burns, Reverend Thomas (1796 – 1871)
Founding father of Otago

In 1843, when the Disruption split the Kirk, Church of Scotland minister for Monkton in Ayrshire Thomas Burns joined the Free Kirk. He agreed with the plan for a Scottish colony in the South Island of New Zealand and was accepted for the position of minister.

Despite early delays, his ship *Philip Laing* arrived at Port Chalmers in April 1848. Burns was a hard worker who helped the young colony of Otago develop, especially the small town that grew into Dunedin, the Gaelic name for Edinburgh. Burns remained the only minister for six years. He travelled around his expanding parish, ignoring the hazards and discomforts of unmade roads and unreliable weather. In many ways it was Burns that kept the community and the idea of Otago together. He was a practical man and a devout Christian, but had a fiery temper.

Not everything worked as Burns had hoped. His dream of a Free Kirk settlement dissipated as soon as the first ships landed a mixed bag of settlers, and the colony had to accept people of different beliefs. The Maori Wars of the 1840s also hampered immigration to New Zealand.

Burns, however, succeeded in guiding Otago to become one of the safest and most attractive of colonies. He was also determined to introduce high quality education. He was elected Lord High Chancellor of the proposed University of Otago, but died before the building was completed. His memory is still kept alive in Dunedin.

Busby, James (1800 – 1871)
Helped draft Treaty of Waitangi

Born in Glasgow, Busby travelled to New South Wales with his father. Returning to Europe, James Busby studied viticulture in France, knowledge that he used later when he attempted to introduce vine growing into both New Zealand and New South Wales.

After a period working for the civil service in New South Wales, Busby shipped back to Britain in 1831, but the government soon appointed him as Resident in New Zealand. At that time New Zealand was not a British colony, and was the haunt of sealers, whalers and other wild men.

In 1833 Busby landed at the Bay of Islands. He bought land at Waitangi and erected a house that was later to become one of the best-known buildings in New Zealand when the treaty with the Maoris was signed there in 1840. As an unarmed man with no legal powers but a host of responsibilities, Busby was in an extremely difficult position, but he tried his hardest to represent the United Kingdom. A Maori attack wounded him in 1834, he was known as *Man o War without guns* and the local British, without any justification, believed him useless.

However, when a Frenchman, Baron Thierry arrived and claimed to be the chief of New Zealand, Busby brought together 35 Maori chiefs and persuaded them to sign a declaration of independence. Although the British government acknowledged the document, they still refused to back Busby with real powers.

Busby still persevered, helping to draft the momentous Treaty of Waitangi that gave the Maoris certain rights in exchange for land. When he was replaced, Busby withdrew to Sydney, but later returned to New Zealand. With the country becoming more established he represented the Bay of Islands in the Auckland Provincial Council between 1859 and 1863, and was instrumental in establishing a newspaper in the rapidly growing town of Auckland.

Byng, Harry (1856 – 1960)
Hairdresser to the King of Hawaii

Born in Glasgow, Byng spent his early life at sea, although he had been trained as a barber. After extensive travelling that included circumnavigating the world a reputed seven times, Byng settled in Washington. While there he recommenced his hairdressing career. His reputation was so high that King Klagas of Honolulu appointed him his royal hairdresser so that in 1887 Byng moved to Hoquaim to open his hairdressing business. He remained there until he died at the age of 104.

Callender, James Thomson (1758 – 1806)
Professional scandalmonger and blackmailer

Born in Scotland in 1758, Callendar was a Scottish nationalist at a time when such views were considered as treason. He also attacked the famous Dr Johnson in print. Indicted for sedition, Callender immigrated to the United States, settling in Philadelphia in 1793. He became a political propagandist and a journalist, but took a dislike to the politician Alexander Hamilton's pro-British views. Callender did not restrict himself to Hamilton's political life, but spread evidence that Hamilton had committed adultery and had misused government funds. Although Hamilton denied the corruption, Hamilton's career was nevertheless ruined.

In 1800 Callender was imprisoned under the new Sedition Act for attacking the government. In his time Callender also libelled George Washington and John Adams, but he is best remembered for his attacks on Thomas Jefferson. Shortly after he was released from prison, Callender requested a position of postmaster but the president, Thomas Jefferson, refused. In retaliation, Callender accused him of a long-standing affair with his wife's half sister, Sally Hemings, something that Jefferson denied, but which modern DNA evidence seems to support. Callender died within a few years, drowned in shallow water, possibly after drinking heavily. Although he seems to have been an unpleasant person, Callender was perhaps the progenitor of modern newspaper journalism, where he exposed the faults of leading personalities of the day.

Cameron, Archibald (1813 – c1890)
Inventor of fire engines

Born on the island of Lismore in Argyll, Cameron immigrated to the United States in 1842. Like many Highlanders, he settled in Charlestown, South Carolina. Cameron was a man of his hands and founded the Phoenix Iron Works, which built steam powered fire engines. At a time when many American buildings were built of wood, Cameron's engines should have proved a boon, but the authorities were too conservative for new technology and stopped the Charleston Fire Engine Company from using the steam powered machines.

In December 1861 a campfire spread to the town buildings and hand pumps, which were all that Charleston had, proved inadequate. Cameron's fire engine saved the day and thereafter became an integral part of the fire fighting service.

Cameron, Charles (1740 – 1812)
Architect of Russian palaces

After studying at Rome, in 1772 Cameron published a detailed book on the architecture of the baths of Trajan and Nero's Domus Aurea. It was this book that caught the attention of Catherine the Great, Csarina of Russia, and she asked Cameron to St Petersburg to work on her palaces. An absolutist ruler, Catherine knew what she wanted and nearly always got her man.

It was Cameron who designed Grand Duke Pauls's Grand Palace of Pavlovsk. Work commenced in 1781 but the building was not complete until 1796. Cameron also designed the interiors of Tsarskoe Selo, about fourteen miles south of St Petersburg. Cameron's interiors became as popular in Russia as Adams' were in Britain. He put great skill into new designs, and with the luxury of vast funds, he could produce splendid work. His style had Roman ornament as a foundation, with discriminating rooms adding surprising contrast.

As well as designing, Cameron taught architecture, until his student Brenna took his place at court. However Cameron took many foreign commissions until royalty again deigned to notice him. Using Robert Adam as a model, Cameron also designed the barracks and naval hospital at Kronstadt in 1805.

Cameron, John (1579 – 1625)
Theologian
Born in Glasgow, Cameron was educated at Glasgow University, but left for the Continent in 1600. After teaching theology at Sedan, Bergerac and Saumur, he returned to Scotland in 1622 as principal of his old university. However his belief in passive Christian obedience was not always popular. Perhaps because of these quiet ideas, he was back in Europe by 1623, again teaching at Saumur. Awarded a professorship in divinity at Montauban, he was once more criticised for his belief in moderate Calvinism.

Eventually one of his enemies tested his passive beliefs by attacking him in the street. Cameron did not resist as he was stabbed to death.

Campbell, Archibald (1787 – c 1830)
Sailmaker to the king of Hawaii
Born in Paisley, in his autobiography, Archibald Campbell's describes himself as a "common sailor." Apprenticed to a weaver when he was ten, in 1806 Campbell signed on an Indiaman to seek adventure. Arriving in Canton, he signed onto an American vessel, which carried him to Japan and Kamchatka, before being wrecked off Alaska. Sailing in a longboat to the Russian settlement at Alexandria, Kodiak Island, Campbell, set off again, to suffer further shipwreck and frostbite that cost him his feet. Having seen enough of the world, Campbell attempted to return home, but instead landed in Hawaii, where he remained over a year. He became sailmaker to King Kamehamela I, building the first loom in the islands. Eventually returning to Scotland

by way of Brazil, Campbell scrabbled for a living, begging and playing the violin in Edinburgh, Leith and the early Clyde steamboats.

Campbell, Colin (c1686 – 1757)
A founder of the Swedish East India Company

Probably born in Edinburgh, where his father was a burgher, in 1720 Colin Campbell also became a burgher of Edinburgh. He lived in London between 1720 and 1723, where he was deeply involved in the financial transactions of the South Sea Bubble. With the collapse of the South Sea Company, Campbell fled to Ostend, where he worked with the Austrian East India Company. At that period Austria owned that part of Europe. Probably realising that the Austrian company was failing, Campbell next moved to Stockholm and by 1731 he lived in Gothenburg, applied for and received Swedish citizenship and from that year onward was a director and a principle player in the Swedish East India Company.

That same year Campbell sailed in the company's first ship to China as Sweden's Minister Plenipotentiary to the Emperor. He kept an immensely interesting diary of the voyage, which only came to light in 1986 and is now in the Gothenburg Museum. Despite the inexperience of the Swedish captain and interference from the Dutch East India Company, the voyage was profitable and the company continued to succeed until after Campbell's death.

Campbell, Sir John Logan (1817 –1912)
Pioneer of Auckland, New Zealand

Born in Edinburgh, Campbell followed his father's profession by graduating as a physician at Edinburgh University. Becoming a ship's doctor, he immigrated to Australia in 1839, but soon moved on to New Zealand, arriving at Coromandel in 1840. Campbell was present at the foundation of the city of Auckland, and, together with his partner, William Brown, opened business premises at the aptly named Commercial Street. He became involved in many facets of Auckland's growth, including the first direct export from that city to the United Kingdom. He sent over Kauri wood for ship's spars, as well as copper and manganese. Although he travelled extensively, Campbell always returned to Auckland, despite having made a small fortune when he became involved supplying material to the Californian gold miners in 1849.

Campbell, Robert (1769 – 1846)
Merchant, the 'father of Australian commerce'

Born in Greenock, Campbell was the youngest son of John Campbell, 9th Laird of Ashfield. In partnership with his brother John, Campbell ran the trading firm of Campbell and Clarke. When one of the company ships was wrecked, he moved from his Calcutta offices to Sydney, New South Wales in 1797, hoping to investigate and exploit the trade of this new colony. John Campbell had not been idle, importing sugar, spirits and cattle to the convict settlement. Robert Campbell, however, was to become known as 'Merchant Campbell' for his talent. In 1800 he moved permanently to Sydney as that city's first 'free' merchant.

With varied interests including banking and politics as well as tax collecting, Campbell was better known for his involvement in rum and sealing. Governor Bligh considered that Campbell was 'just and humane and a gentleman', but he was also a born entrepreneur who challenged the mighty Honourable East India Company. The HEIC's monopoly of trade in the East included Australia, with the laws of monopoly declared that no Australian based company could ship the products of sealing or whaling to Britain. Campbell, however, loaded *Lady Barlow* with 260 tons of seal oil and nearly 14000 sealskins. The oil would be used for street lighting and lubrication in the industrialising streets of Britain, the skins for clothing. To drive the message home, Campbell shipped a further 34,000 skins in a second vessel.

Naturally incensed, the HEIC impounded Campbell's ships and cargo, but when Campbell took legal action, he won the case. He had ensured that Australia could export its goods, thus releasing the colony from some of its convict shackles.

While he exported oil and sealskins, Campbell's most important import was rum. Again he challenged the authorities, for while they restricted his imports to a mere 4000 gallons a voyage, his ships carried anything up to 14000 gallons, sometimes smuggled in lieu of cattle. Not until 1815 did Governor **Lachlan Macquarie** declare Sydney a free port, so traders could openly sail in and out.

Four years later, Campbell, wealthy from lucrative government contracts in cattle importation, was a prime mover in opening Australia's first savings bank, which was intended to help the 'industrious poor' to save. Campbell's interest was so extensive that the Sydney branch soon earned the sobriquet as Campbell's Bank. In 1825 Campbell had become an early settler in the Canberra area, and built a substantial, nearly Scottish style house that he named Duntroon.

As if his political, economic and trading operations were not enough, Campbell was also an agent for the London Missionary Society. He died at Duntroon in 1846, a man successful in all that he attempted.

Campbell, Robert (1808 – 1894)
Fur trader and explorer
Born in Glenlyon, Perthshire, Campbell was the son of a sheep farmer. Joining the Hudson Bay Company, he immigrated to Canada in the early 1830s and worked around the Red River area. Rising to chief factor, Campbell explored around the Mackenzie River area, where he examined the Frances Lake country and discovered and named McPherson Lake after **Murdoch McPherson**, chief factor for the Mackenzie District. Campbell also explored around the Yukon, where he discovered the Upper Yukon in 1848. One of his best-remembered exploits was a 3000-mile walk in snowshoes from the Yukon to Montreal. Retiring from the HBC in 1871, he moved to Manitoba and turned his hand to ranching along with his wife Eleanora Stirling.

Cargill, William (1784 – 1860)
Soldier and coloniser

Born in Edinburgh on the 28th August 1784, Cargill was the son of an alcoholic solicitor whose early death caused the family many problems and caused Cargill to be taken from the Royal High School. Cargill's mother, a woman of strong character, moulded her son into a man. She also gave him a distinctively Christian train of thought that harkened back to the seventeenth century Covenanters more than to orthodox Victorian evangelicalism.

At the age of 16, Cargill became an officer in the 84th Foot. Transferring to the 74th Highlanders, he fought with the future Duke of Wellington against the Marathas, as well as in the Peninsular Wars, being wounded at Busaco. He was later promoted to Captain, the highest rank he ever achieved. Sometime in 1813 he married the Englishwoman Mary Yates in Oporto. Ten of their seventeen children reached adulthood.

Selling out of the army in 1820, Cargill worked as an Edinburgh wine merchant until 1834 and by 1841 was working with the Oriental Bank Corporation in London. At no time in his life had Cargill made much money, and now he thought about emigration. George Rennie, a Scottish politician, promised that Cargill could lead any systematic Scottish settlement in New Zealand. After the Disruption of 1843 split the Church of Scotland, Cargill and Rennie proposed the newly formed Free Church with a plan for emigration, and within two years Cargill headed the idea for a Free Church settlement.

Despite difficulties imposed by the Colonial Office and New Zealand Company, Cargill continued to press his scheme and in November 1847 accompanied two shiploads of emigrants, including the **Reverent Burns**, to Otago. They arrived on the 23 March 1848, with no loss of life on the voyage, which was impressive for the period, and Cargill celebrated their arrival with a sermon that compared them to the Pilgrim Fathers.

The first year was difficult, with a wet winter, no roads or facilities for unloading supplies and a raw land to tame. The Scots argued with the English, with Cargill viperous toward the Anglican William Valpy. Although Cargill was a decent man, he refused to tolerate opposition to his Presbyterian views. More of a patriarch than a democratic leader, Cargill was always steady and held the respect of most of the community. While the Covenanting-style blue bonnet and the plaid he wore may have been endearing to the Scots, the English settlers affected to find them amusing. Although he was a member of the New Zealand parliament, he spoke little and without much effect. He pushed forward his own family, tended toward archaic conservatism and free trade and hoped for an arable society based on class.

Nevertheless, Cargill did help create an Otago that was markedly more pleasant to inhabit than most colonial settlements were. He achieved a balance between families and single settlers, and between men and women. His colony progressed slowly until the discovery of gold brought in a horde of non-Church attending men that altered the whole balance of Otago. Perhaps fortunately, Cargill did not live to see this event.

Carmichael, General (fl 1570)
Russian soldier

Carmichael was a Borderer, reputedly uncle of Sir John Carmichael, one of the best-remembered Wardens of the Scottish Marches. At some stage he travelled to Russia and joined the army of Ivan the Terrible. His natural Border talent for mayhem and military matters stood Carmichael in good stead and in 1570 the Csar appointed him to command 5000 men. He led them against the Poles, apparently with much success, and was later appointed Governor of Pskoff.

Carnegie, Andrew (1835 – 1919)
American industrialist and philanthropist

Born in Dunfermline, Carnegie grew up in poverty as his weaver father saw his position deteriorate during the hungry forties. In 1848 he emigrated with his family to Allegheny, now known as Pittsburgh. Carnegie found employment in a cotton mill as a bobbin boy, and then became successively a telegraphist and a clerk in the railways. In 1859 he was made a superintendent in the Pennsylvania Railroad.

He invested most of the money he earned and in 1865 devoted himself entirely to his financial affairs. At first concentrating on oil, Carnegie then switched to iron and steel. As his money grew, Carnegie bought steel companies, consolidating them into the Carnegie Steel Company, the largest iron and steel works in America. Carnegie used a combination of factors to create his wealth, including business efficiency, excellent subordinates and his knowledge of and co-operation with railways.

Carnegie preferred to create his wealth by increased steel production, rather than by playing the stock market, and survived the depression of the middle 1890s. His company controlled railroads, iron mines, ore ships and coke ovens, but he was not always popular with his workers.

In 1901 the US Steel Corporation bought him out for $250 million. Carnegie then retired to his estate at Skibo Castle in Sutherland. His published writings include *The Gospel of Wealth* that stated rich men were only trustees and should use their money to benefit the public. Putting his own words into practise, Carnegie was one of the most prolific benefactors of the nineteenth and early twentieth centuries. As well as the famous Carnegie Hall in New York City, the Carnegie Institution in Washington and the Carnegie Foundation for the Advancement of Teaching, he funded the Carnegie Endowment for International Peace. Many of the 2800 libraries that he funded were in Scotland, but perhaps his most personal purchase was Pittencrieff Glen in Dunfermline. As a boy he was not allowed to roam in this beautiful place, so he bought the glen, transformed it into a park and handed it to the town of Dunfermline for everybody to enjoy.

Carnegie, Honourable David Wynford (1881 –1900)
Australian explorer and gold prospector

The fourth and youngest son of the Earl of Southesk, Carnegie had little prospect of attaining the family wealth. He was only twenty-one when he travelled to Western Australia to prospect for gold. Instead he caught typhoid, but survived, and heard about the vast unexplored tracts of Australia. Almost as soon as he arrived, Carnegie hoped to take part on an exploring expedition. Four years later **Sir Thomas Elder** sent him to lead an expedition between Coolgardie and the diggings at Kimberley. Carnegie had orders to discover if stock could be driven northward from Coolgardie. Being a digger, he also prospected for gold as he travelled.

Sensibly, Carnegie chose experienced men to accompany him, bought nine camels, loaded them with food and equipment, added galvanised iron water casks and set off.

Carnegie headed almost due north. He travelled in the depth of the Australian winter, hoping to avoid the worst of the heat of the desert. However, the land he described the land as 'the great undulating desert of gravel.' They found water by tracking the Aborigines and using their deep wells, once even straining putrid water through flannel shirts and adding Epsom salts as a purifier. Carnegie admitted that his treatment of the local Aborigines was not always gentle, but excused himself by explaining they 'were doing their best to lay bare the hidden secrets of an unknown region, as arid and desolate as any the world can show.'

They travelled through 1500 miles of barren land but last reached the mining town of Hall's Creek, a metropolis of nine buildings that had a bi-annual wagon connection to the port of Derby. He began the return trip in March 1897, but one man had died in an accident. They travelled a different, unknown route, down Sturt's Creek and into the desert. After 450 miles of sand ridges, Carnegie's men were weary. "One's nerves get shaky from constant wear and tear," Carnegie wrote, but persevered, returning to Coolgardie in the winter of 1897. He wrote of his experiences in *Spinifex and Sand*. Unlike other explorers he had discovered no pastureland, no new rivers, having experienced "one ceaseless battle for water."

Making only the one exploring trip, Carnegie sailed from Australia in 1897 for the even wilder lands of northern Nigeria. There was trouble there as the colonising British attempted to quell local resistance.

In 1900, when he was only twenty-nine years old, a poisoned arrow, fired by a disaffected tribesman, killed him.

Carrick, William (1827 –1878)
Photographer in Russia

Born in Edinburgh, Carrick was the son of a St Petersburg timber merchant. Brought up between Scotland and Russia, Carrick attended the Academy of Arts in St Petersburg, where he studied painting and architecture, but in 1853 travelled to Rome to advance his knowledge of art. In 1856, with the end of the Crimean war, Carrick returned to St Petersburg, where he entered the portrait photography business.

In 1857 Carrick left St Petersburg for Edinburgh, where he studied photography. He also met John McGregor and together they moved to St Petersburg and in 1859 opened a photographic studio. When the quality of their work became known, the Imperial court took notice, and the royal painter Mihaly Zichy became a close friend and business contact.

At first Carrick had numerous clients from the upper and middle classes, but during slack times he took a number of portraits of more humble people, either in the studio or in the street where the people lived and worked. He published the results in 1860 as the *Russian Types*. Carrick hoped that his work would sell on the tourist circuit. In 1871 he left St Petersburg with McGregor, travelling to the Sirnbirsk region, where he photographed people at work. He is remembered as one of the pioneers of Russian photography.

Caskie, Donald (1902 – 1983)
Tartan Pimpernel

Born in Bowmore on the island of Islay, Caskie became a minister in the Church of Scotland. His first appointment was to Gretna Church in Dumfriesshire, where he ministered for five years. He next took charge of the Scots Kirk in the Rue Bayard, Paris.

When the Second World War erupted, Caskie remained at his post when the Germans thrust the allied armies aside and occupied Paris. Although the Vichy French ordered that all Frenchmen collaborate with their conquerors, Caskie was more inclined to help the cause of democracy and freedom.

Joining a number of other refugees, Caskie travelled across France. Suspected of being a spy, he was arrested and nearly shot, but survived to reach Marseilles. Caskie used the British Seaman's Mission as a base to smuggle British civilians out of France, but also helped those British servicemen who had escaped the chaos of Dunkirk.

Known as the Tartan Pimpernel, Caskie worked regardless of his own safety, but was eventually, and inevitably, betrayed. Imprisoned in Italy, he was beaten up and sentenced to death, until a German clergyman spoke for him. He was freed and after D-Day he returned to Scotland. When the Scots Kirk in Paris was rebuilt, Caskie returned to his Paris congregation.

Chalmers, James (1841 – 1901)
Missionary

Born at Ardrishaig in Argyll, in 1865 Chalmers became a Congregational Missionary to the Pacific and worked in Rarotonga in the Cook Islands.

In 1876, highly experienced, he ventured to the even more dangerous land of New Guinea. He explored into Papua, meeting cannibals and tribes who had never seen a white man. Next Chalmers sailed to Samoa and spent time with Robert Louis Stevenson.

In 1892 he returned to New Guinea, working in the fever mangrove swamps where cannibals listened to his preaching as they sucked on the marrow of human bones. On 1901, he was on the vessel *Niue* with a party of Papuan converts who themselves had become missionaries. They were anchored off the island of Goaribi. Hordes of tribesmen left the island in their canoes and gathered on deck, brandished their spears and war clubs and examined the trade goods.

When the missionaries followed the tribesmen up a narrow creek to a native village, Chalmers walked on ahead. He entered a longhouse, along a narrow passage where a tribesman thumped him with a stone club and another cut his throat, then hacked off his head. When the tribesmen sliced him into pieces, the woman added him to a sago stew, the main meal of the day. It was April the 8th 1901, Easter Monday and Chalmers had paid the ultimate price for his devotion.

Chisholm, Erik (1904 – 1965)
Composer

Born in Glasgow, Chisholm studied at what is now the Royal Scottish Academy of Music and Drama then under Herbert Watson at Glasgow Cathedral. He left school at 13, travelling to London to meet various composers and by the time he was 18, Chisholm was composing intricate work. When he was 22 Chisholm travelled to Nova Scotia, where he accepted an appointment as organist and choirmaster at Westminster Presbyterian Church as well as Director of Music at Picton Academy. Perhaps these positions encouraged Chisholm to seek further qualifications, for he returned to Scotland after two years and entered Edinburgh University. He graduated with a Bmus in 1931 and a Dmus in 1934.

From 1929 Chisholm created the 'Active Society for the Propagation of Contemporary Music in Glasgow,' where he presented some spectacular works, many of it rarely seen. From 1930 he also conducted the Glasgow Grand Opera and founded the Barony Opera Company and the Scottish Ballet Society.

In 1945 Chisholm accepted an appointment as Professor of Music at Capetown, South Africa. While there he created a dozen new appointments, more than doubled the number of available courses and introduced a number of new degrees and diplomas. In 1948 he was instrumental in forming the South African National Music Press, which was designed to help unknown South African composers into publication.

Industrious and innovative, in 1951 Chisholm created the Opera School, which premiered works by South African composers and produced Chisholm's own work *Dark Secret* in 1954. Chisholm's broadcasting work spread his fame across South Africa, where he died of a heart attack in 1965. In his lifetime Chisholm wrote over 100 pieces, including 35 orchestral works, nine operas and seven ballets, yet his name is hardly known in Scotland.

Chisholm, Jesse (fl 1865)
Of the Chisholm Trail

Although Chisholm was only Scottish on his father's side, while his mother was a Cherokee, he deserves a mention for his part in opening up the American West. In 1865, guided by Black Beaver of the Delaware Nation, Chisholm drove his wagons and livestock south from where Wichita, Kansas now stands, to Fort Cobb, where he traded with the local tribes.

However, Chisholm was not the first to use this route, for Lieutenant-Colonel William Emory took a military force this way in 1861, and Black Beaver had already guided Audubon, Kearny and Marcy in their expeditions, but Chisholm still gained the kudos for being first.

The trail, across the most accessible fords of the Canadian, Cimarron, Chikaskia, and Ninnescah Rivers to the Arkansas, was marked by Chisholm's wagon wheels and became one of the most famous cattle routes in the west.

Christie, Dugald (c1858 – c1930)
Medical missionary

Born in Glencoe, in 1882 the United Presbyterian Church asked Christie to travel to Manchuria as a medical missionary. Basing himself in Mukden, Christie used his own money to teach medicine to local people. He dedicated himself to the health of the people, particularly during his anti-plague campaign of 1910. Two years later he opened the Mukden Medical College.

The college proved to be Christie's life work. Nine years after its foundation, Christie was in charge of a 140-bed hospital with a trained staff of Chinese surgeons and nurses, plus a British matron. In 1897 the Chinese honoured Christie with the Imperial Order of the Double Dragon, including ceremonial robes, which he wore with great pride.

Christison, Robert (c1830 – c 1890)

Shepherd and overlander

Born and brought up in Berwickshire, Christison and his brother Thomas immigrated to Victoria, Australia, in 1852. Initially the brothers were employed as shepherds at Werribee, where Christison developed his horse riding skills as well as becoming a notable boxer. However, he failed in his attempts to find gold, despite the gold fever that was then overwhelming Australia.

Christison also failed to join the expedition of Burke and Wills that hoped to be first to cross Australia from south to north. The urge for excitement was still strong, so he attended classes for navigation and moved into the wilder parts of Australia. Travelling to northern Queensland, he worked as a shepherd to finance his initial exploration of the countryside. Buying enough stores for a long journey, Christison chose a young aborigine as a companion, selected some quality horses and headed for the unexplored lands to the west.

Following the advice of the Scottish explorer **William Landsborough**, Christison found an area suitable for farming. Naming it Lammermuir, he tried his hand at shepherding. Christison soon found that the district was lively with dingoes and aboriginal tribesmen. At that time, European settlers in Australia habitually treated the Aborigines like wild animals, often shooting them on sight, but Christison attempted a form of kindness.

His kidnapping of an aboriginal child was unethical, but Christison then treated the boy gently and returned him to his tribe. Almost at once, his relations with the local tribes improved. Using Lammermuir as a base, Christison explored the western part of Queensland, but he is better remembered for his drive of 70,000 sheep all the way to Adelaide in 1870. After such an epic trek, it is good to know that Christison made a handsome profit. It is even better to know that the Queensland aborigines are said to have remembered him as a man who treated them with respect.

Clapperton, Captain Hugh (1788 – 1827)

African Explorer

One of twenty-seven children by the same father, Hugh Clapperton was born in Annan, Dumfriesshire. Becoming a merchant seaman at the age of thirteen, his stubborn spirit was proved when he refused to shine the shoes of the ship's master. Perhaps the master was not sorry to lose such a troublemaker when the Royal Navy press-ganged Clapperton. He rose to the rank of lieutenant, and gained praise for his conduct in Mauritius, where he hauled down the French flag. He served in North America during the 1812 war with the United States, commanding a blockhouse by Lake Huron and losing part of a thumb when he carried an injured man across the frozen lake. Clapperton became engaged to a Huron woman, but was sent home in 1817, one of the many able officers to be beached during peace.

In 1821 he and the Englishman Dixie Denham travelled to search for the source of the River Niger. **Dr Walter Oudney** of Edinburgh, who died half way through the journey, nominally led the expedition. Travelling across the Sahara with a caravan of merchants they discovered Lake Chad in 1823, where they separated. Rather than a dark continent, they found cultivated lands and 'civilized, learned, humane and pious people', as Clapperton himself wrote. There was a friendly elite, female stall owners and an impressive souk at Kano. The slave trade, however, was a constant point of dispute between Clapperton and the local Arab chiefs.

Clapperton journeyed to Sokoto, through lands disrupted by war, and was again welcomed. Sultan Bello gave Clapperton a letter for King George IV and spoke of friendship and trade. The return journey was bad, with men in the caravan dying with exhaustion, but things looked up when a sympathetic chief offered Clapperton the pick of his harem. One of the chief's women nursed the explorer back to health.

Clapperton returned to Britain in 1825. Although his exploration had brought some amazing African kingdoms into the public eye, it had not solved the mystery of the source of the Niger.

Less than a year after his return, Clapperton was back in Africa, authorised to open trading relations between Britain and Sultan Bello of Sokoto. This time he landed in the Bight of Benin, where disease ensured that only 'one comes out for forty goes in.' He had hoped to find representatives of the Sultan waiting at the coast, but such people did not exist. Together with Richard Lander and a few others, Clapperton travelled north through the fever belt and the tropical forest. As most of the party died of disease, Clapperton and Lander continued. The natives were friendly, but endlessly curious, so that even the most private functions had to be performed before an interested audience.

First Clapperton, then his servant Lander fell ill. Each nursed the other with genuine tenderness so they became close friends. In time Lander became one of the most successful and least known, of African explorers. As they probed north, their health improved and Clapperton noted a king with two thousand wives. They penetrated to Yorubaland, the first known white men to do so, but were held captive by the "sly, lubberly, fat and monstrous eunuch – Ebo." They swam crocodile infested rivers, were entertained by the naked wives of Yarro, king of the cheery city of Kaiama and were waylaid by the widow Zuma, who sought a white husband. At length they reached Sokoto. The Sultan was not as friendly as he had been, holding Clapperton as a captive until he died of dysentery. A man of great resource, he is hardly remembered today.

Cleghorn, Archibald Scott (1835 – 1910)
Prince of Hawaii

Born in Edinburgh on November 14 1835, Cleghorn was the fifth son of Thomas Cleghorn and Janet Nesbet. When Cleghorn was still a child, the family immigrated to New Zealand, but in 1851 sailed to Hawaii, where Thomas Cleghorn started a store to supply visiting shipping. Two years later he died, leaving his son, then 18, to run the business. A good businessman, Cleghorn opened more shops across Hawaii, but still had time to father three children on a Hawaiian girl. Although he cared for his daughters, he did not marry the mother. Instead he wed Miriam Likelike, who was the youngest daughter of

Chief Kapaakea. Although she was far younger, their marriage was successful.

In 1874 Miriam's brother Kalakua became king of Hawaii and Cleghorn found himself in an elevated place in society. Perhaps he only realised his new status when the birth of his daughter was announced by a salute of cannon on Punchbowl Hill. Given the charming, if long, name of Princess Victoria Kawekiu Lunalilo Kalaninuiahilapalapa Kaiulani Cleghorn, the child was christened at St Andrews Episcopal Church, with an immediate gift of a ten-acre estate in Waikiki. Cleghorn used his gardening skills to beautify his daughter's property, named the estate Ainahau and took up residence.

In 1877 the king died and the heir apparent took Likelike on a tour of the islands, where she engaged in a brief affair with another man. The marriage survived and in 1883 Cleghorn was brother-in-law and advisor to a king. Ignoring a family feud, he enjoyed the coronation, but was more distressed when Mount Loa erupted in January 1887. In Hawaii, such an event presaged the death of a chief. Believing that somebody had cursed her, Lilelike died in February, leaving Cleghorn to bring up their daughter. Kaiulani was unhappy when Cleghorn proposed sending her to Britain for her education, but Robert Louis Stevenson, out of Scotland for health reasons, tried to improve her morale with his tales of Scotland.

Cleghorn travelled with Kaiulani to San Francisco before returning to Hawaii. While she was away the king died and the new queen promoted Kaiulani as heir to the throne. It was now that Cleghorn began to play politics. Unhappy with his sister-in-law's policies, he began to wonder if it would be better for the United States to annex the islands. When this happened in August 1898, Cleghorn realised that his daughter had lost her inheritance. Within six months Kaiulani had died of fever, but Cleghorn married again.

Becoming a member of King Kalakua's Privy Council, Cleghorn was appointed to the Board of Immigration and the Board of Health as well as the Board of Prisons. However, it may be his appointment as Honolulu's first park commissioner that was most important, for he is remembered as the 'father of Hawaii's park system.' As well as nearly creating a royal dynasty, Cleghorn planned Emma Park and Kapiolani Park. He died on November 1910.

Cleghorn, Hugh F.C (1820 – 1895)
Father of Scientific Forestry in India

Cleghorn graduated from Edinburgh University with a degree in medicine and joined the East India Company. While at the Edinburgh assembly of the British Association, he created a Committee to discuss the destruction of tropical forests.

Cleghorn wrote the report in person, and sent it to his superiors. As a direct result, the East India Company created a Forest Department in Madras. In time the Forest Department covered all of British India. In 1867 the government appointed Cleghorn the Inspector General of Forests in India. He is sometimes remembered as the Father of Scientific Forestry in India.

Clerck, Richard (c1570 – 1625)
Swedish admiral

Born near Montrose, Clerck (or Clark, or Klerck) immigrated to Sweden, where he seems to have been a shipbuilder before entering the Navy. Around 1610 he commanded five ships that captured Riga. He was appointed Vice Admiral in 1612 and the following year was in charge of provisioning the Swedish fleet at Stockholm. Despite his high rank, Clerck did not forget his birthplace and sent a fine chandelier to the old parish kirk at Montrose.

Clerck, Richard (1604 –1668)
Swedish Admiral

Born in Eastern Scotland, Clerck followed his uncle into Swedish service. He joined the navy and obtained command of the ship *Swardet,* in which he proved himself a notable fighter. In 1648 the monarch knighted him, and he rose to become an admiral before his death in 1668.

Clunies-Ross, John (1786 – 1854)
King of the Cocos Islands

John Clunies-Ross was born in Weisdale Voe in the Shetland Islands on August 23 1786. He was the son of a schoolteacher, and learned seafaring on local fishing trips. He joined a whaling ship at the age of thirteen, and by the time he was twenty-seven had seen much of the world. When he was returning from the Southern Fisheries, his ship stopped at the Portuguese colony of Timor. Clunies Ross used his experience to exchange his position as third mate and harpooner to take command of *Olivia,* a British brig.

The owner was Alexander Hare, who combined trading with spying for the British and a little exploring on the side. Hare's ambition was to do as little work in as much luxury as possible, preferably in the company of beautiful and compliant women. He had started working toward his dream by gathering a harem of female slaves.

Clunies-Ross spent the next five years working in East Indian waters. His primary task was to attempt to colonise Borneo with unwilling convicts from Java. It was a thankless job, particularly for the settlers, who died in droves from disease. Many of the convicts were guilty of only petty offences, some may even have been kidnapped, but Clunies-Ross ignored their distress in the belief that he was helping the British Empire. Although subjected to numerous invitations from female slaves, Clunies-Ross restrained his desires and even attempted to restrain those of Hare. He also wrote to the government, complaining about Hare's licentiousness.

Back in London to report on conditions in the East, Clunies-Ross escaped from a press-gang by leaping into a nearby house. Elizabeth, the woman who greeted him was the daughter of the merchant who owned the house. Clunies-Ross soon married her and they had a son.

Clunies-Ross and Elizabeth intended to rule a Christian colony on an eastern island. When he continued his seafaring career, Clunies Ross searched for a suitable spot. In 1825 he settled on the Cocos Islands in the Indian Ocean. After a few days of investigation, he nailed the Union Flag to one of the tall coconut trees on Horsburg Island and arranged for his family to join him. Clunies- Ross brought over his wife and their growing family, as well as Mrs Dymoke, his mother-in-law and eight Scottish seamen. Unfortunately Alexander Hare had found his own paradise on the island, and the two colonies were best of friends.

Hare was surrounded by a bevy of forty Malayan slave women. Ironically, Clunies-Ross brother had ferried Hare to Cocos, but now Hare and his harem attempted to push the newcomers out. Clunies-Ross won the skirmish and Hare withdrew to a neighbouring island, where he kept his women locked in a makeshift fortress. Hare's home became known as Prison Island. However, some of the women escaped, and the Scottish seamen had little difficulty in crossing the channel to these Malayan captives. Knowing he could not win by force, Hare tried bribery. When the Scots celebrated St Andrews Day, Hare sent rum and pork across to Horsburg Castle, with the hope that the Scots seamen would stay away.

Clunies-Ross named his settlement New Selma after Ossian's heaven. More practically, he brought modern farming and house building to the Cocos Islands, exploiting the coconut palms for their fruit. In time the population of his kingdom grew, swollen by an exodus of female slaves from the neighbouring island. However, as more slaves crossed to the kingdom of Clunies-Ross, Hare slipped away to Borneo, where he created another seraglio.

As Clunies-Ross's subjects increased, he ruled by the Bible and a form of benign slavery. People who broke his laws were shipped to Java and Clunies-Ross quelled an attempted uprising by two Europeans, who hoped to entice American whalers to the island. The people lived in some comfort, with large houses; even the slaves had better houses than most people in Scotland enjoyed. Clunies Ross ruled his islands as a private kingdom for twenty years. He was 68 when he died. In 1857, three years later, the British government applied Dominion status to the Cocos Islands.

Cochrane, Thomas, Earl of Dundonald (1775 – 1860)

Admiral of Chile and Brazil

Thomas Cochrane may have been the most able ship commander that Scotland produced in the French Revolutionary and Napoleonic Wars. He was born on 14 December 1775 in Eddlewood House, near Hamilton. In June 1793 he signed on the frigate HMS *Hind,* which worked off Norway and Canada. Cochrane then served under Admiral Keith in the Mediterranean, where he received his first command.

Speedy was small and lightly armed, but Cochrane increased her speed and throughout 1800 and 1801 he ran riot off the coast of Spain. He captured Spanish merchantmen, gunboats and privateers, but his greatest success was the capture of the Spanish frigate *El Gamo,* with nine times *Speedy*'s armament and six times her crew. After capturing fifty enemy vessels, Cochrane was himself captured by a squadron of French frigates. Eventually exchanged for French prisoners, Cochrane read moral philosophy at Edinburgh University until the Admiralty appointed him to HMS *Arab,* in which he performed routine patrols.

A change in higher command saw Cochrane appointed to HMS *Pallas,* a 32-gun frigate in which he made his name. Cruising off the Azores, he captured four Spanish merchantmen laden with treasure and evaded three French battleships, only to see the port admiral grab the bulk of his prize money. Cochrane was never popular at the Admiralty. Innovations that he introduced to make convoys safer were ignored, his exploits were belittled and he gradually became resentful.

His nautical career in *Pallas* continued with captures and victories over the French, but a diversion into politics, where he criticised the naval abuses of the government, was unsuccessful. In command of *Imperieuse,* he pricked at the enemy coast, but when he captured two Maltese pirates he found that Admiralty officials part-owned the ships. With his exploits earning him the sobriquet the Sea Wolf from the French, Cochrane was unsupported by higher command at the battle of Basque Roads and began a campaign against naval abuses that cost him his career.

Cashiered for a crime that he did not commit, Cochrane lost his commission. In 1817 he accepted an invitation to create a navy for

Chile, then fighting for independence from Spain. In November 1818, Cochrane, together with his wife and two sons, arrived at Santiago. He had a 300-ton merchant ship with the unwarlike name of *Rose,* two other vessels including the frigate *O'Higgins* and the rank of Vice-Admiral. His initial objective was to eject fourteen Spanish ships out of Lima. Joined by his five-year old son, Cochrane attacked Callao during a festival. His first attack was repelled, so he blockaded the city with his small squadron, releasing chained Chilean captives and capturing a Spanish gunboat.

Cruising the Chilean coast, Cochrane defeated the Spaniards at Huacha and brought home a wad of Spanish money. A reconnaissance of Valdivia resulted in the capture of a Spanish brig carrying wages for the garrison. A subsequent attack was jeopardised when one of Cochrane's frigates ran aground, rendering the gunpowder useless, but Cochrane attacked with the bayonet and the Spanish had lost their main base in southern Chile.

In August Cochrane was wounded twice but still managed to capture *Esmerelda*, the Spanish flagship. When Cochrane realised that San Martin, the Chilean leader and his employer, had no intention of paying his men, he pirated Martin's personal treasure and distributed it to the navy. Cochrane realised that his time in Chile was coming to a close. The Spanish navy was defeated, hundreds of miles of coast had been opened to international trade and the United States had recognised Chilean independence.

Next, Cochrane accepted command of the Brazilian Navy. Brazil was struggling to free herself from the rule of Portugal, which was backed by loyalists in the Northern provinces. With a fleet of three ships, Cochrane's attempt to defeat a thirteen-strong Portuguese fleet off Salvador failed, mainly due to poor discipline. After retraining the best of his men, Cochrane returned to Salvador with a small fleet. Sailing *Pedro Primiero,* his flagship, into Salvador harbour under cover of night, he ascertained the position of the Portuguese fleet, but before he could attack, the Portuguese fled the harbour.

Cochrane skirmished with their fleet. Leaving his followers to mop up the troop transports and merchantmen, he forced the Portuguese fleet to flee. Next he captured Maranham, the wealthiest province of Brazil. He did the same to the province of Para, following this exploit up by defeating an attempted revolt. Returning to Britain, Cochrane found that he was a national hero.

After South America, in 1827 Cochrane lent his support to the cause of Greek independence. To the classically educated British, Greece was a land of romance and heroes. Instead Cochrane found bandits and piracy. His enemies were Turkey and Egypt. He succeeded in destroying an Egyptian warship in Alexandria harbour and another off Navarino, but realised that his efforts to keep the peace between the fractious Greeks were in vain and resigned.

After fighting to clear his name in Britain, Cochrane was reinstated to the Royal Navy and, in 1841, appointed a pension. He also worked on ship engineering, improving rotary screw engines and screw propellers. Six years later he was Commander in Chief of the North American and West Indies station. When he died, in 1860, the government of the day gave him a state funeral and a burial in Westminster Abbey.

Couper, Captain James (c1615 – 1641)
Mercenary

Little is known about Couper's early life or career, but he arrived in the East Indies in the late 1630s as master of a Dutch ship. He seemed to specialise in combined land-sea operations as he led a flotilla of light craft against the Dutch East India Company's enemies. He commanded a force of 130 seamen in 1640, and in September of that year led the Batavian naval flotilla that blockaded the city. In 1641 the 'esteemed Commander James Couper' died.

Couper, James (fl 1660s-1680s)
Mercenary

James Couper was first recorded in Java in 1653, and presumably spent the next few years in the East as he was reported again as a soldier in Java in 1664, at which time he became assistant military commander at Bantam and Batavia. By 1665 he was 'secunde' and in 1672 was a senior merchant. At some period his sister, Elizabeth, and his brother John joined him.

James Couper continued to climb the Dutch ladder, travelling from Commandant at Mataram in Lombok, to Commandant at Indermayo. Before 1680 he commanded the entire area and sat on the Council of Surabaja in Eastern Java. He seems to have feuded with a native named Troenjja, whom he fought in April 1680 at Kartsura and Mataram. The following year Couper defeated another chieftain named Balian Namoud, but lost many men, probably as much from disease as battle.

When a diplomatic solution ended the war, Couper became Governor of the West Coast of Java. In August 1684 he was back in action to suppress anti-Dutch factions, and was further promoted to be Governor of the West Coast of Sumatra, where he negotiated between the Dutch and English East India companies.

Between his official wages and private trade, Couper became very wealthy. In 1687 he returned to Europe as 'Commanding Admiral' of the Dutch Fleet that brought back the treasures and spices of the Indies. Almost as soon as he reached the Netherlands, Couper was appointed to be Conservator of Scottish Privileges in the Dutch Republic. In 1694 Couper, now an Admiral was appointed as the Dutch Consul-Extraordinary to Batavia, but was presumed drowned on the journey.

Craik, James (1730 –1814)
Chief Medical Officer of United States Army

Born near Dumfries, Craik's parents were unmarried, but his father appears to have cared for him nevertheless. Educated at Edinburgh University, he graduated in medicine and joined the British Army as a surgeon. After service in the West Indies, Craik resigned his commission and travelled to Virginia in 1751. In 1754, with the Seven Years War looming, he joined the Provincial Regiment as a surgeon and became friendly with George Washington.

Craik served alongside Washington throughout 1758 and 1759. He settled on an estate at Port Tobacco and in 1760 married Marianne

Ewell, a union that produced nine children. Craik retained an intense loyalty for his new country, siding with the Patriots in 1774 when the British blockaded Boston.

When the Revolutionary War began, Craik became the Assistant Director of the United States Army Medical Department. He tended the wounded immediately after the bloody battles, with one of his patients being the Marquis de Lafayette. Craik's association with the United States army was long lasting, for in 1798, with war with France threatening, he was appointed Chief Medical Officer. It was Craik who attended Washington in his last days, giving rise to speculation that his intended cure actually speeded the President's death. Craik finally left the army in 1800, to live another fourteen peaceful years.

Crichton, James (1560 – 1585)
The Admirable Crichton
Born in Cluny, Perthshire, the son of the Lord Advocate, Crichton was educated at St Andrews University by George Buchanan, one of the leading scholars of the period. He graduated in 1575 and travelled on the continent, where he is said to have been famous as a poet, scholar and linguist. He may have spent two years in the French army, and was reported to have given an oration in Latin before the senate in Genoa in 1579. Crichton was also reported as having participated in a scholastic debate at Venice in 1580 and in Padua the following year.

He became part of the court of the Duke of Mantua, but for all his scholastic skills, his reputation as a swordsman may have been exaggerated, for the duke's son killed him in a brawl. History has remembered him as the 'Admirable Crichton.'

Cuming, Sir Alexander (1680 – 1775)
'Crown King of Tennessee'
Born in Culter in Aberdeenshire, Cuming was university educated. He became a member of the Royal Society as well as a successful merchant. During the 1740s he traded with the Carolinas, partly to collect minerals and plants for scientific purposes, but he also took part in

local politics, as he believed he could convince the hostile Cherokees to switch their allegiance from France to Britain.

Aware of the friendship between Highlanders from Georgia and other Indian nations, Cuming donned Highland dress and marched into Cherokee country. It was said that he brandished his sword at a bemused Cherokee chief and demanded his allegiance to the British Crown. After that act, Cuming was known as 'Emperor of the Cherokee Nation' or, alternatively, 'Crown King of Tennessee.'

His sheer audacity had some success, for Cuming brought a group of Cherokees to meet George II, to whom they presented a collection of human scalps. Nonetheless, Cuming did not retain his popularity. Accused of fraud, in 1773 he was consigned to the debtor's prison, where he died two years later. The town of Cuming in Georgia is his memorial.

Cunningham, Alexander (1814 – 1893)
Soldier and archaeologist, the 'father of Indian archaeology'

After completing his education at Christ's Hospital, Cunningham joined the army of the East India Company. While he rose from officer cadet to major general, Cunningham was employed in various roles, from an engineer during the Sikh wars of the 1840s to heading boundary commissions in Kashmir and Ladakh. At one time he was also aide de camp to Lord Auckland, but all the time Cunningham's interest centred on the virtually untapped archaeology of India.

Cunningham arrived in India in 1833, and by 1834 he had written about the archaeological stupa in the Punjab. In 1837 he was the first Western scholar to examine the Buddhist stupa at Sarnath where the Buddha first preached. Fascinated by the virtually unknown travels of Buddha in India, Cunningham followed his journeying, identifying various hitherto unexamined Buddhist sites throughout northern India.

Even when Cunningham at length retired to Scotland, the authorities asked him back to India, where he led the Archaeological Survey for fifteen years. As well as practical archaeology, Cunningham wrote on the subject, being the first westerner, and possibly the first person, to indicate the depth, complexity and quality of the archaeology of India.

Cunningham, Allan (1791 –1839)
Botanist and explorer

Although born in England, Allan Cunningham was the son of a gardener from Renfrewshire. His working at Kew Gardens and in Brazil, he was employed as a plant collector for Sir Joseph Banks. In 1816 Cunningham sailed to New South Wales. He introduced himself as 'Mr Allan Cunningham, King's Botanist' to **Governor Macquarie**, who encouraged him to join the explorers who were beginning to extend the frontiers of the colony.

As he searched for new plant specimens, Cunningham also explored new territory in New South Wales and around Moreton Bay in Queensland. His first trip inland was with Surveyor-General John Oxley, probing into the country west of the Blue Mountains. Cunningham joined Oxley in following the Lachlan River, hoping to find an inland sea. Instead the river disappeared into a series of marshes. Cunningham, however, was not disappointed. The six-month trek through eucalyptus covered ridges, deep valleys and dry plains allowed him to collect more than 400 different species of plants.

Cunningham divided his time between hunting for plants, exploring and studying the local botany. By 1823 he was a noted explorer, discovering Pandora's Pass, which connected Bathurst, the Liverpool Plains and the Hunter River. Two years later he explored the Liverpool Plains, and then in 1827 he led a party to discover the pasture land of the Darling Downs that made settlement possible in Queensland.

Leaving Australia, he hunted for plants in Norfolk Island and in New Zealand. In 1831 he returned to Kew to classify his many specimens. Although he was offered the position of botanist for New South Wales, he preferred to remain in London, allowing his brother Richard to continue his work in Australia. Unfortunately, Richard disappeared, presumed killed by natives while on an expedition with **Sir Thomas**

Mitchell, and Cunningham took on the position. However, he was not happy, as the job entailed growing vegetables for the governor and supervising the Sydney Botanical Garden. Leaving for New Zealand, he again came back to New South Wales, where he died of tuberculosis. He is remembered by many species of Australian trees, particularly the coniferous genus *Cunninghamia,* as well as his written work, which is held at Kew.

Dalrymple, George (1826 – 1876)
Australian explorer and politician

The tenth son of Sir Robert Dalrymple-Horn-Elphinstone of Logie Elphinstone in Aberdeenshire, Dalrymple left Scotland in the 1840s to become a coffee planter in Ceylon. Tiring of that life, he sailed to Queensland, Australia, where he arrived around 1856.

Having failed in an attempt to buy land in the Darling Downs, Dalrymple's next idea was to create a pastoral settlement deep in the north of Queensland, which at that time was unsettled by Europeans and virtually unknown. Dalrymple set up an exploring expedition to the Burdekin River Watershed, and led it as far as the site of present day Bowen.

In 1860 the authorities made Dalrymple Commissioner for Crown Lands in the Kennedy district of Queensland, and in August of that year he was exploring again, probing to see if Port Denison would be a suitable deep-water port for the area. After that he led an expedition overland and in April 1861 proclaimed a township at Bowen. After a spell as a businessman and land manager on the upper Burdekin River, he became embroiled in a scandal that centred on another man's wife. Although both he and the woman were innocent, Dalrymple was certainly guilty of assaulting a policeman, for which he was fined £500.

In 1864 he was instrumental in establishing the settlement of Cardwell on Rockhampton Bay and the following year he represented Kennedy in the Legislative Assembly. After a position in government he returned to exploring work in 1873, trekking along the Endeavour

River. That was his final probe into the wilds, but Dalrymple was well thought of in Australia.

Davidson, William (1846 –1924)
Father of New Zealand mutton industry

Born in Edinburgh, Davidson was the son of a high official of the National Bank of Scotland. Rather than follow his father into the financial industry, in 1865 he sailed to Dunedin and enrolled as a cadet at The Levels sheep station at Timaru on the Canterbury Downs. After experience as a shepherd, Davidson became the Assistant Superintendent at The Levels, being promoted to superintendent in 1875.

Not content with merely supervising the flocks, Davidson imported Lincoln stud rams and merino sheep and bred them to create the Corriedale sheep, New Zealand's first distinctively developed breed. In 1878 Davidson returned to Scotland as the General Manager of the New Zealand and Australia Land Company, in which position he furthered developed the agricultural culture of New Zealand. It was Davidson who arranged for the first consignment of frozen New Zealand meat to be shipped to the United Kingdom in 1881. He travelled outward and return on the refrigerated ship *Dunedin* to ensure that everything proceeded correctly.

As if that was not enough, Davidson was also a father figure to the New Zealand dairy industry. After being heavily involved in the creation of the Edendale Dairy Company on land owned by the New Zealand and Australia Land Company, Davidson visited Canada and Denmark to investigate their dairy industry. Only then did he have plans for dairy factories drawn up and sent to New Zealand, following that with the recruitment of an experienced Danish butter maker.

In some ways it could be said the Davidson was the father of the New Zealand mutton and dairy business, which was quite an achievement for a man who spent most of his working life in Scotland.

Dawson, Simon James (1820 –1902)
Civil Engineer

Born in Redhaven, Moray, Dawson emigrated to Canada when he was barely out of his teens. He became a civil engineer and in 1853 he was asked to survey the scarcely known territory that stretched between Lake Superior and the Saskatchewan River. Although fur trappers operated in this vast stretch of land, it was not until Dawson's report of 1859 that the Canadian government seriously considered settling these plains.

With his reputation assured, Dawson's next major expedition was in 1868 when he was sent to create a practicable road to the Red River Country. Future travellers would know the 'Dawson Route' well. Two years later, Dawson was called upon to guide Wolseley's small army on their bloodless campaign to the Red River.

As well as an engineer and a surveyor, Dawson was also a politician. From 1875 to 1877 he was a Conservative member of the Ontario Legislature, and from 1878 to 1891 he sat in the Canadian House of Commons.

Dempster, Thomas (c 1579 – 1625)

Scholar and poet

Born in Aberdeenshire, Dempster started his education at Turriff, and then continued at the universities of Aberdeen, Cambridge, Paris, Louvain, Rome and Douai. With such a prestigious selection, it was natural that he should be offered a choice of professorships before settling at Paris University for seven years.

Dempster was known as an excellent swordsman, but his temper let him down and he fought with his own students. Moving to England, he married but as he was a Catholic, found many positions closed to him in a Protestant country. Returning to the Continent, Dempster became a professor at Pisa in 1616. When his English wife was unfaithful he relocated to Bolgna, where he became Professor of Humanities.

There are certain similarities between the career of Dempster and that of the Admirable James Crichton. However his *Historia Ecclesiastic Gents Scrotum* is not to be trusted, as he tends to exaggerate the exploits of Scotsmen, which, of course, are notable enough to stand unaided.

Dickson, Robert (c1767 –1823)
Fur trader

Born in Scotland, Dickson was still a young teenager when he immigrated to Canada. By 1786 he had entered the fur trade, working at Michilimackwac. In common with many Scots of his generation, Dickson seems to have been a natural and became one of the most important fur traders on the Upper Mississippi River.

When the 1812 war with the United States blew up, Dickson used his considerable influence to persuade the local Indian tribes to fight for Britain. He appointed Black Hawk as chief of the five hundred warriors who mustered at Green Bay. Black Hawk took part in the battle of River Raisin, where the Kentucky detachment of the American army was defeated, as well as in the repulse of Major Zachary Taylor.

With the American War ended and Canada secure, Dickson assisted Lord Selkirk when he established the Red River Colony. Perfectly at home in the area, Dickson married a Sioux woman named To-To Win, with whom he raised five children.

Dickson, William (1769 –1846)
Duellist, Canadian politician and town founder

Born in Dumfries, Dickson was educated as a lawyer. He immigrated to Canada at the age of 23, settled in the Niagara area and began work as a lawyer. True to his Border blood, Dickson was able to take care of himself and when he disagreed with an Irish barrister, the two met with pistols at dawn. Despite Dickson killing his man, the duel did not seem to have any adverse effect on his career.

When the 1812 war with the United States began, Dickson enrolled in the Canadian Militia, only to be captured by the Americans before he could prove himself. By the end of 1815 he was a member of the Legislative Council of Upper Canada. That same year he bought land

and founded the township of Dumfries, to which he encouraged settlers. Moving to Galt in 1827, he again supervised the settlement and expansion of the town.

Dinwiddie, Robert (1693 –1770)
Colonial administrator

Born near Glasgow, Dinwiddie was appointed collector of customs for Bermuda in 1727. In this position he showed honesty remarkable for the time, but was perhaps unwise in revealing the corruption of his peers. Eleven years later he became surveyor-general for the southern colonies of America.

In 1751 he became lieutenant governor of Virginia. His honesty in refusing to waive duties payable made him less than popular among the Virginians. However he also attempted to prevent the French occupying the Ohio valley. At that time France and Britain were major colonial rivals in North America, with their European wars transferred across the Atlantic. It was the colonists who suffered most from Indian attack, atrocity and murder. The French were attempting to link their small colony in Louisiana with their larger hold in Canada. If they had succeeded they would have hemmed the British colonials between the Appalachian Mountains and the Atlantic.

Dinwiddie clearly saw the threat and sent scouts to ascertain the number and strength of the French forts. It was Dinwiddie who first gave George Washington a position of authority. Washington was a young surveyor and Dinwiddie sent him to request French withdrawal from the area. Even when backed by troops, Washington had to surrender to superior forces at Fort Necessity. Recognising the Washington had done all he could, Dinwiddie promoted him to colonel.

Due to Dinwiddie's warnings, the British government sent over regular regiments of foot. However Britain insisted that the colonists should contribute funds for their own defence and it was Dinwiddie's task to raise the revenue. When the colonials refused to pay, Dinwiddie suggested that the British government take sterner measures to collect the taxes. He was recalled from America in 1758, by which time the

Seven Years War had broken out, but the tax he proposed was one of the causes of the American Revolution of 1776.

Donahue, Peter (1822 – 1885)
Engineer
Born in Glasgow, Donahue immigrated to New York while a young man. He left for California in the 1840s, settling in San Francisco when the state was still unsettled after the United States-Mexico War.

When the Californian gold rush began in 1849, Donahue tried his luck, but was unsuccessful. Foiled of a quick fortune, he began to repair and manufacture mining equipment. Realising that he had a rare talent with his hands, Donahue also created California's first printing press and steam locomotive. Finally, Donahue helped the safety of a rapidly expanding city by laying San Francisco's first gas lighting.

Douglas, David (1798 – 1834)
Botanist
Born in Scone, Perthshire, Douglas became an apprentice to William Beattie, the head gardener at Scone Palace. Paying for his own education, he learned science and mathematics and by 1817 was the under gardener to Sir Robert Preston at Valleyfield.

After a spell at Glasgow Botanical Garden, he became a collector for the Royal Horticultural Society. In 1824 the RHS and Hudson Bay Company sent Douglas on a plant-gathering trip to North America. He returned the following year, basing himself at Fort Vancouver as he searched and catalogued species of plants and animals that ranged from the California vulture to the California sheep. 'Not a day passed,' he wrote in his diary, 'but brought something new or interesting either in botany or zoology.'

Known as 'King George's chief' by the Chinook natives, Douglas found many previously unspecified varieties of shrubs, trees and herbaceous plants. He carried them to Britain to be catalogued and stored. He was back in America in 1827, crossing the Rockies as he tramped from the west coast to Hudson Bay. Society in Britain accepted him and his ideas, but he was far happier in the wilds, to which he returned for the last time in 1834.

Probably the most significant of his discoveries were the Giant Fir *Abies grandis,* in the western part of North America in 1825 and the Oregon pine, *Pseudotsunga menziesii,* which was later renamed the Douglas fir in his honour. The Douglas squirrel was also named after him. Douglas was killed in Hawaii, when he appears to have fallen into an animal trap and was gored by a bull. From time to time a rumour has been voiced that an Englishman named Gurney murdered the Scots botanist.

Douglas, Sir James (1803 – 1877)
Trader and politician

Born in Lanarkshire and educated locally, Douglas immigrated to Canada at the age of seventeen. By the time he was twenty-one, he was administrating Hudson Bay lands west of the Rocky Mountains. In 1830 Governor **George Simpson** sent him to Fort Vancouver, the furthest west of all Hudson Bay posts. Douglas erected a line of wooden forts to ensure that local Indians, Americans or even Russians did not encroach on the Company's property.

Remaining in the west, in 1843 Douglas created a trading post at Camsoun. With its name changed to Victoria, the post became the headquarters for a vast centre of fur trading that extended beyond the Arctic Circle. Douglas was right in the centre of things when Britain and the United States disputed their respective boundary rights. Despite the American call for 'fifty-four forty or fight,' the 1846 treaty fixed the frontier line at the 49th parallel. Unfortunately that meant that the Hudson Bay Company had to withdraw its southern posts in Oregon. Instead the Company concentrated on British Columbia. Douglas, now vastly experienced, was appointed to head the Western Department. By 1851 he was Governor of Vancouver.

Douglas still had to negotiate the frontier question with the Americans. Although the main boundary was decided, there was a dispute over the San Juan Archipelago. This 200 square mile island group lies between the North American mainland and Vancouver Island. With war threatening, Douglas sent a number of Royal Marines to the north section of the main island, while the American General William Harmey, who had already invaded Mexico without orders, did the same on the south. The two rival military forces remained in garrison for some two decades, never coming to blows, until in 1873 the German Emperor arbitrated in favour of the United States.

Douglas ended his career as Governor of British Columbia and Vancouver, keeping the peace with great skill.

Douglas, Count Robert (1611 – 1662)
Mercenary soldier

Robert Douglas was born in Scotland on the 17th March 1611. When he was little more than a boy, he travelled to the court of Gustavus Adolphus of Sweden, where he became a page. However, Douglas soon followed the example of many Scotsmen and joined the Swedish army, rising to the rank of Colonel by the end of the Thirty Years War.

At that time the mercenary Scottish soldiers had a reputation for being quick tempered and Douglas was no exception. When he quarrelled with the Austrian Colonel Spiegel, the Austrian drew a pistol and shot him. As Douglas fell, wounded, his Swedish companions killed Spiegel. Mercenary soldiers were not always well paid, relying on looting to supplement their income. In the case of Douglas, by 1643 he had not been paid for months and suffered from debt. Nevertheless he still fought for Sweden in the Polish Wars. Douglas took part in the battle of Jankow, where he was in the charge that decided the battle. He also led the centre of the line at the three-day battle of Warsaw.

In the 1650s Douglas was still fighting. In the Livland campaign he captured Willmar and then advanced toward Kurlas, assaulting Mitau. He also defeated General Kimorowsky in 1659. That victory was his last, for he returned to Stockholm with the peace, dying in 1662. Douglas had fought loyally for three Swedish monarchs, never switching allegiance or betraying his trust, which was unusual for a mercenary soldier.

Douglas, Thomas, 5th Earl of Selkirk (1771 –1820)
Coloniser

Born on the family estate in Wigtownshire, Selkirk had experienced something of colonial values when **John Paul Jones** had led a party to raid his ancestral home and steal the family silver. While being educated in Edinburgh University, Douglas met Walter Scott, whose romantic vision of the Highlands so influenced him that he embarked on a Highland tour in 1792. He saw some of the Clearances at first hand, sympathised with the Highlanders and taught himself Gaelic. In 1799 Thomas Douglas inherited the Earldom

In 1802 the new Earl of Selkirk placed 800 Scottish Highland emigrants in Prince Edward Island, mainly as a taster for a much more ambitious plan. Two years later he published *Observations on the Present State of the Highlands of Scotland*, which advocated the planting of Highlanders in the British North American colonies, partly as a defence against possible American attack, partly to alleviate the poverty in the north. Two years later he married Jean Wedderburn

In 1811 he tried out his theories in the Red River Valley in present day Manitoba, Minnesota and North Dakota. The Earl had obtained a grant of 116,000 square miles of land from the Hudson Bay Company, possibly because, through his wife, he now held a large number of their shares. Selkirk's land was far to the west of any existing Canadian settlement and the Earl had learned of its existence by reading **Alexander Mackenzie**'s book about his exploring expeditions.

The first group of selected Highlanders, led by Miles MacDonnell, sailed across from Stornoway. 21-year-old **Archibald MacDonald** led the second party from Thurso. The crossing was rough, the reception at Hudson Bay forts rougher and the march from the Bay to Red River a nightmare of frost, rapids and sheer distance.

Two groups of people were unhappy at this Highland invasion. The first was the North West Company, who also claimed the land as part of their fur trading empire. The second were the local Metis, mixed breed French, Scots and Indians who lived by hunting and trading. In 1816, led by Cuthbert Grant, a part Scottish Meti, they attacked and killed 21 of the Highlanders, but the colony continued.

In 1817 Selkirk personally visited the Red River Settlement, bringing a force of mercenary soldiers with whom he began a private war with the North West Company. In time the North West Company merged with the Hudson Bay, and Selkirk's Red River Colony grew into Winnipeg, with the Highlanders merging with the larger community. Unfortunately, Douglas did not live to see the climax of his dream.

Douglas, William of Nithsdale (d1390)
Crusader

In the fourteenth century, many Scots took part in the Northern Crusades against the Prussians. One such was Lord William Douglas of Nithsdale. He was experienced in the endemic border warfare of the time and married to Egidia, daughter of King Robert II. He seems to have been respected by both Scots and English knights and may even have commanded their combined fleet that left for Danzig.

However, with the natural enmity between Scots and English, it was not surprising that Clifford, an English knight, challenged him to a fight in single combat. According to folklore, when Douglas arrived at the destination, Clifford did not appear but sent a group of paid assassins who attacked Douglas. There are a number of versions of what happened, but it seems that Douglas and his servant were killed, with Douglas fighting "lyke ane lyon."

The death of Douglas seems to have especially enraged the French, allies of the Scots, and a French knight named Boucicault challenged any Englishman to fight, but they refused.

Douglas, William (fl 1620s)
Dutch soldier, engineer and inventor

Perhaps one of the most ingenious Scots of his day, Douglas has been largely forgotten by history. Joining the Dutch in their struggle for independence from the Spanish, Douglas rose to Captain of a company, but it was his inventive mind rather than his military skills that most benefited the cause of freedom.

Among the inventions that he proposed was a combination of pike and musket that appeared to be a forerunner of the musket and bayonet. He also created an artillery piece that could fire five shots in the time a conventional piece could fire two. Although members of the Council of State were impressed, they decided not to press ahead with this new technology. They did, however, pay substantial moneys to Douglas for his efforts.

Drysdale, Anne (1792 – 1853)
Farmer

Born in Fife, Drysdale farmed in Scotland before immigrating to Australia for the sake of her health. She arrived in Melbourne in March 1840, and within a couple of months had set up house with Dr Alexander Thomson of Geelong. It was Dr Thomson who helped her obtain a land grant of 10,000 acres at Bozungoop.

By August 1841 Drysdale was farming with the Englishwoman Caroline Newcomb. As well as running an efficient operation, their farm was noted for its neatness and comfort. It was one of the few in the area to boast a piano as well as having gravelled paths through the garden and cheerful conversation. In 1843 they bought the Coryule run, which they also ran with great skill, acquiring the freehold in 1848. Drysdale wrote a fascinating diary about her pioneer life, mentioning trouble with dingoes and details of sheep shearing and baling.

Duff, James, 4th Earl of Fife (1776 – 1857)
Spanish general

Born in Scotland, James Duff was the eldest son of the Honourable Alexander Duff. He was university educated and when his wife died in 1808, he joined the Spanish army that was resisting Napoleon Bonaparte. He rapidly rose to become a major general and fought at the victory at Talavera in 1809, where he was wounded. The following year he helped defend Cadiz, where he again suffered wounds.

A grateful Spanish government awarded Duff a knighthood in the Order of St Ferdinand, and when he became Earl of Fife in 1811 he retired to Scotland.

Dunbar, Earl Patrick of (c1200 – 1248)
Crusader

Earl Patrick of Dunbar was one of the leading Scots of the thirteenth century. In the 1240s he was noted for his generosity, having reputedly once burned down his own kitchen rather than disgrace himself by being unable to feed all his guests. After a major Islamic assault on the Holy Land, in 1247 Earl Patrick decided to go on Crusade. Before he left, his wife invested in a mediaeval insurance policy when she founded a Trinitarian hospital at Dunbar, which order was dedicated to ransoming Christian prisoners from the Moslems.

Despite his good intentions, and his wife's forethought, Earl Patrick did not return to Scotland. He died of disease at Marseilles, before sailing to Outremer, the Holy Land.

Dunsmuir, Robert (1825 –1889)
Coalmaster, politician

Born in Hurlford, Ayrshire, Dunsmuir was the son of a coalmaster and grew up in the coal industry. At the age of 22 he married Joanna White from Kilmarnock. In 1850 the couple emigrated to British Columbia, where the Vancouver Coal Company utilised Dunsmuir's mining skills. He located a rich seam of coal at Wellington, and the subsequent mine became a major employer that helped the infant colony find its financial feet. Dunsmuir's bank balance also showed some considerable benefit.

Using his new wealth, Dunsmuir invested in railways, becoming President of Esquimalt and Hanaimo Railway. He also became financially involved in a number of local businesses. In 1882 Dunsmuir was elected to the Legislative Assembly of British Columbia, becoming President of Council four years later. The magnificent mansion, known as Craigdarroch Castle, which now stands in downtown Victoria, may be the most enduring monument to British Columbia's first million-aire. Unfortunately Dunsmuir died before his castle was complete, but the building was converted into a museum and can now be viewed by the public.

Dyer, Henry (1848 – 1918)
Pioneer of Japanese engineering

Born in Bothwell, Lanarkshire, Dyer served an apprenticeship in a Glasgow engineering works before entering Glasgow University in 1868. He was the first Scotsman to win the coveted Whitworth Scholarship and graduated five years later. Dyer had the best ever academic record of any engineering student, so it was no surprise when he was handed the position of Principal and Professor of Engineering at the newly founded Imperial College of Engineering of Tokyo.

At that time Japan was undergoing a dramatic change from a mediaeval to a modern nation, and Dyer was right at the forefront. He created engineering studies that combined the practical with the theoretical in a six-year course. To enhance the practical side, Dyer was instrumental in founding the Akalane Engineering Works, which was Japan's largest engineering establishment and supplied the nation's public works.

Students trained by Dyer were responsible for many of the engineering feats that categorised late nineteenth century Japan. When he believed that they would benefit from further training, Dyer sent his students to Glasgow or other British universities. In 1882 Dyer left Japan, with high praise following him. The college appointed him Honorary Principal but the Emperor topped that honour by awarding him the 3rd class of the Order of the Rising Sun, the most distinguished Japanese order for the foreign-born.

Ironically, Dyer could not obtain a suitable position in Britain, although in 1886 he became the governor of the Glasgow and West of Scotland Technical College. Well known in Japan, Dyer never received the recognition he deserved in Scotland, but he was instrumental in bringing Japan into the modern world.

Eckford, Henry (Harry) (1775 – 1832)
Naval designer
Born in the small village of Irvine, now part of Kirkpatrick Fleming, Eckford sailed to Quebec at fifteen years old. Six years later he headed south to New York, where he began work as a shipbuilder. Within ten years he was building his own ships and in1820 he became Naval Constructor at the Brooklyn Navy Yard. At first he concentrated on fast, extremely strong, sailing ships, but with the new invention of steamboats he built *Robert Fulton* in 1822. This ship was famous for making the first steam voyage from New York to New Orleans and Havana.

Edgar, James (fl 1890)
First department store Santa Claus
Not a great deal appears to be known about James Edgar, yet he changed the face of Christmas for generations of children. Certainly Scottish, he immigrated to the United States and settled in Brockton, Massachusetts. He does not appear to have made much money, so in 1890 the Boston Store employed him as the first ever department store Santa Claus. A tall, plump man with a white beard, Edgar loved children and his booming laugh made him popular. Hundreds flocked to the store, some even coming by rail from Rhode Island, so other stores soon latched on to the idea.

Elder, Sir Thomas (1818 –1897)
Entrepreneur who introduced camels to Australia
Born in Kirkcaldy, Fife, the son of a shipowner and merchant, Elder immigrated to Adelaide in 1854. Working with his brother Alexander, who had already established Elder and Company, he financed copper mining in South Australia, then, with **Robert Barr Smith**, founded Elder, Smith & Company.

As this new company expanded to become one of the largest wool broking firms in the world, Elder bought huge areas of land, in South Australia, Queensland and Western Australia. He realised that transport was one of the major problems in the often-drought conditions of the bush, so imported over a hundred camels and their Afghan drivers. Basing them at Beltana Station in South Australia, he used the camels as breeding stock to raise native-born beasts. Elder's camels proved exceptionally useful during the construction of the Overland Telegraph between Adelaide and Darwin in 1872. Explorers also used camels on their arduous treks into the interior.

Elder eventually owned an area of land in Australia larger than all of Scotland, but he did not keep his wealth to himself. A noted philanthropist, in 1874 he donated £20,000 to establish Chairs of General Science and Mathematics at Adelaide University. Between 1883 and 1897 he handed over a further £80,000 to fund music and medical schools. His will included magnificent sums for Working Men's Homes and Adelaide Art Gallery, while he also expended wealth on Methodist, Anglican and Presbyterian churches.

Elder also provided the finance for various explorers, such as Warburton, Ross and **Carnegie**, who were primarily searching for pastoral land. Appointed GCMG in 1887, Elder was one of the most commercially successful Scottish emigrants to Australia.

Elliott, Gilbert, 1st Earl of Minto (1751 – 1814)
Politician, Governor General of India

A Borderer and a friend of Walter Scott, Gilbert Elliot was the first Scot to control British India when in 1807 he was appointed Governor General of India. At that time the Napoleonic Wars were at their height, Britain still worried about invasion and India was growing in importance in British minds. Elliot had to ensure that all French influence over the sub-continent was eradicated, while maintaining and possibly expanding British influence.

He succeeded brilliantly. In 1810 he sent expeditions that conquered Mauritius and Reunion, from where French warships had harassed British trade. The following year he sent an army to conquer Java, the principal island of the Dutch East Indies at a time that the Netherlands was an important ally of France. Elliott also opened embassies in Persia, Lahore and Kabul in Afghanistan, creating an alliance against possible French pushes from the Middle East. Not only that, but he ensured peaceful internal frontiers by creating a treaty with Sind, whose Amirs were notably troublesome.

Elliott's internal policies were not so successful. When missionaries began to issue religious tracts that may have offended the Hindu majority, Elliott imposed censorship to preserve the East India Company's principles of religious tolerance. However sensible this action, there were people in Britain who accused him of interfering with the Christian enlightenment of the heathen. In 1813 the Prince Regent lent his considerable weight to have Elliot removed and the Earl of Moira, a personal friend of the Prince, to take over in his place.

Elphinstone, Admiral John (d1785)
Russian Admiral

One of the Scots who transferred from British to Russian service after the Seven Years War, Elphinstone played a major part at the battle of Chesme. However, Empress Catherine preferred to give credit to the Russian Alexis Orloff. Coincidentally, Elphinstone and Orloff were rivals for the amorous interests of the Empress, but Catherine chose the Russian over the Scot.

However, Elphinstone rose to high command in the Russian Navy and spawned generations of Elphinstone seamen.

Elphinstone, Mountstuart (1779 –1859)
Colonial administrator and historian

Mountstuart Elphinstone was the fourth son of Baron Elphinstone. At the age of seventeen he entered the Bengal civil service. He became Assistant to the British resident at Poona and travelled in Sir Arthur Wellesley's train to speak with the Mahratta princes. At that time the hard riding Mahrattas were a powerful force in India and a serious threat to the Honourable East India Company.

Elphinstone was a notable member of Wellesley's staff at the battle of Assaye. He was then appointed resident at Nagpur. In 1808 he became the first British envoy to the turbulent city of Kabul in

Afghanistan. Although he was sent to create an Afghan alliance, his efforts failed when a new Afghan leader rejected the British treaty.

After 1810 he was the resident at Poona, dealing again with the Mahrattas. When war eventually and inevitably broke out, Elphinstone took command at the battle of Kirkee and defeated the Mahrattas. He ended the Mahratta War in 1817, as well as organising and governing the new lands won for the Honourable East India Company.

Between 1819 and 1827 Elphinstone was governor-general of Bombay. In this position he vastly improved the administration of the territory and modernised state education throughout the sub continent.

Turning down the position of Governor-general, Elphinstone retired to Britain in 1829. His published works include *History of India* and *Rise of British Power in the East.*

Erskine, Dr Robert (1687 -1718)
Physician to the Csar

A son of Sir Charles Erskine of Alva, Erskine studied in Edinburgh and Paris before travelling to Russia around 1704. He became one of a long line of Scottish physicians who worked at the Russian court. Erskine accepted the appointment of head of the Ministry of Medical Affairs, and in 1712 moved his offices from Moscow to the recently founded city of St Petersburg.

Paid a handsome salary of 1500 ducats, Erskine made great improvements to the Imperial Dispensary, and as well as supplying the army and navy, sold drugs to the rest of Russia, which raised funds for the Csar.

However, Erskine was more than just a doctor and an administrator. He was also a diplomat, travelling to the lands of the Tartars. In 1716 Erskine accompanied the Csar on a tour of Denmark, the German states and the Netherlands, as well as being present at the wedding of Tsarina Yekaterina Ivanovna. He also accompanied Csar Peter to Paris in 1717, possibly corresponded with Scottish Jacobites, but died young at Koucheserski. In his will, Erskine left his British possessions to his mother, and his Russian to the poor.

Fairweather, Ian (1891 – 1974)

Australian painter

Born in Bridge of Allan, Ian Fairweather fought through the First World War in the British army. In 1920, with the war over he discarded his rifle in favour of a paintbrush when he signed on at the Slade School of Art in London. Fairweather preferred Oriental art, developing a style in which Chinese brushwork mingled with a more traditionally European culture.

Leaving the art school, Fairweather travelled widely from 1924, visiting his old enemy of Germany as well as Canada and the more exotic locations of India, China and Japan, before settling in Australia. When the Second World War erupted, Fairweather once again donned uniform. He served as a Captain with the British army in India between 1940 and 1943, when he was invalided out to Australia.

Although Fairweather continued to paint, he was not content with a quiet life. In 1952 he constructed a raft, in which he sailed from Darwin to Indonesia. The voyage took so long that he was presumed drowned and his obituary published. He travelled around the islands for a few months, and then returned once more to Australia. Never a traditionalist, Fairweather built himself a shack on Bribie Island off Queensland, where he lived and worked until his death.

Falconer, Hugh (1808 – 1865)

Botanist and palaeontologist

Born at Forres, Falconer studied medicine at Edinburgh University and obtained an appointment with the East India Company as a doctor in Bengal. By 1832 he was the Keeper of the Saharanpur Botanical Garden, but his duties allowed him time to wander through the Siwalik Hills, where he found many fossils.

Probably more important for the future of India, it was Falconer who first grew tea in the country, beginning what became a major industry. By 1842 his health was declining so he returned to Britain, where he worked with Indian fossils in the British Museum and wrote about Indian palaeontology and botany. It was during this period that he produced the work for which he is best remembered, *Fauna Antiqua Sivalensis.*

In 1847 he was back in India as Professor of Botany at Calcutta while also superintending the Calcutta Botanical Garden.

Fergus, Robert (1815 – 1897)
Father of Chicago's printing industry

Born in Glasgow, Fergus emigrated to Milwaukee when he was 24 years old, but decided that he preferred Chicago. Fergus became a printer and is recorded as the 'Father of Chicago's printing industry'. As well as printing the first city directory of the city, he also produced the *Fergus Historical Series* of books.

Fergus died young, killed while crossing a railway line in Evanston during a thunderstorm.

Ferguson, Arthur (1880? – 1938)
Confidence trickster

In the 1920s Ferguson began to sell historical buildings to the Americans, starting with Nelson's Column in London, which he sold for £600 to a family from Des Moines, Iowa for their back yard. He also sold Buckingham Palace, accepting £2000 as a deposit, which was twice as much as he made for Big Ben. Immigrating to the United States in 1925, he mortgaged the White House to a Texas cattleman for a mere $100,000 a year, and nearly succeeded in selling the Statue of Liberty to an Australian. However, he was too audacious to remain free, the Australian reported him to the police and Ferguson served five years in prison before settling in Los Angeles, where he returned to his old life.

Finlayson, Roderick (1818 –1892)
Founder of Victoria, Canada

Born in Lochalsh, Ross, Finlayson immigrated to North America in 1837. Working for the Hudson Bay Company, he started as a clerk but in 1839 was ordered across the Rocky Mountains to the Pacific coast. For the next few years Finlayson travelled around the region, operating from Fort Simpson on the Mackenzie River. In 1843 he was back on the coast, being heavily involved in the foundation of Fort Victoria.

Finlayson was to spend many years at Fort Victoria as he built the remote frontier post into a thriving community. Promotion came steadily. He was Chief Trader in 1850 and Chief Factor in 1859. Two years later and now regarded as a fixture in Victoria, Finlayson was elected as member of the Legislative Council for Victoria Island. He left the Company in 1872 and lived out the rest of his life on comfortable retirement.

Fisher, Andrew (1862 – 1928)
Coal Miner and Australian Prime Minister

Born into a coalmining family, Fisher worked down the pit from the age of ten. By the time he was seventeen he was such an effective Trade Union secretary that the mine owners blacklisted him. He immigrated to Queensland in 1885, where he worked underground in the Gympie mines. Despite his Union activities, Fisher was a quiet man, self educated and modest, with genuine concern for the most vulnerable in society. Fisher again became active in the Trades Union movement.

The 1880s and 1890s were difficult years in the Queensland mines, with the government and mine owners locked head to head with the unions. Fisher was involved in the creation of the Labor Party and entered the Queensland state assembly in 1893. As the representative for Gympie, Fisher tried but failed to push through a Workman's Compensation Bill although he was more successful with a Factory and Shops Act. In 1901 he was a member of the first federal parliament, when he fought Labor's corner against both Free Traders and Protectionists. Becoming a government minister under Watson, Fisher was now in the forefront of the Labor Party.

In 1907 Fisher was elected leader of the Australian Labor Party, initially supporting the Protectionists in return for some concessions, but in 1905 he led the party onto its independent feet. He was Prime Minister for seven months between 1908 and 1909, again between 1910 and 1913 when he was the first Labor Prime Minister to win an election. During this term Fisher improved the Old Age Pension, introduced a maternity allowance, regulated working hours, introduced land reforms and modernised the defence forces. He was Prime Minister again between 1914 and 1915.

When the First World War began, Fisher promised to help 'the Mother Country... to the last man and the last shilling.' Nevertheless, he opposed conscription in 1916. Between 1916 and 1921 Fisher was the Australian High Commissioner in London. He died in London in 1928, where he was buried.

Fleming, Mrs Ann Cuthbert (d1860)
Poet and educator
Born in Scotland, Fleming immigrated to Canada around 1815. She published two volumes of poetry, of which *A Year in Canada* is arguably the better.

Fleming also founded a school for women in Montreal, and then published three books that were widely used in Canadian schools. Married to James, she was a stalwart and much respected member of the Montreal community.

Fleming, Sir Sandford (1827 –1915)
Canadian railway engineer
Born in Kirkcaldy in Fife, Fleming studied engineering and surveying before becoming an apprentice at John Sang Engineers and Surveyors in Kirkcaldy. Together with his brother David, he immigrated to Canada in 1845, at the height of the Hungry Forties.

Arriving at Montreal, the Fleming brothers sailed up the St Lawrence to Peterborough. At that time there was no map of Peterborough, so Fleming surveyed the town and made his own, following up by surveying other towns in the area. Skilled surveyors were in demand, and a railway company soon employed him. The Red River Railway Company was next to approach him, and Fleming spent the next ten years working for them. During that period he had the dream of helping build a railway right across Canada.

By 1867 he was chief engineer of the Inter-colonial Railway, a position he held until 1876. One of his major successes was to persuade the railways to build steel bridges rather than the traditional wooden variety. Wood was more readily available, and wooden bridges were cheaper and easier to build, but were also vulnerable to fire. Fleming was also instrumental in persuading the world's nations to accept Standard Time, mainly because his railway passed through several time zones.

As Chief Engineer of the Canadian Pacific Railway between 1872 and 1880, it was Fleming who surveyed the Yellowhead and Kicking Horse Pass among other routes. Lastly, Fleming was also a prime mover in the Australian Pacific Cable that created a telegraph and telephone link across the Pacific between Canada and Australia.

Fleming, Williamina (1857 – 1911)
Astronomer

Born in Dundee, Williamina Fleming was made a pupil teacher at the age of 14 and six years later married James Fleming, with whom she immigrated to the United States. They settled in Boston, but shortly after split up, leaving Williamina Fleming pregnant and alone in a strange land. However, Scotswomen were in demand as domestic staff for their education and honesty. Professor Edward Pickering, Director of Harvard College Observatory, employed the 22-year old as a cleaner.

The professor must have been a good employer, for Fleming named her son Edward Pickering Fleming in his honour. She must have been an equally good employee, for he promoted her to general clerk. Fleming seemed to have found her niche in the observatory and before she was twenty-six she was responsible for the photographic library. The 19th century development of photography had enabled astronomers to study the stars in more detail than ever before and while his countrymen were taming the West, Pickering was exploring the final frontier of space. As Fleming studied the maps and classified the stars, she gained knowledge and skill to become the most notable female astronomer of the century.

At a time when female scientists were a rarity, Fleming lectured to her peers at the Chicago World Fair of 1893. Speaking about 'A Field for Woman's Work in Astronomy,' Fleming did not just theorise, but employed women in her library.

By 1899 Fleming was the first female Curator of Astronomical Photography at Harvard. She had an all-female staff of twelve, who she ruled with an iron discipline as she sought for perfection that few could find. These women worked long hours as they pored over the 190,000 photographic plates that were gradually unlocking the secrets of the heavens. Each of the tens of thousands of stars had to be catalogued and positioned. The woman who had left formal education at fourteen had progressed to complex mathematical equations, lecturing and personnel skills, while still caring for her son.

Lacking computers or calculators, Fleming analysed thousands of unrelated facts as she prepared the *Harvard Annals* for publication. Overall, Fleming classified 10351 stars, but also made other contributions to science. She discovered a third of the 22 then known novae, 52 nebulae and 222 variable stars. In 1912 her *Stars having Peculiar Spectra* was published, possibly the best astronomical work written by a woman up to that date.

In 1906 Fleming became the first ever United States citizen to become an honorary member of the Royal Astronomical Society, as well as an Honorary Fellow of Wellesley College. French and American Astronomical societies also vied for her membership and after her death in 1911; the Astronomical Society of Mexico awarded her a medal for her amazing work.

Forbes, Bertie Charles (1880 – 1954)

Magazine proprietor

Born in New Deer, Aberdeenshire, Forbes immigrated to the United States as a young man. In 1904 he began a career in New York journalism, in which he became famous. Forbes began to publish the *Forbes*

Magazine of Business, which became one of the most respected magazines in the United States. His son continued the business as Forbes, a self made millionaire, retired. He was buried in New Jersey but later his body was brought back to New Deer for reburial.

Forbes, General John (1710 – 1759)
Soldier, founder of Pittsburgh
Born in Fife, John Forbes was trained as a physician but preferred the military life. Joining the army in 1735, by 1745 he was lieutenant colonel of the Scots Greys, fighting in Europe during the War of Austrian Succession. At the end of 1757, with the Seven Years War in full swing, Forbes was appointed brigadier general, taking part in the expedition against Louisburg in North America.

Known as 'The Head of Iron' for his stubborn nature, Forbes made his mark in North America. As Washington's commander, he allowed the Colonial colonel time to woo and win Martha Custis as his wife. In 1758 he commanded the force that took Fort Duquesne, where George Washington led the Virginians. British forces under General Braddock had suffered a severe defeat in the area, with Colonials and Highlanders tortured and killed by the Indians and French. George Washington had escaped the slaughter. The area was of vital importance, for the French intended creating a line of forts from Upper Canada to the mouth of the St Lawrence that would cut off any British westward expansion.

By the time he entered the wilderness, Forbes he was severely ill and had to be carried in a litter, but still directed the operations that defeated the French and captured the fort. Forbes altered the name to Fort Pitt, after William Pitt, and made treaties with the local Indian tribes before returning to Philadelphia.

Forbes-Mackay, Alastair (1878-1914)
Soldier, surgeon and explorer
Born in Argyll, Forbes-Mackay served in the Boer War as a soldier, where he fought beside Baden-Powell. Joining the Navy as a surgeon, Shackleton included him in the South Polar Expedition of 1908-1909.

He had a double function in the Antarctic, for his primary task was to look after the shaggy Manchurian ponies, while his surgical duties were secondary.

While in the Antarctic Forbes-Mackay climbed Mount Erebus and in 1909 he was also part of a three-man party that was first to reach the Southern Magnetic Pole.

Forbes-Mackay was included in Stefansson's Arctic expedition of 1914, when he died.

Forrest, John (1873 – 1932)
Botanist and plant collector
Born in Falkirk in Stirlingshire, Forrest was trained as a pharmacist in Kilmarnock, then at the herbarium at the Royal Botanical Garden in Edinburgh. While working in Edinburgh, Sir Isaac Bayley Balfour selected him to collect plants from China. His remit was more for decorative than scientific purposes, for the plants were destined for a Liverpool merchant who wanted to create a garden of exotic plants.

In 1904 Forrest travelled to the virtually unexplored Chinese province of Yunnan. It was an excellent choice, for this region is prolific with plants such as rhododendrons, gentians and primulas. Forrest returned many of his specimens to Edinburgh to be identified. On his seven expeditions to China between 1904 and 1932, he took an impressive number of photographs, which are held in the Royal Botanical Garden in Edinburgh.

While working in southwest China, Forrest operated from a French Christian mission. There was the occasional drama, as in 1905 when Tibetan bandits attacked the French mission. In the ensuing massacre, 68 of the 80 occupants were killed, but Forrest escaped. Dressed as a Chinese native, he survived hunger and privation for three weeks, knowing that the alternative was slavery or death.

To finance his expeditions, Forrest persuaded people to sponsor him. In return he would bring back plant seeds for his sponsors or name newly discovered plant species after them. He became probably the foremost plant collector of the early 20th century.

In all Forrest collected some 31,000 specimens, many of which are now common in Britain's gardens. The Royal Botanical Garden in Edinburgh benefited most, having the largest collection of Chinese plants outside of China. However, Forrest did not just collect plants. He was also interested in mammals, birds and insects. The golden-breasted fulvetta bird has the Latin name of *alcippe chryosotis forresti* in his honour.

Having just completed his seventh and last expedition in 1932, Forrest died of a heart attack at Tengchong. He was only 58 years old.

Fortune, Robert (1813 – 1880)
Horticulturist

Born in Edrom, Berwickshire, Fortune's first position was at the Edinburgh Royal Botanical Garden. From there he moved to the Horticultural Society in Chiswick. In 1843 he travelled to the Far East, particularly China, for the London Botanical Society. Fortune perceived that Shanghai would become 'a place of vast importance.'

First and foremost, Fortune was a plant collector, discovering many new species, which he subsequently brought into Britain. However he was also instrumental in introducing tea planting into the North West Provinces of India.

Among his discoveries were the double yellow rose, the Japanese anemone and the fan palmed *Chamaerops Fortineii*. He published *Yeddo and Pekin* in 1863.

Fraser, Peter (1884 – 1950)
Prime minister of New Zealand

Born in Fearn, Easter Ross, Fraser was apprenticed to a carpenter but continued to educate himself, becoming particularly interested in economics and politics. When he was only sixteen years old, Fraser was secretary of the Fearn Liberal Association. He joined the Independent Labour Party in 1908 and two years later immigrated to New Zealand.

Fraser worked as a labourer in the docks and became involved in union activity. In time he became President of the Auckland Labourers Union. Joining the New Zealand Socialist Party, Fraser moved to Wellington and became secretary of the Social Democratic Party.

Life in New Zealand was not always smooth, for Fraser was arrested for a breach of the peace, and then became heavily involved in creating the Labour Party. At a time when the cream of New Zealand's manhood was fighting at Galipolli, Fraser protested about any New Zealand involvement in the First World War. In 1916 he was arrested for opposing conscription, and jailed for a year.

In 1919 Fraser was elected MP for Wellington and the following year he married Janet Munro. He became party president and proved his pragmatism by dropping some Labour policies that were opposed by the majority of New Zealanders, despite Union objections.

When Labour came to power in 1935, Fraser was appointed Minister of Health and then Minister of Education. Rising to lead the party, he was elected Prime Minister during the crucial years of 1940 and 1949. As such he guided New Zealand through the Second World War and in the immediate aftermath. Perhaps Fraser abandoned some of his principles when he introduced conscription and press censorship, and lengthened working hours, but desperate times were grim and the Japanese were more of the threat to New Zealand in 1942 than the Germans had ever been between 1914 and 1918.

In 1944 Fraser was given the freedom of Edinburgh. He said "I want to thank the people of Edinburgh and Scotland for their overwhelming hospitality extended to our boys from New Zealand when they were privileged to come here in the darkest hour that was the greatest in the history of the United Kingdom. There is nowhere on earth our men are received with greater friendship or are more at home than in Scotland."

Fraser brought New Zealand a new respect in the world stage and was re-elected after the war, when he also began to address Maori issues.

Fraser, William, (1784 –1835)

Colonial administrator

As a young man, William Fraser joined the Honourable East India Company. After graduating from Fort William College in Calcutta in 1806, he became Assistant to the Resident at Delhi. At a time when there was little division between Indian and Briton, Fraser was fascinated by Indian culture. He was a political agent during the Nepal War of 1814/15, being wounded at Kalunga and founding one of the earliest regiments of Gurkha troops.

Fraser's next assignment was as Commissioner to the Sultan of Garwhal, but he was also commissioned into **Skinner**'s Horse. He was perfectly suited to that superb body of cavalry, being noted as "half Asiatick in his habits but in other respects a Scotch Highlander." Fraser lived in the Indian manner, dressing and behaving as a Mughal noble with a harem of local women, a brood of half Scottish, half Indian children and enough affection for the local culture to converse with Ghalib, perhaps the greatest Urdu poet of his time. If more men had acted like William Fraser, the horrors of the Mutiny may never have occurred.

Frickleton, Samuel VC (1891 –1917)

New Zealand soldier

Born in Scotland, Frickleton immigrated to the town of Blackball in Westland while young. He was a coal miner and joined the army when his adopted country became involved in the Great War. Frickleton became a Lance Corporal in the 3rd battalion, New Zealand Rifles. In July 1917 he was as Messines when two German machine gun nests were harassing his regiment. Single-handed, Frickleton attacked and the citation for his Victoria Cross spoke of his 'magnificent courage and gallantry' in subduing both machine guns. Unfortunately, Frickleton was killed later that year.

Gallagher, Thomas (1851 – 1925)

Doctor and terrorist

Born in Glasgow of Irish ancestry, Gallagher graduated in medicine. He immigrated to the United States, where he worked as a doctor in

Brooklyn, New York in 1875. Simultaneously, he joined the Fenian organisation that was intent in causing trouble in Canada.

Returning to Britain in 1883, he was involved in a terrorist bombing campaign in London, for which he was arrested. Released in 1896, Gallagher was judged insane and later committed to a secure sanatorium in New York, where he died.

Galt, Sir Alexander Tulloch (1817 – 1893)
Politician

Alexander Galt immigrated to Canada in 1835. Galt was a director of the British American Land Company and made money on the South Alberta coalfield as well as founding the town of Lethbridge, Alberta with its original name of Coalbanks.

Entering politics, Galt became finance minister between 1858 and 1862 and again between 1864 and 1866. He was also High commissioner in Britain between 1880 and 1883 and became known as one of the 'Fathers of Confederation.'

Garden, Mary (1874 – 1967)
Soprano

Born in Aberdeen as Mary Davidson, Garden's, parents took her to the United States as a young child. After studying music in Chicago and Paris, she was called upon to take the title role in Charpentier's *Louise* at the Opera Comique due to the illness of the lead. Her performance was so successful that it formed the basis of her subsequent career.

In 1902 Garden took the role of Melisande in *Pelleas et Melisande*, and the following year the composers Massenet and Erlanger created roles specifically for her. Between 1902 and 1903 she was prominent at Covent Garden, playing Salome, Carmen, Juliet and Violetta.

From 1907 until 1927 Garden sang at the Chicago Grand Opera. She also directed the opera from 1921 to 1922. In 1939, Garden returned to Scotland, where she spent the rest of her life.

Gardiner, Frank (1830 - 1895)

Australian bushranger

Born as Francis Christie, Gardiner left Scotland at the age of five. His family settled in the Australian bush, where Gardiner grew up learning how to ride and shoot. Even as a youngster, he was wild, stealing horses and cattle, so that it was no surprise when he became a bushranger in 1861. Gardiner was the leading light of the bushranging gang to which the famous Ben Hall belonged. In 1861 his gang robbed a gold convoy at Eugowra Rocks, escaping with £12,000 of gold and banknotes. Gardiner fled to Queensland, where he ran a store until the police traced him. Convicted and sentenced to 32 years in jail, he was released after eight years, provided he left the colony. He sailed to California and bought a saloon in San Francisco, where he is presumed to have died.

Gascoine, Sir Charles (d 1806)
Russian Ironmaster

Born in Scotland, Gascoine was the son of Woodroffe Gascoigne and the Honourable Grizel Elphinstone. Gascoigne had been manager of the Carron Iron Works when the company hit financial difficulties. It was **Admiral Greig** of the Russian Navy, who suggested to the Empress Catherine that Gascoigne could be useful.

Gascoigne and his key workers crossed over to Russia, constructed an ironworks at Petrozovodsk and took over the mines at Olonetz. More successful in Russia than in Scotland, Gascoigne was created a Councillor as well as a Knight of St Vladimir and died a rich man in St Petersburg.

Gibson, John (fl 1808)
Prussian Political agent

John Gibson was the brother of Sir James Gibson Craig of Riccarton. He worked in Potsdam in the early nineteenth century, but became a member of the Prussian court. Gibson was with King Frederick William III when he fled to Konigsberg in 1807. He also tutored the Crown Prince, later King Frederick William IV, in English, and was deeply involved in Tugenbund, a secret society dedicated to organising Prussian resistance against Napoleon Bonaparte.

When the Napoleonic wars were finished, Gibson seems to have travelled to Rome, where he acted as an unofficial political spy for Prussia.

Gilbert, Captain David, (fl 1600)
Mercenary and adventurer
A mercenary soldier, Gilbert served first Csar Boris Goodunov, and then was one of the 300 strong bodyguards to his successor, the 'False' Dmitri. When the second Dmitri assumed power, he intended to drown 52 foreigners, including Gilbert. The Scot was one of a group who swam the Oka River to plead for their lives with Dmitri's Polish wife, Maryna Mniszek.

Pardoned, Gilbert allegedly fought for Poland, raiding in Russia. When the Russians captured him, King James VI pleaded for his life. Gilbert was again reprieved and travelled back to Britain, but later sailed again to Russia, where he vanishes from recorded history.

Gille-Brigde Albanach (fl 1218)
Crusader and bard
A Gaelic bard, Gille Brigde is chiefly remembered for his poem *A ghilli, gabhus an anstiur* that describes the men of the Fifth Crusade sailing between Acre and Damietta. 'Lad who takest the helm; you travel often to unknown lands,' he wrote. Gille Brigde had travelled from Scotland, presumably by sea, and seems to have remained with the crusading army for the duration of the campaign. The return journey was by land. His companion, the bard Muiredhach Albanach, wrote the memorable line 'Far is Rome from Lochlong', which smacks of homesickness when abroad.

Gilroy, John, (1794 – 1869)
First English speaking resident in California
Born John Cameron in Scotland around 1794, John Gilroy was a seaman who landed at Monteray in 1814. Changing his name from

Cameron to Gilroy, that of his mother, he was baptised Juan Bautista Gilroy. In 1821 he married Maria Clara, and became a merchant in soap, onions and meal from his own mill. Hearing of his hospitality, settlers came to the area, and the United States Army appropriated his horses during the American invasion of the 1840s. The town of Gilroy, California is named after him.

Glass, Corporal William (1786 – 1853)
'Governor' of Tristan da Cunha

Glass was born at Kelso in the Scottish Borders. His first position was as a gentleman's servant to a landed family in Alnwick in northern England. According to folklore, he was jilted by a girl and joined the Royal Artillery, being posted to the Cape of Good Hope at the age of 19. He was employed as an officer's servant, promoted to corporal and in 1814 married the thirteen-year-old Maria Magdalena Leenders. Glass's officers must have held a high opinion of his character to allow his marriage, whether Leenders was Cape Dutch or, as was rumoured, of Cape Coloured origins.

1816 Glass and Maria were sent to the island of Tristan da Cunha, in charge of Hottentot artillery drivers. The island's garrison was intended to thwart any French attempt to release Bonaparte from St Helena, but when the army withdrew, Glass decided to remain behind. His officers granted permission and he became the patriarch of this tiny colony. His wife, not yet sixteen and their year old child also remained on the island.

Glass was a member of the Church of England, renowned for his generosity. His family expanded to sixteen children, all of whom survived, which is remarkable in itself, and he entered in a partnership with two civilians to own and run all that was valuable on the island. They agreed to share everything, including labour, and to have a settlement of equals. Glass continued to govern the island on these lines as the shipwrecked seamen and others joined the settlement. He is remembered as a gentleman who wore a Scots bonnet and who welcomed each new arrival to his island.

Glen, James (1701 – 1777)
Colonial Governor

Born in Linlithgow, Glen studied Roman law at Leiden in the Netherlands. A local councillor, he was sometime Provost of Linlithgow as well as Keeper of the Royal Palace and of Blackness Castle. He was also involved in customs duties.

Glen's appointment to the governorship of South Carolina may have been due more to influence than to ability; for he said that the Earl of Wilmington had 'procured for me the governorship of Carolina.' Presumably his marriage to the illegitimate daughter of the earl helped. It is also possible that his sister, a mistress of the then Prime Minister, Sir Robert Walpole, could have spoken for him.

Glen proved a successful, long-lasting governor. He managed Indian Affairs very well, creating a peace treaty between the Iroquois and the Catawbas, and between Catawbas and Natchez. He also purchased land for the expanding colony from the Cherokees, while always arguing for the royal prerogative in what was a royal colony.

Gloag, Helen (1750 – c1792)
Empress of Morocco

Helen Gloag was born near Muthill in Perthshire. At nineteen, she decided to immigrate to the American colonies. When Moorish corsairs captured Helen's ship she was taken to the port of Salle and became the slave of Ibn Abdullah, the Sultan of Morocco, who soon promoted her from concubine to his fourth wife and Empress.

Gloag used her position to help fellow captives. When corsairs snatched the English woman Mrs Crisp in Minorca, it was probably Gloag that obtained her release. Gloag seems to have had great authority with the Sultan, perhaps even persuading him to introduce William Lempriere, an English doctor, into the country. Unfortunately, Dr Lempriere did not meet Gloag, who may have been at Fez, where wives over thirty were put out to grass.

It is possible that it was also Gloag who persuaded the Sultan to ban the export of African slaves from the country, long before European nations prohibited the slave trade. The Sultan also began to release British subjects that had been captured at sea. Sallee rovers no longer ranged from Malta to Iceland in their quest for captives. Instead, the Sultan modernised the economy of his country by entering trade agreements with Britain.

Gloag brought up her two sons as best she could, and kept in touch with her Scottish relatives. However, circumstances deteriorated in 1790 when Sultan Mohammed died. Gloag might have hoped that one of her sons would take the throne, but instead Mulai Yazeed, a half brother, hacked his way to power. In the inevitable civil war, Gloag sought to save her sons by sending them to one of the Christian monasteries.

The British took an interest in Moroccan affairs, particularly as there was a British woman involved. The Royal Navy prepared for action and a British officer crossed to investigate. However, assassins murdered both of Gloag's sons before the British arrived, so instead the Navy helped Yazeed raid the Spanish colony in Ceuta.

By 1793 Yazeed was dead. It is unlikely that we will ever know Gloag's fate, but her place in history is assured, for few Scotswomen have risen to be empress of a foreign nation.

Glover, Thomas Blake (1838 – 1911)
The Scottish Samurai

Born in Fraserburgh, Thomas Blake Glover was the son of the Chief Coastguard. After his education he found employment as a merchant with Jardine Matheson, travelling the world at a time when the frontiers were expanding and optimism was at a peak. He settled in Nagasaki, Japan, shortly after that nation opened her doors to the West and at the age of 23 started his own company. In 1863 he built his house, which remains the oldest western building in Japan. Glover rose to prominence in Japan, helping to industrialise the country and enabled the samurai remove the Shogun, their military leader.

After ordering three ships for the fledgling Japanese Navy from Aberdeen, Glover created his own shipbuilding company by importing the Kusuge dock from Aberdeen. This company developed into the Mitsubishi Company. He also brought the first railway and mechanised coalmine to Japan, while recommended that young Japanese should be educated in modern practices, sending many to Britain. His brewing company grew into the largest in Japan.

Marrying a Japanese lady named Tsura, whom many believe to be the original Madam Butterfly, Glover was the first non-Japanese to be awarded the Order of the Rising Sun, and the place where he lived, known as Glover Garden, is a major tourist attraction.

Goldie, John (1793 –1886)
Naturalist
Born in Kirkoswald in Ayrshire, Goldie was always interested in nature, and worked at the Botanical Garden in Glasgow, where Sir William Hooker taught him botany. In 1815 he married Margaret Dunlop with whom he spent much of his life.

Goldie's first major botanical expedition was in 1817 when he visited North America, returning two years later. Later trips took him to Siberia and Russia, but it was to Ayr in Upper Canada that he brought his family in 1844. He is chiefly remembered for his *Diary of a Journey through Upper Canada and Some of the New England States in 1819* and his discovery of the Canadian plant *Aspidium Goldianum* that was named after him.

Gordon, Patrick (1635 – 1699)
Russian General
Patrick Gordon was born in Auchleuchries in Aberdeenshire. At a time when religion divided Scotland, the Gordons were Catholics and Stuarts. Sent abroad to complete his education, Gordon began training as a Jesuit priest, but after two years at a Catholic Prussian college he slipped secretly away and joined the Protestant Swedish army. He was nineteen years old. In 1656 Gordon took part in the Swedish war with Poland. When the Poles captured him outside Warsaw he changed his allegiance to join them, only to rejoin the Swedes when they took the city. Back in the Swedish army, he was captured again while foraging,

and only the interception of a Fransiscan monk saved him from being executed.

When peace broke out in the north, Gordon offered his sword to Austria, who refused the honour, and then to Russia. Legend claims that he exaggerated his CV, and the Russians employed him as a major in the army. He joined the army of Csar Alexis, which already had a Scottish Legion among its mercenary troops. A pragmatic man, Gordon led his men to quell rioting Muscovites so effectively that the Csar promoted him to lieutenant colonel. In early 1665 he married Catherine Von Bockhoven, a fellow Catholic whose contacts among the foreign residents would have been invaluable.

The Csar seemed to trust Gordon, sending him as envoy on a trade mission to Charles II in London. A few years later the Csar sent Gordon as envoy to Scotland. When he was not engaged in diplomatic missions, Gordon learned all he could about the art and science of war, ballistics and fortifications. He also adapted himself to merge with the suspicious Muscovites. When his wife died, Gordon married again, to Elizabeth Roonuer, and their union proved successful and enduring.

In 1677 Russian armies clashed with Turkish forces along the Dnieper River and Gordon played a notable role. As commander of Kiev, a city-fortress that defended Ukraine from Poles and Turks, he was promoted to Major General and Chief Engineer, one of the most important foreign-born soldiers in the Russian army. There was trouble at court, however, as Csar Alexis died, then Csar Theodore. Csarina Sophia took power as regent until her brother Peter became of age. Sophia refused Gordon permission to return to Scotland. She did, however permit him to travel to England, where King James VII wrote him a request to leave Russian service. Still Sophia refused. Instead Gordon had to sign a document stating he would never leave Russia.

Another Turkish war in 1687 was less successful, with half the Russian army lost in a bad defeat. The Russian commander, Galitzen, still accepted rich awards, as did Gordon, albeit with some guilt. Now a full general, Gordon clearly saw that there was trouble brewing between supporters of Peter and Sophia. No friend of the Csarina, Gordon still fought his best, but could do little when the Russians suffered another defeat in the Crimea.

When Gordon supported Peter against his sister, the new Csar made the Scot his military advisor. Csar and general became friendly, with Gordon helping coin the term 'Peter the Great', and the Csar making him a Rear Admiral. However, Gordon was never to return home. The Glorious Revolution put the protestant William of Orange on the British throne, and William would never have accepted the Jacobite Gordon back in Scotland.

Gordon's last campaign was a success. Due to Gordon's strategy of building fortresses to block and capture the town of Azov, Peter gained control of the Dnieper Cossacks and enlarged the boundaries of Russia.

Two years later Gordon was again in the saddle as he defeated an attempted revolution by Sophia's supporters. That was his last military campaign. He spent his final months supporting the cause of Catholics in Russia and died in 1699, with the Csar attending his Moscow funeral.

Gordon, Admiral Thomas (c 1680 – 1741)
Russian Admiral

Born in Scotland, Gordon was a captain in the tiny Scottish Navy at the time of the 1707 Union. Although he was appointed a captain in the Royal Navy, Gordon's Jacobite past counted against him and he left, to live for a while in the Netherlands. From there he entered the Russian service of Peter the Great, becoming a Captain-commander of the Russian Navy in 1717.

Two years later Gordon was a Rear Admiral, and by 1721 he was in command of the Kronstadt squadron of six battleships, three frigates and two small vessels. With this force he skirmished with the Danish Admiral Sievers. Personal tragedy hit that same year when his wife, Margaret Ross, died, to be buried near the grave of the Csar's sister in St Petersburg. In 1724 Gordon captured Danzig for Russia and three years later became Governor and Commander in Chief at Kronstadt.

Resigning this position, he was reinstated in 1733, and continued there until his death in 1741.

Gowans, William (1803 – 1870)
'Eccentric Antiquarian of Nassau Street'

Born in Lesmahagow, Lanarkshire, William Gowans immigrated to the United States in 1821, where he worked on a Mississippi flat boat. When he was 25 he established a bookstall in New York, while living with the family of Edgar Allan Poe. Unfortunately, Gowans was more of a book collector than a businessman, and kept most of the books, leaflets and pamphlets that he purchased. Eventually settling on a site in Nassau Street, he also re-published historic books on Americana, but could be extremely rude to those customers to whom he took a dislike. When Gowans died, he had nearly 300,000 books in his shop, with eight tons of pamphlets and leaflets that were sold as waste paper.

Grant, George (c1840-1878)
Introduced Aberdeen Angus cattle into the United States

Born in the Highlands, Grant seemed a natural entrepreneur. While he was working in the cloth trade, Prince Albert became terminally ill. Grant immediately invested heavily in buying black crepe. When Prince Albert died, Grant nearly monopolised the frenzy of mourning that erupted across Britain.

Grant hoped for land of his own, but with money at his back, he wanted something grander than just a small farm. After reading literature that extolled the American West, he crossed the Atlantic and toured the prairies, searching for a site for an estate and a new colony. By 1872 he had bought some thirty thousand acres of prime grassland in western Kansas.

With the land purchased, Grant advertised for settlers from Scotland. He hoped to found a colony, but also to make money with quality sheep and cattle raising. Unfortunately, Grant died before his dream could rise to fruition. The Scottish colony dissolved before a mixture of drought, grasshoppers and Russian settlers.

On the credit side, Grant has been recognised as the man who first introduced Aberdeen Angus cattle to America.

Grant, James Augustus (1827 –1892)
Soldier and explorer

The son of a minister, Grant was born in Nairn and educated at Marischal College, Aberdeen. Joining the Indian Army at the age of nineteen, he rose to the rank of Colonel, taking part in the battle of Gujerat in the Sikh War and being wounded during the siege of Lucknow in the Indian Mutiny. He was also involved in the Abyssinian campaign of 1868, but it was his African explorations of 1860 to 1863 that made him famous.

Together with the Englishman, John Speke, Grant travelled to find the source of the Nile. He made significant botanical discoveries on the journey, during which he suffered an infected leg and was virtually abandoned by Speke for months. On his return he wrote an account of his adventures *A Walk Across Africa*. When Speke died in tragic circumstances, Grant became one of the most important authorities on African exploration.

In character, Grant was more modest than most explorers. General Gordon had little time for 'that old creature, Grant', but Gordon was a paragon, especially, perhaps, in his own eyes. Modest Grant was, but he had gained a medal through bravery in the terrible battles of the Mutiny, and had survived hardships in Africa that would have killed a lesser man. If he lacks the colour of some other explorers, he matched them in bravery and endurance. More importantly, he also survived to live a long life.

Greig, Sir Samuel (1735 – 1788)
Russian Admiral

Like so many Scottish seamen, Greig was a Fife man, born in Inverkeithing. His father was a shipowner, so Greig, after a rudimentary education, spent his youth working in the coasting trade. Sailing small vessels along the East Coast and in the North Sea, Greig learned navigation and seamanship. He signed into the Royal Navy as a master's mate and took part in the capture of Goree, a French held island off West Africa.

Under the overall command of Admiral Hawke, Greig served in *Royal George* in the Seven Years War at the blockade of Brest and the important battle of Quiberon Bay in European waters. Further afield he saw action at the capture of Havana, one of the major Spanish bases in the Caribbean.

When the war ended in 1763 the Royal Navy reduced its manpower and there were few prospects for a penniless Scots master's mate with no connections. However Catherine the Great, Empress of Russia was actively recruiting naval officers so Greig transferred to Russian service. His service record ensured that he was immediately accepted as a lieutenant, and soon became a captain. Within six years he commanded a squadron in the Mediterranean, where Russia faced her ancient Turkish enemy. Greig was instrumental in defeating the Turkish fleet at Cesme in 1770. Lieutenant Drysdale, another Scot, commanded his flotilla of fire ships.

Not surprisingly, Catherine promoted Greig to Rear Admiral and when in 1773 he defeated a force of ten Turkish ships with a far smaller force, Greig became a Vice Admiral.

However great his achievements in war, it was probably Greig's peacetime accomplishments that were more significant. Catherine appointed him grand admiral and governor of Kronstadt St Petersburg's naval base. He also became Knight of the Order of St Andrews, St George, St Vladimir and St Anne. Between 1774 and 1778 he reorganised, trained and disciplined the Russian Navy. He found it a third rate service, not to be compared to the Royal Navy of Hawke. After his reforms the Russian Navy was in far better condition, able to defeat the Turks and compete with the Swedes in northern waters.

Greig also introduced many Scottish officers into the Russian navy, which proved awkward when Catherine joined the Armed Neutrality against Britain during the American Revolutionary War. Sweden, however, was Russia's main enemy in the north. Greig led the infant Russian navy against the powerful Swedes near Hogeland in the Gulf of Finland. It was a day of vicious gales that tested the nerve of both Swedes and Russians in the island-scattered gulf as they cannonaded each other until night ended the battle. Both sides withdrew; Greig threw a number of inefficient Russian officers into prison and sailed out again, seeking the Swedes.

Blockading them in their base at Svenborg, the naval base of Helsinki, Greig remained at sea. He died on duty and was awarded a state funeral. He is remembered as the father of the Russian Navy, and his son, Alexis created the Russian Black Sea fleet that faced the British during the Crimean War.

Hallidie, Andrew Smith (1836 – c1890)
Inventor, builder of San Francisco's first cable car

Born in Dunfermline, Hallidie immigrated to California in 1853. Although he was unsuccessful in his search for gold, he became a prosperous inventor and engineer. In 1855 he constructed a flume that spanned the middle fork of the American River, following that by building various flumes and suspension bridges in the Pacific area over the next twelve years.

Around 1857 Hallidie became the first steel-wire rope manufacturer on the west cost, and in 1867 he invented a rigid suspension bridge. He was also the creator of the Hallidie Ropeway, which made cable railroads possible. Hallidie's method of hauling streetcars up steep slopes by an underground endlessly flowing cable became common throughout the United States. In 1873 Andrew Hallidie built the first cable car in San Francisco and he was also involved in founding that city's first public libraries.

Hamilton, Alexander (1755 – 1804)
Controversial secretary of the US Treasury

Hamilton was born illegitimately to a Scottish father named James Hamilton and a woman named Rachel Lavien in the island of Nevis in the Caribbean. His father left when Hamilton was ten, but a clergyman raised funds to educate him in the American colonies, where in 1777 he became an aide-de-camp to George Washington. Present at the battles of Monmouth, Germantown and Brandywine, Hamilton married Elizabeth Schuyler in 1780. The marriage produced eight children.

Hamilton was an important force in creating the Constitution and was the first United States Secretary of the Treasury. He created an effective financial strategy that put the United States on its feet. However, as leader of the Federalist Party, he was opposed to Thomas Jefferson, who was one of the men who accused him of misusing treasury funds. Nevertheless, it was another political opponent, Aaron Burr, who challenged Hamilton to a duel after losing an election to be governor of New York. Burr's shot killed Hamilton.

Hector, Sir James (c1840 – 1900)
Canadian explorer

Born and brought up in Edinburgh, Hector discovered one of the first and best passes through the Canadian Rocky Mountains. Named Kicking Horse Pass, it became the route of the Canadian Pacific Railway through the Rockies. Moving to New Zealand, Hector became the Director of the Geological Survey of that country.

Hepburn, Sir John (1598 – 1636)
Mercenary soldier

As the younger son of the family, John Hepburn had to make his own way in the world. When he heard that Sir Andrew Craig was recruiting soldiers, Hepburn, at 22 years old, was quick to volunteer. Craig was drumming up an army for Frederick, the Elector Palatinate of Bohemia in the war between Protestant and Catholic, Habsburg, Sweden and France.

Although Hepburn was a Catholic, he had no scruples about fighting in the Protestant cause, perhaps because the Elector was married to Elizabeth, the daughter of King James VI of Scotland. The enemy was the Emperor Frederick the Second of Austria and Craig found 1500 volunteers in a Scotland plagued by peace.

Inexperienced as he was, Hepburn was soon commanding a company of pikemen, that acted as bodyguard to the Elector. By November of that year the Scots were in action at the Battle of White Hills, facing an Austrian advance. They must have wondered why they had bothered as the Elector dug in his spurs and fled. Used to commanders who led from the front, the Scots cut their way free and searched for a leader of higher quality. Gustavus Adolphus, the King of Sweden, was a natural choice. He was Protestant, a warrior and he was building up a formidable fighting army.

Gustavus was one of the greatest military modernisers of his age, changing the old style unwieldy masses of infantry into mobile battalions of pikemen and musketeers. He also trained his cavalry to charge home with the sword rather than canter forward and discharge their pistols. While Hepburn could only agree with these reforms, he was less sure about the King's dislike for ornate clothing and flamboyant uniforms. Like many Scots, Hepburn enjoyed stylish dress, and like many of his generation, he was extremely vain.

Gustavus evidently tolerated this fault in Hepburn's character, for in 1625 he promoted the young Scot to command one of his Scottish regiments. As such, Hepburn took part in the Swedes ongoing war with Poland. Hepburn led his regiment in the relief of Mirtau near Riga, fighting in the forefront as 3500 Swedes and Scots repelled a 30,000 strong Polish army. Arranging his regiment around a prominent rock, Hepburn faced attack by Cossacks and Polish cavalry. 'Scottish arms,' the horsemen yelled, 'cannot abide the bite of the Polish wolves.'

In this case it was the Polish wolves that were bitten as Hepburn's Scottish infantry defended themselves for two dour days of blood and valour. With one in seven of his men dead, Hepburn would be relieved when the Poles eventually withdrew, with terrible casualties. It was a fine victory but only the beginning of Hepburn's career.

In 1627 Hepburn was present when Gustavus invaded Prussia. Again the Scots were in the forefront of the fighting, as they were when Gustavus attacked Lovinia. Peace with Poland left Gustavus as master of the Eastern Baltic, with one of the most successful armies in

Europe. Swedish garrisons in Prussian ports ensured a constant flow of tax revenue to the Crown, but when Cardinal Richelieu, of *Three Musketeers* fame, offered Gustavus 200,000 ducats a year if he invaded Germany, the Swedish king agreed.

Once again the Scots found themselves facing the Austrian Empire, but this time they were battle experienced and well led. Colonel Sir John Hepburn, in his gilded half armour was recognised as being among the best of them.

There were four Scottish regiments present when the army of Gustavus crossed into Pomerania in June 1630. Rather than a single regiment, Hepburn now commanded this Scottish Brigade that took the place of honour on the right of the line. Before his thirty-first birthday, Hepburn's Green Brigade was famed as one of the best fighting formations in Europe. In March 1631 they advanced into Pomerania, heading for Frankfurt –on-Oder. It was a tough fight as Hepburn stormed across the fosse, through the moat and over the high stone wall. With the gate blown in, Colonels Lumsden and **Monro** led the forlorn hope that took the town. Hepburn was wounded in this battle that shook all Europe, for there had never been such a surprise attack on a defended town.

The fighting and the victories continued. Hepburn led the Green Brigade in the charge that decided the battle of Breitenfeld. It was Hepburn's Scots who won the battle of Donauworth, but they took casualties in a black day at Nuremberg. Perhaps frustrated after his failure, perhaps harbouring resentment, Gustavus turned on Hepburn for his fancy armour and Catholic religion. Hepburn, whose pride matched his bravery, withdrew from Swedish service.

A mercenary without an army, Hepburn followed the old Scots route to France, where Richelieu and Louis XIII were pleased to renew a fragment of the Auld Alliance. Recruiting a further 2000 Scots, Hepburn augmented his regiment with Scottish soldiers who had long fought for France and got ready to renew the struggle with Imperial Austria.

The French marched into Lorraine, with Richelieu admiring Hepburn's military skill while jesting at his Scottish candidness and pride. Hepburn's men fought well, with Hepburn, as usual, irritating his allies by his arrogance while awing them with his courage. As the French and Scots prepared to assault Alsace, Hepburn rode to the front to check the breach for himself. An unknown defender, probably realising the importance of the man in the decorative half-armour, shot him in the neck.

Hepburn was buried in Toulon Cathedral, with an epitaph that stated 'the best soldier in Christendom and consequently, in the world.' It would have been interesting to see if Hepburn's presence during the soon-to-occur Civil Wars in Britain would have eclipsed Cromwell, Leslie and Montrose.

Hunter, John (1737 – 1821)
Naval officer and Australian administrator

Born in Leith, Hunter attended Aberdeen University, where he studied theology. At the age of 17 he joined the Royal Navy. After steady, if unspectacular promotion, in 1786 he became second captain on *Sirius*, the flagship of the First Fleet that was to create a penal colony in New South Wales. Hunter was now vastly experienced and more humane than many of his compatriots.

Arriving in New South Wales in 1788, the colonists realised that the land was not flowing with milk and honey. Rather than rich grassland there was scrub and eucalypt, peopled with tribesmen who brandished spears and shouted '*warra warra*,' "go away, go away!" Hunter helped prepare a plan of the proposed settlement at Sydney Cove, where the Governor's House, Hospital and church were carefully marked. Hunter also sailed around Cape Horn to Cape Town to obtain provisions to keep the colony alive. After a global circumnavigation, he returned to Sydney with a full cargo of wheat, flour and barley.

Hunter returned to Britain in 1792 but was back in Australia in September 1794, this time as the second ever Governor of the colony. He had to struggle to assert his authority over a domineering military presence, and to push Government policy in a colony that was already heading in its own direction. One of the many abuses that he attempted to quash was the illegal import of spirits. In the process he made bitter enemies and was recalled in 1800.

Nevertheless, during his time in office he sent Bass and Flinders on valuable voyages of exploration, and also ordered expeditions into the interior to locate new zoological and botanical specimens. His efforts saw an increase in the amount of land under cultivation and a rise in population. Hunter's journal is an invaluable guide to the early colony as well as an indication of the life and habits of the native peoples before and during the early contact with Europeans.

Hunter, Sir William Wilson (1840 – 1900)
Statistician

Born in Glasgow, Hunter was educated in Glasgow, Paris and Bonn. In 1862 he entered the Indian civil service, recently modernised after the Indian Mutiny and the collapse of the East India Company. Between 1866 and 1869 he was the superintendent of public instruction at Orissa, when he wrote *Annals of Rural Bengal* and *A Comprehensive Dictionary of the Non-Aryan Languages of India*.

From that position he was promoted to secretary of the Bengal government, then to secretary of the Government of India. In 1871, at the age of 31, he became director-general of the statistical department of India. It was Hunter who produced the colossal census of India in 1872. He retired in 1887, returned to Britain and wrote about India.

Jack, Gilbert (1578 –1628)
Academic

After graduating from Marischal College in Aberdeen, Jack travelled to the Lutherian University at Helmstadt, and then to Herborn, which offered him a position as lecturer. However, Jack decided to move on to Leiden in the Netherlands, where he studied medicine and lectured in philosophy.

In 1605 Jack became Professor of Logic, being appointed a 'Professor Ordinarus' in 1612. As well as philosophy, Jack lectured in physics, attaining his own chair in that subject in 1617. His teachings of metaphysics was not officially sanctioned by the university, but proved popular with his students. He married a Dutch woman, and between them raised ten children, and in 1621 refused an offer to teach moral philosophy in Oxford.

A leading scholar and humanist, Jack also wrote on medical matters and despite a dispute over his unorthodox humanist views that resulted in a temporary loss of his chair, taught at Leiden until his death.

Jardine, William (1784 – 1843)
Opium smuggler and businessman

Born at Lochmaben in Dumfriesshire, Jardine gained a diploma in medicine from the Royal College of Surgeons in Edinburgh. In 1802, at the age of eighteen, he joined the Honourable East India Company as a surgeon's mate. Jardine was proficient enough to rise to surgeon on a later voyage, but as trading was more profitable than the salary of a surgeon, Jardine went into partnership with a Bombay Parsee, bought a ship and entered the opium trade between India and China.

It was as the agent of the Parsee that Jardine first arrived in China in 1819. Although China had officially banned the opium trade, many mandarins co-operated with the British and other foreign merchants that openly defied the law. A good number of mandarins were addicted to opium, and their war junks would appear to threaten from a distance while allowing trade to continue unhindered. The Indian opium trade had probably begun in the 18th century and by the 1820s was so profitable that it has been estimated that one seventh of the East India Company's trade was in opium.

By 1830 Jardine had become the *Taipan*, or leading house, of the opium traders. Two years later Jardine and **James Matheson** set up a partnership that was to dominate Eastern trade for decades. At that time the British had no scruples about trading in opium, which Jardine referred to as 'the safest and most gentlemanlike speculation I am aware of.' Given the difference between the armament on a British vessel and a typical Chinese junk, the trade was certainly safe.

In 1833 the British government ended the centuries- long East India Company monopoly of the China trade, partly due to pressure from William Jardine and Kirkman Finlay of Glasgow. The firm of Jardine Matheson took full advantage as they began to export silks, rhubarb and cotton. In 1834 Jardine Matheson was also exporting tea for Melrose's of Leith.

China, however, continued to restrict trade, until Jardine Matheson and others encouraged the British government to declare war by claiming that the Chinese had persecuted them. Using his political and economic clout, Jardine requested the British government to force a passage up the Pearl River, but Britain lost prestige when two Royal Naval frigates ran aground. It was Jardine who campaigned for war and free trade, which meant the freedom to trade opium against the laws of China. As Charles Elliot and the Chinese authorities sought a compromise, the traders saw some of their profit dissolve in the smoke of burning opium. They pressed harder for war.

The cynical Opium War of 1839 to 1842 opened many Chinese ports to European shipping, and gained Hong Kong for the Empire. Jardine Matheson opened up trading centres in Hong Kong and Shanghai. Jardine also began a long lasting banking operation in London.

Jardine created a name for himself as an implacable businessman. The Chinese knew him as 'iron headed old rat,' and the British treated him with more respect than friendship. He was a natural businessman with a deep interest in politics and an appearance of arrogance, but once past the barriers he was a loyal friend.

Johnson, Ronald (1908 – 1961)
Speedway racer

Born at Duntochter, near Clydebank, Johnson immigrated to Australia in 1914 along with the rest of the family. Settling on a farm at Dwellingup in Western Australia, Johnson was more interested in mechanics and motorbikes than schoolwork. Riding a Harley Davidson

'peashooter' motor bicycle from the age of 17, Johnson soon graduated to the Claremont Racing track as a speedway rider. He quickly
became one of the finest riders in Australia and in 1928 accompanied
a group of Australians who exported the sport of speedway to the
United Kingdom.

By 1931 Johnson was World Champion and captain of the south
London New Cross Speedway team. He retained that position until
he was badly injured in 1949. One of the first speedway superstars,
Johnson enjoyed the trappings of his fame, with suits from Saville Row
and company from Hollywood to royal palaces. Not content with fast
bikes, Johnson also owned a luxury yacht. Unfortunately his lifestyle
took its toll. His two daughters left him even before his money ran out,
and his wife left shortly after. His speedway injuries barred him from
active service, but he did his bit for democracy as a stretcher-bearer
during the Second World War. Thereafter he found employment as an
aero engine mechanic, finally returning to Australia where he eked
out the final years of his life with no money and no motorbike licence.

He is remembered by the film *Once a Jolly Swagman*, where Dirk
Bogarde took the starring role, and the Ron Johnson Memorial Trophy,
which is raced for at Claremont, Western Australia.

Johnston, Gabriel (c1698 – 1752)

Colonial Governor

Born in the Scottish Lowlands, Johnston was educated at Edinburgh
and St Andrews University, where he also taught oriental languages
before moving to London in 1727. Six years later he was appointed
Royal Governor of North Carolina.

Johnston had a difficult time controlling the colony, which had been
used to low taxes and lax government, and struggled against vested
interest and unhelpful politicians. However, by encouraging immigration, particularly from Ulster and Scotland, he succeeded in tripling
the population from 30,000 to 90,000 souls. He also codified the laws
and erected coastal protection against pirates, French and Spanish.

In 1740 Johnston married Penelope Gollard, a woman who had accumulated much wealth by her previous three marriages. When she died, he married Frances Bunton, with whom he spent the remainder of his life.

Johnston, Major George (c1770 – c1840)
Soldier

Born in Annandale in Dumfriesshire, George Johnston entered the army. One of the first military men in Australia, he became a Major in the New South Wales Corps, a regiment that was primarily designed to keep the convicts in order. In 1793 Johnston obtained a grant of land in the colony, which he named Annandale. A noted womaniser, Johnston fathered six children to various mothers.

In 1804 many of the Irish convicts in New South Wales had been transported for taking part in the 1798 rebellion. The thousands of Irish who were transported were not treated well. In March 1804 many Irish convicts rebelled again. Grabbing whatever weapons they could, they marched on Sydney, singing Irish rebel songs and intent on vengeance. It was Major Johnston who led around sixty of the New South Wales Corps to confront the rebels.

Splitting his force in two, Johnston took thirty to Toongabbie and on to the Hawkesbury River. He met the insurgents at a small knoll.

The convict leaders, Phillip Cunningham and William Johnston stepped forward, hoping to parley. At once Major Johnston had them seized, then ordered his vastly outnumbered men to fire a volley and charge. The redcoats scattered the insurgents in minutes, with Major Johnston in the forefront. Twelve convicts were killed in the skirmish, three later hanged and others suffered variously.

Major Johnston was also instrumental in the Rum Rebellion of 1808, when he arrested Governor Bligh, of *Bounty* fame, because of his despotism. For six months Johnston acted the part of lieutenant governor, but when Bligh reached Britain, Johnston was expelled from his exalted position. He was later court martialled and removed from the army.

Johnston, Sir Reginald Fleming (1874 –1938)
Sinologist, tutor to Emperor of China

Born in Edinburgh, Johnston was educated at Edinburgh University and then at Magdalen College, Oxford. At the age of 24 he became a Hong Kong cadet, where he made a name for himself as an intelligent educator. Between 1919 and 1925 Johnston was a tutor of the Emperor of China. He was fascinated by Chinese culture and history and travelled extensively throughout the area.

Johnston, Samuel (1733-1816)
Creator of the 'Bloody Riots Act'

Born in Dundee, Johnston was the nephew of **Gabriel Johnston**, governor of North Carolina, who encouraged the family to immigrate to the colonies. Arriving in South Carolina in 1735, Samuel Johnston was educated at Yale, later studying law. An attorney by 1756, he was also elected to the Lower House of the general assembly where he represented Chowan Country from 1759 to 1775.

Johnston invested in land, buying a plantation that he named Hayes and in 1770 married Frances, with whom he had nine children, although only four reached adulthood.

Appointed governor of South Carolina, Johnston created the 'Bloody Riot Acts' that imposed the death penalty for illegal assemblies. Nevertheless, Johnston agreed with the American Revolutionary ideas, but rather than force, hoped for legal redress of the grievances. When it became obvious that a major split was inevitable, he threw his hat into the Revolutionary ring, being elected to the first three Provincial Congresses, being president of the third.

In 1780 he was a delegate on the Continental Congress, becoming a United States Senator after independence, as well as a Supreme Court Judge.

Jones, John Paul (1747 – 1792)
Father of the United States Navy

John Paul Jones was born as John Paul in 1747, son of a gardener beside the Solway Firth. At thirteen he went to sea and by the time he was seventeen was third mate of the slaver *King George.* After a couple of years he left the slaving trade and became master of the brigantine *John,* in which ship he had the ship's carpenter, Mungo Maxwell, flogged. When Maxwell later died, John Paul was imprisoned until an enquiry discovered that the carpenter had died of an unrelated fever.

After spending time in the Irish Sea, John Paul returned to the Atlantic as master of *Betsy.* Killing a mutineer, he fled to land he had inherited in Frederickshaven, Virginia and changing his name to John Paul Jones.

Shortly after the outbreak of the American Revolution, Jones joined the Continental Navy. As first lieutenant of *Alfred,* an ex-merchant ship of 30 guns, Jones was involved in action against HMS *Glasgow.* He acquitted himself well and was first appointed commander of *Providence,* then of *Alfred,* which he turned into a renowned commerce raider. However, when Jones became embroiled in naval politics he was removed from his command. He was idle for months until the naval hierarchy presented him with the 20-gun *Ranger.*

Based in France, in April 1778 Jones sank two British merchant ships in the Irish Sea. Foul winds spoiled an attempt to board the sloop HMS *Drake* in Belfast Lough, so Jones headed for Whitehaven, attacking the harbour with his two ship's boats. Jones spiked the guns of both defending batteries and withdrew, burning an unfortunate fishing boat by way of farewell.

In terms of major warfare, Jones' incursion was a pinprick. In terms of national prestige it was a disaster. To a nation whose boast was 'Britannia Rules the Waves,' any naval setback was of psychological importance. But Jones was not finished. On 23 April 1778 he anchored in Kirkcudbright Bay and attempted to kidnap the Earl of Selkirk. When it became obvious that the Earl was not at home, Jones' men stole his silver. Next day *Ranger* met HMS *Drake* in a straight fight. Within an hour Jones had soundly defeated the British and sent the captured sloop to Brest.

In August 1779 he put to sea as captain of the 40-gun *Bon Homme Richard,* the most powerful ship of a small squadron that included another American vessel and six French ships including the frigates *Alliance* and *Pallas.* After creating consternation in the Forth, Jones cruised down the British East Coast, hoping to capture the Baltic convoy. The frigate HMS *Serapis,* commanded by Captain Pearson, and the smaller *Countess of Scarborough* escorted the convoy. On the evening of 23 September 1779, the rival squadrons met off Flamborough Head. With the French proving more adept at commerce raiding than fighting, the combat condensed into two individual ship-to-ship contests. While *Pallas* closed with *Countess of Scarborough,* Jones engaged *Serapis.*

After an exchange of fire, Jones manoeuvred to close and board. When the vessels collided, *Bon Homme Richard*'s accurate musketry prevented Pearson from using his deck guns, but still the British had the edge. Now came a request for the American to surrender, and the celebrated reply.

"I have not yet begun to fight."

Bon Homme Richard had been reduced to a shambles, with some of her crew pleading to surrender, but *Serapis* was also badly damaged and on fire. It seemed that both ships would be destroyed until an American seaman ended the stalemate by tossing a grenade on to a pile of cartridges on the deck of *Serapis.* The resulting explosion caused terrible slaughter and *Serapis* surrendered.

Jones had won a notable victory but two days later *Bon Homme Richard* sunk. Jones took *Serapis* into the Texel. Although the glory had gone to Jones, Pearson's stand had enabled the Baltic convoy to escape. Perhaps if Jones had commanded a faster ship he might have evaded *Serapis* and cut out some of the merchantmen, thus damaging Britain's lifeline. Instead he created an enduring legend.

Jones travelled from the Texel to Paris and then to the United States. He was recommended to command *America,* at 70 guns the largest ship in the United States Navy, but instead she was handed over to France. The frustration mounted as Jones did not receive the prize money he had earned and his attempt to gain promotion to Rear Admiral failed. Disillusioned, he left the American Navy and returned to Europe.

Russia was always open to hungry naval officers and from useful service against the Turks as Rear Admiral in the Black Sea fleet; Jones was posted to the Baltic. From here things slid downhill. After an accusation of rape, Jones left Russia and died in Paris in July 1792 from jaundice and pneumonia. He is often remembered as the father of the United States Navy.

Keith, Francis Edward James (1696 – 1758)
Prussian Field Marshal

Born in the castle of Inverugie near Peterhead, Keith was a younger son of an ancient family. After an elementary education, he attended Aberdeen and Edinburgh University, where he pondered a career in law before deciding to become a soldier. He was on his way to London to become commissioned in the king's army when his brother George, Earl Marischal, persuaded him to join the Jacobite cause instead. Keith took part in the abortive battle of Sherrifmuir, and left Scotland when the 1715 Rising collapsed. Unable to sign on for the Swedish or Russian army, he moved to Paris to study mathematics.

When war broke out between Spain and Britain the Spanish planned an attack on Scotland, using disaffected Jacobites. James Keith was an officer in the 1719 expedition, which ended in the defeat at Glenshiel. Again he fled the country, enlisting in the Spanish army. He proved a good soldier, rising to colonel and fighting against Britain in the siege of Gibraltar. However, as a Protestant he could not reach general rank so he transferred to Russian service. Within a short time he was commanding the royal guards, and during the Polish War of 1733 he distinguished himself in the siege of Warsaw.

Promoted to Major General, Keith rose to command the Russian army in the Ukraine. Fighting disease as well as Poles, Turks and Tartars, Keith was wounded at the successful siege of Otchakoff in 1737. "I would rather lose ten thousand of my best soldiers than Keith," the Empress Catherine is reported to have said. The musket ball in his thigh turned septic, but a Parisian surgeon removed the cause and Keith returned to active service. In 1740 he was sent as an envoy to

London. Despite Keith's Jacobite history, George II received him, so Keith belatedly accepted that the Hanoverians were the established monarchs of Great Britain.

Promoted to be Governor of the Ukraine, Keith survived a change of rulers as he declined bribes and dispensed fair justice. In 1741 he was back at war, with Sweden the new enemy. Again Keith proved his skill, firstly by victory at Helsungforts, then by capturing the Aland Islands. Appointed the Russian ambassador to Stockholm, he was an honest, if direct, diplomat, but high placed Russians became jealous of his success.

By 1745, Keith was commander in chief of the Russian army, but peace was concluded before he could test his skill against the Prussians. There is a possibility that Empress Catherine took a fancy to Keith, for she is reported as saying that he was the only man who could "bring up a future heir of the throne." Perhaps this statement influenced the Russian elite to turn against Keith and in 1747 he transferred to Prussian service. King Frederick the Great appointed Keith a Field Marshal as well as Governor of Berlin.

Keith immediately made his mark by beginning a system of wargames in the Royal Military Academy and commanded the Prussian army during the 1756 invasion of Bohemia. Successful at the battle of Lobositz, he led 32,000 men at the less memorable battle of Prague, executed a neat defence of Olmutz and was instrumental in the victory against massive odds at Rossbach. In 1758 Keith was with the Prussian right wing when the Austrians launched an attack through thick mist. Heavily outnumbered, he sent a message to the king. "I shall hold out here to the last man and give the army a chance to assemble. We are in the hands of God and I doubt whether we shall see each other again."

His prediction was true. Mortally wounded, Keith refused to leave his men and died on the field. The Croats stripped and plundered his body but the Austrians, more chivalric, returned it to the Prussians. Frederick the Great was the chief mourner at his funeral.

Keith, Thomas (1786 –1815)

Scottish soldier, one of the last Mamlukes

Edinburgh born, Thomas Keith was an armourer with the 78th High-landers in the abortive expedition to Al-Mansoura in Egypt in 1807. Captured and enslaved by the Turks, he converted to Islam under the name Ibrahim Aga, fought a duel and was sentenced to death but escaped and became a commander of the Mamluke cavalry, the most feared of the local fighting men. At the age of 26 he became the first man into the breach during the conquest of Medina during the war between the Ottoman Turks and the Wahhabis. For a short time Keith was treasurer to the Pashsa and was made governor of this holy Muslim city. In this position he had a small garrison under him. In 1815 he commanded the Ottoman rearguard, but was ambushed by an armed band, and killed four of his attackers before being hacked to death. He was one of the last ever Mamlukes

Keith, William (1839 – 1911)

Landscape artist

Born in Old Meldrum, Aberdeenshire, at the age of 12 Keith immigrated to New York with his mother. His first position was as an apprentice engraver, and then he worked for *Harper's weekly*, who sent him to California in 1858. Deciding that he preferred the sunshine of the southwest to the unpredictable weather of New York, Keith returned to California a year later, this time intending to settle.

Working as an engineer in San Francisco, he began to paint. He studied in Europe, but always returned to California. An artist and naturalist, he created black and white sketches of the American West Coast and the Sierras of California before progressing to some impressive landscape paintings. He was a good friend of **John Muir**, with whom he co-operated in some of his more famous canvases, as Muir escorted Keith to some of the finest views in the Sierra Nevada.

Some of Keith's works did full justice to the scale of the New World, with his *California Alps* measuring ten feet by six. In all Keith is estimated to have produced over 2000 sketches and paintings, but lost most when the 1906 San Francisco earthquake destroyed his studio.

Famous in his time, he is still highly regarded as the best Californian landscape artist of the period.

Kennedy, Alexander (1837 – 1936)
Pastoralist and pioneer

Born in Dunkeld, Perthshire, Kennedy worked with livestock in Scotland until he was twenty-three, when a migrant scheme lured him to Queensland. He arrived at Gladstone in November 1861 and obtained a position on Peter MacIntosh's sheep run at Rio on the Dawson River. Next Kennedy became manager of the Wealwandangie station on the Comet River, until an agricultural depression forced the station to close.

By now Kennedy was experienced with Australian conditions, and bought 1400 acres near Rockhampton, where he attempted to grow sugar. Unfortunately, the station was not suitable for that crop, so he accepted the position as manager of the Lorne station near Tambo.

In 1871 he married Marion Murray, and their son Peter was the first white child born on the Barcou River area. Kennedy then bought another small run, but again returned to Rockhampton. Constantly searching for a suitable property, Kennedy rode west; exploring the unknown hinterland, and then in 1878 he took two partners and bought nearly 400,000 acres of land at the Buckingham Downs.

Gathering their livestock, the partners and their families overlanded the 700 miles to their new land. On arrival, they lived in tents until they chopped down trees to build huts, and then found the natives hostile. Nevertheless, Kennedy had a business to run and a family to keep, so in 1879 he set out on another epic trip when he overlanded 300 bullocks to Adelaide, following that with a succession of treks from his remote station to places where he could sell his cattle.

Despite Aborigines killing one of Kennedy's partners in 1884, he continued to farm and even expanded his ownership as his herds swelled. The following year he was a member of the Cloncurry council. By 1892 he owned 50,000 head of cattle and 1200 square miles of land. Even in old age, Kennedy continued to pioneer. He was one of the original directors of Qantas, the Australian airline and a founder of the Company account. As late as 1922, when he was well into his 80s, Kennedy became the first passenger to fly in a scheduled airline in Eastern Australia.

There cannot be many people who helped to colonise a country, opened up its back lands and played a part in establishing its national airline.

Kerr, Deborah (b1921)
Dancer and actor

Born in Helensburgh, Argyll, as a girl Kerr was more interested in dancing than in acting. She changed to acting during the late 1930s and worked in the British film industry through the Second World War. However it is her Hollywood classics that really made her name, more particularly *From Here to Eternity* and *The King and I*, which told the true story of a western woman working in Siam. In 1994 Hollywood recognised Kerr's talents with a Lifetime Achievement Oscar.

Kerr, Walter Montagu (1852 – 1888)
Explorer

A grandson of the 6th Marquis of Lothian, Kerr is one of the unknown Scotsmen who helped open up the world. Between 1883 and 1885 he travelled from the Cape Colony to the Great Lakes of Central Africa. He had intended to reach the Scottish mission at Livingstonia, but when the station was deserted he had to be rescued by an African Lakes Company steamer.

A hunter as much as an explorer, Kerr wrote of his adventures in *The Far Interior*. He mentioned the slave trade, but also spoke of slaughtering the indigenous wildlife. He wrote about progress "dissolving the clouds of storm and strife from the face of this unhappy land." Such progress would ensure that his type of adventure could never be repeated.

Lagman, King of Man and the Isles (fl 1096)
Crusader

When the Byzantine Empire suffered a major defeat at the hands of the invading Turks at Manzikert in 1071, it called for mercenaries from western Christendom to bolster its defences. Instead it got the First Crusade, a host of fighting men from all Europe, who were less interested in rescuing Byzantium than in restoring the Holy Land from its Moslem conquerors.

Some of the Crusaders came from Scotland, including Lagman, king of Man and the Isles. It seems that after defeating his rebellious brother, he had blinded him but his conscience demanded an act of piety. Renouncing his kingdom, Lagman took the Cross. His party might have been those described as "groups of Scots, ferocious among themselves but elsewhere unwarlike, with bare legs, shaggy cloaks" and "copious arms."

Lagman would have joined the assembled crusaders in Normandy, but although there were Scots who survived the horrors of mediaeval travel to march across Asia Minor, it is not known if Lagman was among them. However, in 1105 the King of Scots was the owner of a camel, so possibly some Scots returned in triumph.

Laing, Alexander Gordon (1793 – 1826)
African explorer

Born in Edinburgh on 27 December 1793, Laing was teaching before he was sixteen and was educated at Edinburgh University. He joined the army at the age of seventeen, serving in the West Indies and Honduras. After becoming an officer in the Royal African Corps, he was sent to West Africa as aide-de-camp to Major General Charles Macarthy. While he was based in Sierra Leone, he began to push for command of an exploratory mission inland.

When the governor of the colony sent him on an expedition to quell slavery and smooth the way for trade, Laing took the opportunity to search for the source of the Niger, which was one of the most mysterious rivers in Africa. He reached the town of Falaba, only sixty miles from where the river began. Laing recorded that the natives were too superstitious to draw water from the source. More ominously, King

Assana of Falaba was hostile and prevented his progress. Laing also took part in the Ashanti War, against one of the most dangerous tribes in Africa. He fought bravely in a campaign where Macarthy was killed and his skull decorated as an Ashanti drinking bowl.

In 1825 the government sent Laing to explore the source of the Niger and locate the supposedly rich city of Timbuktu. At that time there was a strong belief that the Niger and the Nile were the same river. Laing tarried for a brief courtship with Emma Warrington, daughter of the British consul and after only two days of unconsummated marriage he left Tripoli, crossing the Sahara Desert. He thought the Arabs "a set of greedy vagabonds," but the inhabitants of Ghadames full of "kind and hospitable acts." Betrayed by Sheikh Babani, who had been paid to bring him across the desert, Laing was attacked by Touareg tribesmen.

Badly wounded, Laing staggered a further 400 miles to a friendly camp to recover. He entered Timbuktu on 13 August 1826, after spending a year on the journey. He found the city in ferment, but spent weeks with the merchant elite. Leaving Timbuktu on the 22 September 1826, but was murdered by tribesmen. His journals were never recovered. A man of superhuman strength and bravery, Laing is now almost forgotten.

Lamont, Johann Von (1805 –1879)
German astronomer
Born in Braemar, Lamont travelled to the Scottish seminary in Ratisbon in 1819. By 1835 he was director of Bogenhausen Observatory. In 1852 he was appointed Professor of Astronomy at Munich. Although he taught, he continued to study the skies, cataloguing some 34,000 stars.

Despite these endeavours, Lamont is best remembered for his work on terrestrial magnetism. He founded a magnetic observatory at Boghausen in 1840, and nine years later published *Handbuch des Erdmagnetismus.*

Lang, Gideon Scott (1819 – 1880)
Pastoralist and writer

Born in Selkirk in the Scottish Borders, Lang was one of three brothers that immigrated to Melbourne in 1841. Acting together, the Lang brothers bought land on the Saltwater River, and then moved to Buninyong, where they had to break in untouched bush land.

Lang made two trips inland, searching for good farmland. On both trips he relied on Aborigines for help, and he gained a respect for their culture and accomplishments that was almost unique in its time. In 1845, the year of his first exploration trip, Lang wrote *Land and Labour in Australia*, in which he said that after eight years free occupation, a squatter should be permitted to buy his land. Twenty years later he published *The Aborigines of Australia*, which argued for decent treatment for the people who had helped him.

Lang, Doctor John Dunmore (1799 – 1878)
Minister and Australian politician

Born in Greenock, Lang was educated at the parish school in Largs and then at Glasgow University. In 1820 the Presbytery of Irvine licensed him as a preacher. In 1823, on the advice of his brother who lived in Australia, Lang travelled to New South Wales to bring Presbyterianism to the still raw colony. Only one year later he was instrumental in establishing the Scots Church in Sydney, although it was another two years before the building was complete for worship. Lang was the first minister.

In 1835 Lang started a weekly newspaper, but he was so forthright in his writing that he was frequently taken to court. Four of the cases he lost ended in him being imprisoned for libel or debt. Privately, Lang also castigated the colonists, writing of them as a "generation of vipers...thieves and adulterers." Devout in his religion, he had little time for the rampant immorality and drunkenness that seemed so prevalent in the colony.

Lang and **Sir Thomas Brisbane** argued over official support for the Scots Church. However, Lang was also deeply concerned in helping the newly arrived immigrants, and pushed for skilled artisans to leave Scotland for Australia; he looked for respectable, hardworking Presbyterians. He also promoted education, hoping to build a Presbyterian College in Sydney. When the Colonial Office granted him a loan, he chartered a ship, located fifty-four Scottish artisans and shipped them to Australia with the guarantee of a year's steady work. That was only the first of his nine recruiting voyages between Australia and Britain. While locating the best people for Australia, Lang also helped alleviate the poverty and unemployment he saw in Scotland.

As if that was not enough, Lang was also a prolific writer, with over 300 published works, mainly pamphlets. His attack on Irish immigration *Popery in Australia* was not his most popular. Both in his writing and his speech, Lang was noted for his rancour to anyone he opposed or disliked.

Despite his aggressive stance on many subjects and his constant attacks on authority "men who seem so utterly bereft of reason as if they had been indiscriminately taken from the cells of a mad house", Lang was three times elected into the legislative council. He was also a member of the legislative assembly from 1859 until 1869. The best-known Scot in Australia, Lang was respected, and over 3000 people clustered to his funeral. One journalist wrote that Land did "more to advance the prosperity of this country than all other men put together."

Larnach, Donald (1817 – 1896)
Financier and banker

Born in Caithness, the son of a purser in the Royal Navy, Larnach immigrated to Sydney in 1834, joining his brother, John. Within a short while he was manager of a steam flourmill, which he bought in 1842. Larnach also speculated in finance and bought town lots in Sydney and Bathurst, while investing in rural property on the Lachlan River. He was an effective merchant and was fairly prosperous when he married Jane Elizabeth in August 1845.

That same year, Larnach became the auditor of the Bank of New South Wales, advancing to director in 1846. When he was promoted to General Manager, Larnach tidied up the 'Old' bank and in 1852, he became president of the revamped 'New' Bank of New South Wales.

In this position he guided the bank toward buying gold after the gold strikes in Victoria. At the same time he worked as a magistrate.

Larnach became Managing Director of the bank in 1854. There was a hint of scandal the following year when his brother John was accused of financial malpractice, but Larnach's offer to resign was rejected. Working in London, Larnach floated loans for the New South Wales government on the Stock Exchange, while becoming skilled in moving capital for the best interests of the colony and the bank.

Larnach was one of the finest financiers in early Australia, and helped the country properly exploit the gold booms of the 1850s to build for the future.

Law, John of Lauriston (1671 – 1729)
Financier, gambler, founder of the Bank of France
Born in Edinburgh, the son of a goldsmith and financier, Law was educated at the Royal High School. Enjoying gambling as much as orthodox financial speculation, he travelled to London to make his fortune. Unfortunately Law had the common Scottish fault of a quick temper and in 1694 killed a man in a duel over a woman.

One year later, Law escaped from jail and sailed to Europe. Studying banking finance in Amsterdam, he continued his amorous career by seducing a married Frenchwoman and running to Genoa. Using a combination of his charm, financial acumen and gambler's nerve, Law became rich in Genoa and Venice.

Returning to Edinburgh in 1703, he preached the gospel of paper currency to a people who liked the solid warmth of gold, particularly after the disaster at Darien. When the Scottish parliament rejected his ideas, Law returned to less conservative Europe. Following his gambler's luck, Law made and lost a fortune and settled in Paris. In 1716 Law and his brother founded a successful private bank, Law's prosperity was so impressive that in 1718 Philippe, Duc d'Orleans and regent of France, followed his idea for a national bank of France. The next year Law stepped further into financial speculation when he set up a joint-stock company to develop lands along the Mississippi valley. Law termed his Mississippi Scheme 'the system', and bought over the land and trading rights of the Mississippi Valley. If it had worked, Law's system would have made his company as large as the Hudson Bay Company or even the Honourable East India Company. Instead he created a French Darien scheme.

To create wealth, Law had to bring people to the Mississippi, but the French seemed reluctant to emigrate from their home. Those who did venture to the New World tended to remain near the coast, where the city of New Orleans now sits. To increase the flow of emigrants, Law became an eighteenth century spin-doctor, depicting the swampland of Louisiana as a gold-rich land where all that prevented settlers from drinking the milk was the presence of so much honey. Once again Law's gambler's charm worked as thousands of Europeans, worn down by war and poverty, boarded ships for the New World. Those that escaped ship fever found wearisome swamps and voracious mosquitoes.

It had been Law's intention to sell shares to investors and rake in taxes and money.

This Mississippi Scheme made Law a vast fortune. He adopted French citizenship and became a Roman Catholic. The following year he became Comptroller General of Finance for France. Like many gamblers, Law's luck did not hold. When the Mississippi Scheme collapsed, leaving hundreds stranded in Louisiana, a mob burned down his house. The intense dislike from the French people drove Law away from the country and he died in Venice in 1729.

Learmonth, Dr Basil Livingstone (1874 – 1940)
Medical Missionary

Educated in Edinburgh University, Learmonth journeyed through Russia to Manchuria, where he began missionary work in 1897. At first he was based at Ximin, but in 1915 he moved to Pekin, where he married a fellow Scottish missionary.

Learmonth worked in China for over 40 years, becoming the medical officer at Yanjing University. His was a life of dedication and hard work rather than of spectacular achievement, but the Chinese people so appreciated his efforts that when he retired in 1937 they presented him with a jade ruyi. Not a tall man, Learmonth was upright, slender and dignified, typifying the best type of the many Scots who made their lives abroad.

Learmonth, William (1815 – 1889)
Pastoralist

Of Scottish Border stock, Learmonth was educated at the Royal High School in Edinburgh but was only nineteen when he immigrated to Australia. He arrived in Van Dieman's Land in 1834, to be employed by a legal firm. However, the abundance of land soon encouraged him to turn to sheep farming. His first station was Williamwood, near the present day Evandale, and he proved so successful that by 1839 he ran nearly 14000 sheep. He had married Mary in 1837 and for a while seemed set to settle in the area. However an agricultural depression drained away his money and in 1848 he sailed from Tasmania to seek his future on the Australian mainland.

Investing in cattle and horses, Learmonth first acquired land at Darlot's Creek, but moved to the Portland area, where he took over 39,000 acres of land in a station that he named Ettrick. He did not permit Mary and their three children to join him until he felt that the station was safe. Learmonth was an excellent pastoralist, so Ettrick grew into one of the premier stations in the district. Although the local tribes were known to spear cattle and threaten men, Learmonth lived there until 1880. He was also the first mayor of Portland in 1863.

Leslie, Field Marshall Alexander, 1st Earl of Leven (c1580 – 1661)
Soldier

The illegitimate son of the captain of Blair Atholl Castle, Leslie took to soldiering as a young man. After service in the Netherlands, he followed the thousands of Scots who fought for Gustavus Adolphus of Sweden. Like so many of his name, he had a long career with the

Swedes, being knighted and rising in rank to General. Some of his exploits have been remembered. For instance in 1628 he led 5000 Scottish and Swedish soldiers into Stralsund, relieving a siege by the famous Wallenstein. After bringing in supplies, he commanded the garrison in place of the Scotsman Captain Seaton. During a masterly defence, Wallenstein was frustrated and forced to withdraw.

Leslie commanded the Baltic ports for Sweden and in 1631 returned to Britain to recruit more mercenaries. The following year, as joint commander of the Scottish and English forces, he helped take Frankfurt on the Oder, which he afterward governed. Thereafter he fought at Lutzen and in 1636 was promoted Field Marshall, in which position he relieved the siege of Hanau. He also led the Scots and Swedes to victory at Wittstock, and afterward commanded in Pomerania.

When the Covenanting troubles began in Scotland, Leslie was one of the first to return home, bearing two artillery pieces and two thousand muskets for the blue-bonneted armies that were about to march over the Border.

Leslie was responsible for organising the Covenanting army that was victorious at Newark. As the Earl of Leven he was instrumental in the victory at Marston Moor and at the capture of Newcastle. He was less successful in the campaigning in Scotland in 1651, possibly because of religious interference. Captured by Cromwell, he was released on parole; Leslie was one of Scotland's most famous and successful commanders, as well as a field marshal for Gustavus Adolphus.

Leslie, Sir Alexander of Auchintoul (1566 –1661)
Russian general

Sir Alexander Leslie first arrived in Russia in 1631 on a diplomatic mission from King Charles I. Sent to Sweden; he hired thousands of mercenaries for the Russian army, as well as blacksmiths, wheelwrights and other skilled artisans. On his return to Russia, Leslie seems to have been given command of a regiment of these foreign troops.

Although many mercenary Scots later returned to Scotland, Leslie remained in Russia, rising to Colonel, marrying and fathering a son named Theodorus. Further promotion to General followed, and Leslie also became Governor of Smolensk

Leslie, David (1839 –1874)
African trader and hunter

Leslie arrived at Natal, South Africa as an eleven-year-old child, and within three years he was so proficient in Zulu that he was acting as a Zulu interpreter in the courts. In February 1858 he employed a number of Zulu porters, supplied each with a bundle of trade goods and set off to trade and hunts in Zululand. As he had no money to spare for a wagon, he walked in front of his porters.

Trading blankets for cattle, Leslie also hunted elephant and buffalo, meeting veterans of the wars of Zululand and always being welcomed. His first two-month expedition netted him a profit of £156, with which he bought a wagon. Obtaining trading rights from Mpande, the Zulu king, he employed a number of hunters, and engaged in a private feud with rival traders.

As his profits grew, in 1871 Leslie was one of the first European traders to visit Tongaland, which he did by sailing up the uSuthu River in a half-decked boat. Plagued by mosquitoes, he sweetened Noziyingili, the Tongan king, with rum, and then traded around the kingdom for seven fruitful months. Despite a dispute with the Portuguese that cost him much of his profit, Leslie retired to Durban and then Britain, where he died the following year.

Leslie, James (c1635 – c1695)
Mercenary and nobleman of Austrian Empire

Born in Scotland, James Leslie moved to Imperial Austria, where he commanded the 24th Galizuan Regiment that became known as Leslie's Regiment. In 1666 he married a Liechtenstein princess, with the ceremony witnessed by the Emperor Leopold of Austria. The couple lived in the Lesliehof in Graz.

A fine soldier, Leslie was also a diplomat. He rose to be Field Marshall in the Imperial service and fought at the defence of Vienna against the Ottoman forces in 1683. Leslie was successful in a number of battles against the Turks in Croatia-Slavinia and Hungary. In 1684 he and his regiment were heavily involved in the capture of Buda.

Leslie, Norman (fl 1360)
Crusader

Norman Leslie and his brother Walter took part in the Prussian Baltic Crusade of 1356. Returning to Scotland, the brothers were recruited by agents of King Peter of Cyprus who hoped to recover Jerusalem for Christendom and, incidentally, for his own kingdom. By 1364 the Leslie brothers were in Florence, witnessing a contract between that city and the White Company, a group of English mercenaries.

The brothers sailed to Rhodes and from there to Alexandria, arriving with the Crusading fleet in October 1365. Although the Crusaders took the city at least one Scots knight died in the forefront of the assault. This knight may have been Norman Leslie. After a day's looting, the English contingent of the Crusaders retreated to the ships. It seems that the Scots, French and others were willing to stay and defend their conquest, but they were too few in number and withdrew.

Leslie, Walter (1606 – 1667)
Mercenary

The younger son of the baron of Balquhain in Aberdeenshire, Leslie travelled to the continent while still in his teens. Although he was a Protestant, Leslie was one of the Scots who fought for the Habsburg or Imperialist cause against the Swedes, French and assorted Protestants during the Thirty Years War. He rose to command a regiment of mingled Scots and Irish, with whom he fought around Nurnberg. When a Swedish attack faltered around Freystadt, Leslie's regiment was included in the force that hoped to cut off the Swedes retreat.

While most of the Imperialists withdrew before the Swedes, Leslie's regiment stood to fight, which eventually led to Leslie and his lieutenant, John Gordon being captured. The two Scots spent some months at Nurnberg with the Scots **Hepburn** and Munro who were fighting for Sweden, before being freed to rejoin the Imperials. In 1632

Leslie obtained command of a unit of Imperialist dragoons at Eger in Bohemia, an important border post. He remained here for two years.

When news came that Wallenstein, one of the most important Austrian commanders, planned to desert to the enemy, Leslie was given orders to assassinate him. It seems that Leslie organised the murder with some skill, although it was an Irishman named Devereaux who carried out the actual deed. Wallenstaein's body was carried away in Leslie's private carriage. When he brought news of the successful murder to Vienna, the Austrians awarded Leslie the position of imperial chamberlain, as well as command of two regiments, with the associated pay and perks. Thirdly, and more importantly, Leslie also gained the lands and castle of Neustadt in what is now the Czech Republic.

Despite his new position, Leslie remained a fighting soldier, playing a large part in the Battle of Nordlingen in 1634. Leslie was later made a Count of the Holy Roman Empire after he claimed that his family had been associated with the Empire for six centuries. He married Anna Franziska Von Dietrichstein, one of the Bohemian elite and rose higher in the military and social scale so that in 1650 he was a Field Marshall watching over the Croatian-Slavonian military frontier.

Leslie spent the next few years building up his possessions, but apparently could not build up a family. In 1655 he drew up an entail that left his now extremely extensive properties to his nephew, James Leslie. In 1656 he moved into another castle at Oberpettau in Slovenia. Nine years later, together with James Leslie and Francis Hay of Delgaty, Leslie was sent as ambassador to Constantinople to ratify a peace treaty between the Empire and the Ottoman Empire. Rowed down the Danube in a fleet of 36 highly decorated galleys, Leslie travelled overland from Belgrade. Again his mission was a success and he returned with gifts and 60 freed Christian slaves. It was his last official duty, but he did see his nephew James Leslie safely married to a Liechtenstein princess.

Leiden, John (1775 – 1811)
Poet, traveller, Orientalist

Born at Denholm, Roxburghshire, in a small cottage Leiden was the son of a farmer. After an elementary education at Denholm, Leiden studied theology at Edinburgh University. Significantly, he also studied a clutch of languages including Spanish, ancient Icelandic Arabic and Persian. In 1796 he obtained his licence as a preacher but failed to find a parish.

A good friend of Walter Scott, in 1799 Leiden wrote the three-volume *History of African Discoveries*. He also helped Scott with *Border Minstrelsy* while also writing for the *Edinburgh Magazine*.

By 1803 he was contemplating exploring Africa in person, but instead he obtained the position of assistant surgeon in Madras. He took his qualification in surgery within six months and travelled east. An amazingly accomplished linguist, Leiden learned 34 languages and became first a professor, then a judge in Calcutta. He translated the Gospels into five languages. Acting as Lord Minto's interpreter, he travelled to Java, newly conquered from the Dutch, but died of fever at Batavia. Although he is probably best remembered for his ballads, his true genius was probably his translation skills.

Lining, John (1708 – 1760)
Physician and scientist

Born in Lanarkshire, Lining studied medicine in Scotland and perhaps also at Leiden University before immigrating to Charleston, South Carolina around 1728. He established a successful medical practice in the town, becoming a doctor for the poor of St Philips Parish as well as acting as port physician. Lining, however, was as much a scientist as a doctor and experimented with physiology, botany, climatology and even electricity.

Although Lining was most interested in botany, he was more influential in metabolism and meteorology, which he linked to his intense study of yellow fever. Contemporary belief theorised that yellow fever was affected by climatic change, so when a major outbreak hit Charleston in 1748, Lining recorded climatic variations and determined that there was no connection. He also ascertained that the disease was contagious, but failed to establish that mosquitoes were involved. His *History of Yellow Fever* was the first scientific study of the disease.

Lining was also involved with experiments with electricity, some of which he discussed with Benjamin Franklin. Lining may have conducted kite-flying tests even before Franklin.

While not practising medicine or working on his scientific interests, Lining founded the St Andrews Club of Charleston and became president of the Charleston Library Society. He was also a Justice of the Court of Common Pleas. He married Sarah Hill in 1750 but produced no children. Four years after his marriage he contracted gout, retired from medicine and concentrated on growing indigo on his estate.

Little, Andrew (c1875 – c1939)
The Sheep king of Idaho

Born in Moffat, Andrew Little landed in Boise with the clothes on his back and a black and white collie dog. Settling in Caldwell, Idaho, he and the collie began to farm sheep for 'Scotch Bob' Aikman. Rather than money, Little accepted payment in kind, and began to raise his own flock. In 1901, when he thought himself wealthy enough, he returned to Scotland, found a wife, whistled up seven of his brothers and returned, clan-handed, to the Boise Basin.

In time Little was the richest sheep farmer in the West, known as the Sheep King of Idaho because of the 165,000 sheep that he ran in the Boise Basin. He was also termed the **Andrew Carnegie** of the West. It was said that a letter sent to 'Andy Little, USA' would be delivered unerringly; such was his reputation and fame.

Livingstone, David (1813 – 1873)
African explorer and missionary

Born in Low Blantyre, Lanarkshire, Livingstone became a worker in a local cotton mill at the age of ten. After reading a religious pamphlet he decided to become a missionary, and studied Greek, theology and medicine at Anderson's College, Glasgow, following this with a medical degree. Intending to work in China, he met **Robert Moffat**, the Scottish head of an African mission in London. Moffat persuaded him that Africa was the ideal place to work. At that time the Opium War made China unfruitful for any missionary work.

In 1840 the London Missionary Society ordained him and Livingstone travelled to Moffat's mission in Bechuanaland. His career nearly ended when a lion mauled him, but he recovered and married Moffat's daughter Mary. An attempt to Christianise the native people of the Transvaal failed when the Boers objected to his use of African missionaries, so Livingstone journeyed north. Despite being ravaged by fever, he discovered Lake Ngami and began to concentrate as much on exploration as on missionary work.

With one of his prime objectives was to open trade routes across Africa, he spent the years 1852 to 1856 travelling in appalling conditions. Despite the hardships, Livingstone collected a mass of information about the continent and its people. One of his major discoveries was the Victoria Falls on the Zambesi River as he promoted 'commerce and Christianity' as the answers to Africa's ills.

Livingstone's return home was rapturous, and his *Missionary Travels* was an instant success. He gave public lectures to vast crowds, calling on the British people to carry the flag and Christianity to the unenlightened. "I go back to Africa to make an open path for commerce and Christianity," he told the undergraduates of Cambridge, "do you carry out the work which I have begun."

In 1858 the government appointed him leader of an expedition to explore the Zambesi River. This time he also investigated the Shire and Rovuma Rivers, discovering Lake Shirwa and the large Lake Nyasa. It was on this expedition that Livingstone decided that Lake Nyasa would be an important base for missionary and commercial operations, despite the objections of the Portuguese who claimed that part of Africa. In fact Arab slave traders were the true power as they probed into Central Africa from their coastal headquarters, often with the connivance of the Portuguese.

In 1862 Livingstone's wife Mary died. The following year he travelled westward from Lake Nyasa into unknown lands, and sailed to

Bombay before returning to Britain. Now as much a political figure as a missionary, he published *The Zambesi and its Tributaries*, which threw light on the Portuguese influence on the slave trade. He also hoped to raise funds for mission work on the Rovuma River.

Established as the world's leading African explorer, Livingstone was in demand. The Royal Geographical Society requested that he return to Africa to explore the central watershed and discover the source of the Nile. Accordingly, in March 1866 he landed at Zanzibar and probed westward. In 1867 and 1868 he discovered Lake Mweru and Lake Bangweulu, but the trek was appalling. He withdrew to Ujiju to recuperate, and then hacked westward again. When he located the River Lualaba he celebrated, believing it to be the Nile. In fact it was the Congo. Again returning to Ujiju, sick with fever, Stanley met him in perhaps the most famous minute in the history of African exploration.

Refusing to give up until he had unravelled the geography of Africa, Livingstone pushed back to Bangweulu, but hardships and disease caught up with him. He died in Old Chitambo in Zambia. It is a mark of the loyalty of his African companions that they carried his body to the coast. He was buried in Westminster Abbey, a long social stride from his beginnings as a mill worker. Many people have belittled Livingstone's work, claiming that he converted few people and discovered little that the Portuguese did not know before. However, Livingstone opened his results to the world, treated the Africans with a respect that few of his contemporaries or successors could match and fought to destroy the slave trade. There have been few braver missionary-explorers in history.

Livingston, Robert (1654 – 1728)
Politician and merchant

Born in Ancrum in the Borders, Livingston was the son of the Reverend John Livingston, who was persecuted for his Presbyterianism. In 1663 the family sought sanctuary in Rotterdam, where Robert Livingston began to work as a trader.

In 1672 Livingston's father died and he returned to Scotland, but the following year immigrated to the Puritan colony in Massachusetts. By the end of 1674 he had settled in Albany, then a frontier town with a strongly Dutch population. Livingston continued with the trading skills he had learned in Rotterdam, exploiting his position as a Dutch speaking Scotsman with a foot in both camps. In 1679 he cemented the Dutch connection when he married Alida Schuyler van Rensoelaer, whose had blood links with most of the prominent families in the colony.

Livingston acquired massive lands in New York State and, exploiting his family and intermediary connections to the full, entered local politics. A member of the New York Assembly from 1709 to 1711, and 1715 to 1718, he was Speaker in 1718. Livingston, like so many Scots, was also expert in his dealings with the indigenous peoples. It was Livingston who first made the alliance with the powerful Five Nations confederation that proved so important to British policy. To do so, he made a 500 mile journey to the heart of the Iroquois lands at a time when that nation was one of the most feared in North America.

In 1722 Livingston held a conference on Indian affairs. Governor Burnett of New York, **Governor Keith** of Pennsylvania and **Governor Spotswood** of Virginia, joined him in Albany; it was a clan gathering of the Scots who controlled early colonial America. Three years later, Livingston retired, but he left behind a dynasty that became one of the most powerful families in New York State.

Lloyd, Frank (1888 – 1960)
Actor, film maker
Born in Glasgow, Lloyd was twenty-two when he immigrated to Canada. After a few years he moved south to California, where he found work in the fast growing film industry. At first Lloyd acted in westerns, but made his mark when he turned to directing.

Logan, Captain Patrick (1792 – 1830)
'The Beast of Brisbane'

Born in Scotland, Logan became an ensign in the 57th Regiment of Foot when he was eighteen years old. That regiment was one of the most harshly disciplined in the army and the experience must have altered the young officer. Logan saw much of the world during the latter stages of the Napoleonic War, fighting in Spain and France, then faced the Americans during the 1812 War. After a spell on garrison duty in Ireland, he was sent to Australia to help control the convicts.

In 1826 Logan was appointed Commandant of Moreton Bay in the 'deep north' of Australia. Logan soon established a reputation for sadistic violence. A convict song of the period speaks of "where Captain Logan... had us mangled on his triangles at Moreton Bay." Logan was known as the 'Beast of Brisbane', but he was responsible for condemned criminals who lived in an isolated station where there was no help or support from higher authority.

With a convict population that grew from 100 to 1020, Logan attempted to build up the new colony. He planted hundreds of acres of wheat and maize, laid out the plan for the future city of Brisbane complete with barracks for the redcoated soldiers, stores, hospitals and cottages. He worked tirelessly and drove the convicts hard. He kept them in irons, flogged them relentlessly, and often added years to their sentence. Disease struck the colony; the crops failed and Logan retaliated against Aborigine attacks with armed patrols. Folklore claims that he displayed the stuffed skin of an aborigine as a warning to others.

An ex-convict named Hall hoped to bring Logan to trial for his tyranny, but the Commandant was posted to India. Before he left he engaged in some exploring work and a party of Aborigines ambushed him. When his body was discovered, elated convicts claimed that they had killed him, and for some time afterward there were tales of his ghost haunting the colony.

Lyle, Peter (c 1770 – c 1825)
Barbary pirate

A Glasgow man Peter Lyle sailed from Leith to the Mediterranean. Around 1795 he was working as mate on a vessel named *Hampden* when he was accused of theft. Slipping ashore at Tripoli, he asked for sanctuary and converted to Islam. With his name changed to Murad Rais he was operating as a corsair in 1796, capturing a brace of American prizes. After a spell in Egypt, Lyle was appointed Admiral of the Tripoli Marine, and made it one of the most efficient piratical concerns in the world. In 1797 he defended Tripoli against a Danish frigate.

Lyle was not always successful. The Scotsman, Commodore Campbell of the Royal Navy, temporarily captured him in 1799, by which time Lyle had married the Pasha's daughter. When the United States and Tripoli were at war, USS *Essex* attempted to blockade Lyle at Gibraltar, but Lyle shipped his crew out on a British ship and returned to Tripoli. In 1803 Lyle boarded and captured the US frigate *Philadelphia*, where he suspected the American commander, Bainbridge, to be a coward. The Americans later managed to destroy the vessel in Tripoli harbour.

A man of contrasts, Lyle also loved flowers. He died and was buried in Tripoli.

MacAlister, Charles (1765 – 1832)
Designer of the fastest ship afloat

Born in Campbeltown, Argyll, MacAlister was bred to the sea. He immigrated to North America when he was young. Establishing himself in Philadelphia, he rose to become master of several merchant vessels, and moved into ship owning. Eventually owning a number of vessels, he traded with Europe and the East Indies. Around 1810 he designed the ship *Fanny*, which was renowned as the fastest merchant vessel afloat.

MacAlister also entered finance, becoming president of the Insurance Company of the State of Pennsylvania and founded the Mariners Chandlers of Philadelphia.

MacAskill, Angus (1825 – 1863)
The world's tallest, non- pathological giant

Born in Harris, Angus MacAskill was small as a child. He was still young when he accompanied his parents when they immigrated to Cape Breton Island and settled beside other Gaels in Norman MacLeod's colony at St Ann's Harbour. By the age of 14 Angus was known as Gille Mor, Big Boy, as he was growing fast, and knocked out a bully with a single punch.

Already known as the Cape Breton Giant, Angus worked on the family farm, with his great strength a formidable asset. When he reached his full height he was 7 feet 9 inches tall, with a pleasant personality, although well able to take care of those who wished to torment him. As well as farming, he was also a fisherman, able to set a forty-foot mast into a schooner single handed, or tip a half-ton boat on her side.

When bad times hit Cape Breton, Angus agreed to tour North America as an exhibit. On one trip to the western states of America, a couple of would be train robbers ran at just the sight of him. On another occasion Angus lifted a 140-gallon puncheon of whisky and drank from the contents. Building a shop in Englishtown, Cape Breton, Angus settled down, becoming known as a fair and generous man.

MacDonald, Archibald (1792 – c 1840)
Fur trader, settler

Born in Glencoe, Archibald MacDonald was only 21 when he was put in charge of 94 emigrants for **Lord Selkirk's** Red River settlement. They left Thurso for Orkney, where they boarded two ships bound for Canada. Despite typhus and icebergs in the Hudson Strait, the ships deposited the emigrants on the shores of Hudson Bay.

They survived the shocking northern winter and, having built sledges, moved to York Factory to the music of the pipes. From York Factory the emigrants borrowed boats and headed for Lake Winnipeg. It was summer of 1814 before they arrived at the Red River settlement.

Two years later MacDonald withdrew his settlers northward as the local Metis attacked, until Colin Robertson from Perthshire persuaded them to return. A further attack in 1816 left 21 colonists dead or wounded. Joining the Hudson Bay Company, MacDonald later served as a fur trapper in the Oregon Country. He had at least two women in his life, the first a Chinook, with whom he had a son named Ranald. When she died he married an Englishwoman. Ranald was raised with his half-brothers, sent to work in a bank but ran away to sea. When **George Simpson** sent him to Japan as an agent of the Hudson Bay Company, he learned the language, but his wandering spirit drove him to the Australian gold fields before he became a farmer in Canada.

MacDonald, James (1906 – 1991)
Voice of Mickey Mouse: Sound Effects Artist

Born and educated in Dundee, James MacDonald immigrated to Philadelphia in the United States. Obtaining work with the Walt Disney Corporation, he became a dance band drummer, before switching to sound effects. MacDonald worked with Disney for forty years, creating audio effects such as the waterfall in *Snow White.*

However, MacDonald also used his own voice. From a chief yodeller in *Snow White,* he progressed to becoming Sneezy and the Chipmunks. His most high profile voice was *Micky Mouse,* which he took over from 1947.

Macdonald, Sir John Alexander (1815 – 1891)
First Prime Minister of Canada

Although his family came from Sutherland, Macdonald was born in Glasgow. The family immigrated to Canada, living in Kingston, Ontario. Macdonald chose a legal career and in 1836 was called to the bar. A notable lawyer, he became a Queen's Councillor.

When he entered the political arena, in 1844 Macdonald was chosen as the Conservative representative for Kingston. He advocated strong British links, which was important so soon after the 1835 rebellion. He rose to leader of the Conservative Party, fighting to maintain the French seigniorial tenure in Quebec. After forming a coalition with the Liberal party, in 1856 he was elected premier of Upper Canada.

In 1867 he championed the British North America Acts and led the first government of the newly created Dominion of Canada. Under his leadership Canada purchased the North West Territory from the Hudson Bay Company and in 1870 created the province of Manitoba. The following year he concluded the Treaty of Washington and began constructing a transcontinental railway to unite the impossibly scattered towns and territories of Canada. Accusations of political and financial irregularities forced him to resign, but he still managed to out-argue the Liberal **Alexander Mackenzie** on Free Trade.

Macdonald married splendidly, with Agnes Macdonald a strong, colourful character in her own right. One of her more endearing eccentricities was to have a seat specially constructed and attached to the cowcatcher in front of a train. She would sit there as the train rattled through the unparalleled Canadian scenery.

Working as Minister of Justice and attorney general of Canada until 1873, he was Prime Minister for a second time between 1878 until he died in 1891. Macdonald is undoubtedly one of the most important figures in Canadian history, for he helped bring about the confederation of the various parts of the nation and developed the almost empty northwest. He also ensured the creation of the Pacific and the intercontinental railways.

Macdonald, Sir Murdoch (1866 – 1957)
Civil engineer

Scottish born, Murdoch Macdonald was trained as an engineer with the Highland Railway Company. In 1898 he left Scotland to work for the Egyptian government, which was closely associated with the British Empire.

Macdonald became one of the leading civil engineers in Northern Africa, creating such structures as the original Aswan Dam and the irrigation works at Gezira. He was also responsible for the Sennar Dam in the Sudan. After a spell in politics, Macdonald left Egypt in 1922 and returned to Britain. He set up a consulting firm that worked throughout the Middle East, the United Kingdom and Greece.

MacDonald, William (c 1830 – 1910)
Overlander, farmer

Born in Cromarty, MacDonald immigrated with his family to New South Wales in Australia in 1838. Starting with very little, the Mac-Donalds gradually increased their land holdings, the father, Donald working beside his wife and sons. His sons became expert at prospecting, sheep shearing and tracking as they explored further and further out from their farm.

When they brought back tales of their discoveries to their father, old MacDonald yearned for the huge spaces of the north and west. He had the idea of first obtaining a lease for land around the Kimberleys, then droving cattle from his present farm. He proposed that it would be a family trek, the MacDonalds and their Mackenzie cousins.

In March 1883 the combined MacDonald – Mackenzie overland trip began. They had 46 bullocks, 60 horses and 670 cattle. Bullocks drew the two wagons that held their provisions and enough spare gear to last two years. As always in Australia, the climate was the main enemy. At first there were floods, with high rivers that impeded the passage of cattle. Then, as they moved into Queensland, drought slowed them. So many cattle required a great deal of grazing, so it was no wonder that the landholders on their route baulked at allowing them to cross their land. As well as a cattle tax to get into Queensland, there were attacks by hostile natives. The MacDonalds persevered, following the track of thunderstorms to catch water, arguing with other droves, known as mobs in Australia, combating disease and drought. Crocodiles attacked the cattle as they crossed the northern rivers, the natives became more hostile, but the MacDonalds continued.

The family hired hands to help, but only the MacDonalds started and finished the entire three-year overland. Willie MacDonald guided the surviving 370 head of cattle into their new pasture in June 1886. After having endured so much, he never moved again, working his animals until his death in 1910.

MacElhone, Harry (c1880 –1958)
Proprietor of Harry's New York Bar

Born in Dundee, Harry MacElhone has some claim to being the greatest cocktail mixer in history. In 1911 or 1912, he bought the existing New York Bar in the Rue Daunou near the Opera in Paris, which became famed as Harry's New York Bar. A genial man, he encouraged his barmen to create new cocktails, of which some forty came from his bar. It was Fernand 'Pete' Petiot, one of his barmen, who invented the Bloody Mary in 1921, while Harry himself may have created the French '75 after a First World War artillery piece, Sidecar in 1931 and the White Lady while at Ciro's Club in London in 1919. His son, Andy, invented the Blue Lagoon in 1972.

Harry's Bar became very popular among the literary world, with Ernest Hemingway, Irwin Shaw, Malcolm Cowley and Elmer Rice among the clientele. James Bond, 007, also knew the place well. Harry served the first hotdog in France in 1925, and George Gershwin was often at the piano, while James Joyce sang. Harry seconded Hemingway during his boxing match with the Canadian novelist Morley Callaghan. Mae West, Katherine Anne Porter and Jeanne Moreau also visited.

During the Second World War, Harry's became an officer's club, and was equally well used by US servicemen after the liberation.

MacGregor, Gregor (c1790 – 1845)
Soldier, confidence trickster

Gregor MacGregor was the grandson of Gregor MacGregor, Laird of Inverardine and a veteran of the Black Watch. MacGregor also joined the Black Watch, albeit for only a short while, for when he was 20 he sailed to Caracas to join Simon Bolivar's struggle for independence from Spain.

An earthquake in 1812 devoured all MacGregor's possessions, but other Scots, such as Colonel Campbell, who commanded a regiment of riflemen and Mackintosh the saddler, helped him through the lean times. In Bolivar's army, MacGregor displayed an astonishing talent mingled with raw courage and a cunning that his namesake Rob Roy would have recognised. He rose to become a General of Cavalry, then a General of Brigade and before six years had passed he commanded a division. Life could hardly have been sweeter when Simon Bolivar presented MacGregor with the Order of Liberators, except when he married Bolivar's niece, Donna Josepha.

Experienced with infantry and cavalry, MacGregor took to the sea. Using the tactics of the old time buccaneers, he captured entire towns on the Spanish occupied coast and headed north to the Mosquito Coast of what became Nicaragua.

It was now that MacGregor began to play for himself. He met an indigenous native chief who offered him an area of land. It is unclear what MacGregor offered in return, but the Clan Gregor was always blessed with a silver tongue. With the papers to the Mosquito Coast signed and safe, MacGregor returned to Europe. On the voyage the Highland transformed himself into His Serene Highness Gregor I, Prince of Poyais, while Donna was now a Princess.

The tongue that had charmed an Indian chief was equally effective at the Court of King George IV, for MacGregor's credentials were accepted almost without question. Choosing his subordinates, MacGregor awarded them the Illustrious Order of the Green Cross and ordered an impressive wad of Poyais bank notes printed with the MacGregor motto, *Is Rioghal Mo Dhream*, My Blood is Royal. He also had pamphlets printed, showing all the wonders of his mythical kingdom. If it was not quite beyond the rainbow, it was certainly not Kansas, nor the Mosquito Coast. People read in awe of the splendours of MacGregor's capital, with its splendid streets and wonderful buildings.

Next, MacGregor obtained a loan for £200,000 based on the riches of Poyais. He claimed that gold and precious stones, silver and stands of timber all waited on the banks of the Caribbean. MacGregor travelled to Edinburgh, where he and Donna were painted in all their splendour, and then he sprung his trap. MacGregor called for Scottish emigrants to fill his country and the Scots, forgetting the lessons of Darien, rushed to exchange their currency for MacGregor's Poyais notes.

Two shiploads of Scots suffered on the Mosquito Coast, other vessels left Leith. Hundreds died in the tropical hell, of heat, malaria and despair, and it was only through the efforts of John Young, the Scottish Colonial Agent at British Honduras that the death toll was not higher. When the British authorities accused him of fraud, MacGregor denied all charges as he moved to France and attempted the same scam.

The French of 1825 proved as gullible as the Scots of 1822, and Macgregor pocketed his £300,000 loan. However, when he returned to London in 1827, he ended in prison. Talking himself free, he sailed to France, again saw the inside of a cell and again charmed himself out. By 1830 he was in Venezuela, where he was remembered as a liberator and welcomed as a friend.

MacGregor, John VC.MC.DCM. (1889 - 1952)
Canada's most decorated soldier

Born near Nairn, John MacGregor had apprenticed as a stone mason when he immigrated to Canada in 1909. He made his way across the country from east to west, labouring and working as a cowboy. On one occasion he was paid with a horse. After In 1915 he was working as a trapper in upper British Columbia when a ranger informed him about the First World War. "The King needed me" he said, and walked five days across country to enlist. Initially rejected and deemed unfit, he tried again, being accepted as a private soldier in Vancouver. He then began an amazing military career. Serving in the Second Canadian Mounted Infantry, MacGregor was a sergeant when he won the DCM at Vimy Ridge in April 1917, a lieutenant when he won the Military Cross for leading a trench raid at Hill 70 and a captain when he won the Victoria Cross at Cambrai. In this latter exploit he defeated twelve Germans single handed, fighting with the bayonet. He also won a bar to his MC at Quievran, in the last month of the war.

Known as Jock, MacGregor worked as a fisherman, then married and had two sons. When the Second World War started, he enlisted as a private but was soon promoted to be colonel of the 2nd Canadian Scottish Regiment. He trained soldiers throughout the war and died of cancer in 1952. His son, James MacGregor, won the DFC during the Second World War.

Mackay, Donald, First Lord Reay (1591 – 1649)
Mercenary soldier

Born in his ancestral lands, Mackay became head of the clan in 1614. Raising a clan regiment, he fought for Christian IV of Denmark in the long European wars. The Mackay Regiment earned the title of the 'Invincible Regiment.'

With an influx of recruits in 1628, Mackay became Lord Reay and joined the service of Gustavus Adolphus the following year. A decade later, Mackay returned to Scotland. He took part in the Civil Wars, was captured and imprisoned in Edinburgh Castle but freed after the battle of Kilsyth. Exiled in 1649, Mackay died in Bergen.

Mackay, John, (c1759 –1822)
Fur trader and explorer

Born in Kildonan, Mackay immigrated to Canada in 1776 and, in common with so many of his contemporaries entered the fur trade. He also moved south and between 1795 and 1797 explored the Louisiana Territory for Spain, who then controlled much of that part of the Americas.

Many years later the American explorers, Lewis and Clark, used Mackay's maps for their much more famous journey.

Mackenzie, Sir Alexander (1764 – 1820)
Canadian explorer

Born in Stornoway on the island of Lewis, Mackenzie is one of the giants of North American exploration. In 1779 he joined the Northwest Fur Company, the rival to the Hudson Bay Company. Working at first from Toronto, he was sent to the Detroit area and proved himself astute in outmanoeuvring his United States rivals.

Impressed by his abilities, the Northwest Company ordered him to explore even further Northwest. In 1778 he established Fort Chipewayan on Lake Athabasca. Using this point as a base, on the 3rd June 1789 he shoved off in a flotilla of birch bark canoes with his brother and a handful of companions. Travelling along the river that would later be named in his honour, the explorers reached the Great

Slave Lake in six days of steady paddling. The lake was iced over, but was free of mosquitoes, which normally plagued the land. Even better, the guides assured Mackenzie that the woods and prairie was rich in fur-bearing animals. They continued north as summer brought heavy clouds and biting insects.

The native guides were unwilling to travel through the lands of the rival Red Knife tribe, and even more reluctant to meet the feared Inuit of the far north. However, the midnight sun heartened them, and Mackenzie used bribery to persuade their chief to continue. They reached the Arctic Ocean on the 15th July and, after Mackenzie marked the spot with a post, he tried the local fishing. It was not as good as expected. The journey back taxed even their powers of endurance, and Mackenzie reported that his route was not a navigable northwest passage. In 1792-1793 he became the first known European to cross the Rocky Mountains and canoe to the Pacific Ocean.

Mackenzie, however, was more than just a hardy traveller. As he moved through hostile territory, he kept careful note of his latitude and longitude and even recorded his name and the date on rocks. One inscription has been marked with a plaque. It is on a rock in Dean Channel, not far from Vancouver, and reads *Alexander MacKenzie, from Canada, by land, the twenty-second of July, one thousand seven hundred and ninety-three*

It was because of pioneers of Mackenzie's stock that both ends of his trail now lie in Canada. In 1812 Mackenzie married a young woman of his own name. He also acquired an estate in Avoch

Mackenzie, Alexander (1822 – 1892)
Stonemason, Newspaperman, Prime Minister of Canada
Born in Logierait in Perthshire, Mackenzie was brought up in Dunkeld. He immigrated to Canada at the age of twenty and worked as a stonemason and building contractor. Expanding his interests, in 1852 Mackenzie became editor of a Liberal paper, while simultaneously studying politics. In 1861 he was a Liberal representative in parliament.

By 1867 he was leader of the opposition in the first parliament of the Dominion, where he faced **John Macdonald**. He was Prime Minister between 1873 and 1878. As a Liberal, he three times turned down the opportunity of a knighthood. Perhaps too cautious for a rapidly changing Canada, Mackenzie was known as an honest, hard working man.

Mackenzie, Colin (1755 – 1821)
First surveyor General of India

Born in Stornoway, Mackenzie father was the town's first postmaster and he was educated locally. An outstanding mathematician, he became a customs officer. Mackenzie developed an interest in logarithms that led to a contact with Lord Napier, whose ancestor had invented the system. With Napier's encouragement, Mackenzie joined the Madras Engineers, one of the regiments of the Honourable East India Company and at the age of 28 left to study logarithms in southern India. He was never to see Scotland again.

While in India, Mackenzie developed a keen interest in the life and history of the Indian people. As there was no formal interest in the history or prehistory of the country, he became one of the first people to collect artefacts from the derelict historical sites that were prominent in the landscape. Mackenzie sent thousands of carved stones, coins and other artefacts back to the British Museum, including early carvings of Buddha. He was one of the first Europeans to visit the Buddhist site at Amrawati and the first to recognise its importance. As well as rescuing many artefacts from decay and destruction, Mackenzie made hundreds of detailed drawings of objects and carvings that have since been lost.

Based at Fort St George, that became Madras, Mackenzie visited the site at Mamallewam. Although he was a pioneer in the preservation of historical artefacts, Mackenzie was also a serving soldier. As an engineer, he took part in operations against Tipu Sultan of Mysore. Mackenzie was present at the final battle of Serangipatam, where the Scottish general Sir David Baird assaulted the town with the 73rd and 74th Highlanders.

With Mysore incorporated into the East India Company's territories, Mackenzie was sent to map the land. His work was painstaking, as he also surveyed the country, learning of the language, culture and people. Mackenzie forged close relations with his team of Brahmin draughtsmen. He was the first European to investigate Jainism, including some of that religion's most holy sites.

Pragmatic and scrupulous in his work, Mackenzie always supported his subordinates, whatever their race and religion, for he had no thought of racism. He was one of the few people of his time to actively employ the Anglo-Indian community, who were then seen as beyond the pale of society. Marrying late in life, he kept in touch with his relatives in Stornoway, although he never managed to return home.

Perhaps, of course, India was his home, for he served forty years with the East India Company, eventually rising to become the first surveyor general of the country. He died in Calcutta and is remembered only by a plaque in a graveyard in Lewis. His most enduring memory is the many thousands of artefacts that he donated to the British Museum.

Mackenzie, George Henry, (1837 – 1891
Chess champion, soldier

Born at North Kessock, near Inverness, Mackenzie was an officer in the British army before immigrating to the United States, where he joined the United States Army. Although he is not remembered for any outstanding military feat, he was the American chess champion between 1871 and 1880, and the World chess champion in 1887.

Mackenzie, Kenneth (1797 – 1861)
King of the Missouri

Born in Ross and Cromarty, Kenneth Mackenzie became friendly with **Alexander Mackenzie** the explorer and in 1818 he immigrated to North America. Working from St Louis, he traded for the Columbia Fur Company, with an area that extended from the source of the Mississippi to the Great Lakes and the Missouri. When the Columbia Fur

Company merged with the American Fur Company in 1827, Mackenzie assumed control of the entire Upper Missouri district.

This was a dangerous land, a real Wild West where local tribes wielded the power, but Mackenzie built wooden forts and fortified trading posts and traded with the tribes on his own terms. Some knew him as 'King of the Missouri,' others as 'Emperor Mackenzie' but few disputed his law.

In 1834 he overstepped the mark by constructed a personal distillery at his headquarters at Fort Union. Forced out of the country for breaking Company rules, Mackenzie travelled to Europe and learned the art of wine making. Rather than living in the west, he then chose to live in the great American cities as an importer of fine wines.

Mackenzie, Murdo (1850 – 1939)
Cattleman

Born near Tain in Easter Ross, Mackenzie was educated at Tain Royal Academy. After working at the Tain Bank, he became the assistant factor at the Balnagowan estate of Sir Charles Ross. In 1876 he married Isabella MacBain, with whom he fathered five children. In 1885, while Mackenzie was working as an insurance agent with the local bank, a representative from the Prairie Cattle Company Ltd approached him with an offer of a job.

The Prairie was an Edinburgh company that had been formed five years previously. It was the first British ranching company to own land in the American West, and is known as the 'mother of the British cattle companies,' with capital of £100,000 and a prospectus that promised dividends of between 25 and 50% per annum. When the owners asked Mackenzie to manage their cattle business, he accepted. Taking his wife and family, Mackenzie moved to Trinidad, Colorado, from where he managed all three divisions of the company. As well as Colorado, he managed ranges in Texas and New Mexico, acting as the US agent while raising and shipping cattle. An excellent manager, Mackenzie had his own mind, so in 1850, when one of the owners overturned his decisions, he resigned.

The following year the Matador Land and Cattle Company of Dundee appointed him manager of its ranch in the Texas panhandle. More willing to move jobs than upset his family, Mackenzie relocated the Matador's American headquarters from Fort Worth to Trinidad. He was not overly happy about the quality of some of his staff, so employed Scotsmen that were experienced with cattle and who shared his work ethic. Mackenzie was a professional cattleman, not a manager in the rip-roaring Hollywood mould. He did not carry a gun and banned his cowboys from drinking and gambling.

His ideas, however, worked and under his strict management the Matador Company expanded. He bought more land in Texas and expanded into Wyoming, North and South Dakota and into Saskatchewan in Canada. While other operations concentrated on numbers of beasts, Mackenzie was more interested in quality. From 1892 he worked on improving his breeding stock by purchasing Hereford cattle and removing any inferior animals from his herds. It took a decade for his policy to achieve success, but from 1902 Matador cattle received awards at livestock shows up and down the American West.

Mackenzie was also in great demand. From 1896 he was the representative of a number of cattlemen's associations. From 1901 to 1904 he was president of the Texas and South West Cattle Raisers Association. In 1905 he was president of the Colorado branch of the American Cattle Growers Association. In 1908 he joined the board of directors of the American Hereford cattle Breeders Association and two years later Roosevelt appointed him to the National Conservation Committee. Roosevelt also thought that Mackenzie was the most influential of Western cattlemen.

Despite all these honours, Mackenzie still sought new challenges, so when the Brazil Land, Cattle and Packing Company offered him the manager's position, he accepted. Taking his family, Mackenzie headed for Sao Paula, to manage over two million acres of land with the associated livestock. In 1918, after achieving his aims there, Mackenzie returned to the United States, this time to settle permanently. By 1918 he was in Denver, again managing the Matador Company, a position he held until his retiral in 1937. Interestingly, the ownership of the Matador remained in Dundee, and the Texas ranch continued to operate until 1955.

As well as a cattleman, Mackenzie became Director of the Federal Reserve Bank at Denver from 1923 to 1935. His place in Western history was assured when he was mentioned in the Hall of Fame in Oklahoma City. In face and character he was the epitome of the Scottish farmer, average height, shrewd and steady, but he tamed his own section of the West by personality and professionalism.

MacKenzie, Thomas (1854 – 1930)
Prime minister of New Zealand

Born in Edinburgh, Mackenzie was only four when his parents immigrated to New Zealand. He was educated in Dunedin and at the age of twenty travelled to Wellington to join the Survey Department. Three years later he moved back to Otago, serving on Balclutha Borough Council from 1881 to 1887, including a spell as mayor. From 1887 to 1896 MacKenzie was represented Balclutha in parliament. In that period he also led a government inquiry into the produce trade with Britain and was a member of the tariff commission. After a few years out of politics, he became member for Waiherno in 1900, a position he held for a number of years.

In 1908, as Liberal member for Egmont, MacKenzie became Minister of Industries and Commerce, then Minister of Agriculture, Tourism and Health Resorts. In 1912 he briefly became leader of the Liberal Party and Prime Minister. A high commissioner in London, MacKenzie was the New Zealand delegate at the Versailles Peace Conference. For the last ten years of his life, MacKenzie was on the Legislative Council.

Mackenzie, William Lyon (1795 – 1861)
Canadian Politician and insurgent

Born near Dundee, Mackenzie and his mother immigrated to Canada in 1820. Working as a merchant in Upper Canada, he became aware of frustration toward the government. Between 1824 and 1834 he published the *Colonial Advocate* in Toronto, which was remorse-lessly aggressive toward government policies, particularly those of the monied families who dominated the York area. When his politi-cal opponents smashed his printing press, Mackenzie won his suit for damages, bought a larger press and continued his activities.

In 1828 he was elected to the provincial parliament for York. He lasted only two years in the position, being ejected for libel against the assembly. He returned to Britain in 1832, the year of the Great Reform Act, to find his stance popular. Back in Canada, he was mayor of Toronto in 1834. Three years later he published a declaration of independence for Toronto and demanding a republican government for Canada.

That same year, in alliance with a French Canadian named Pap-ineau, he raised a small army of discontents and attacked Toronto. When a larger force threw him back, Mackenzie fled to Buffalo in the United States. On the 13 December 1837 he occupied Navy Island in the Niagara River and announced a provisional government.

The Canadians were aware that an American steamer, *Caroline*, had been supplying Mackenzie's insurgents. On the 29th December the Canadians burned this vessel. With an international incident loom-ing, and sabres being menacingly rattled, Mackenzie retreated to New York. Rather than welcome him, the United States authorities promptly threw him into jail for a year.

Despite his adventures, Mackenzie returned to Canada in 1849 and soon became a Member of Parliament. He was incorruptible, refusing bribes or governmental positions that were intended to keep him quiet. At a time when Queen Victoria was almost deified, he referred to her as "Victoria Guelph, the bloody queen of England."

Mackenzie died in Toronto. The grandfather of Mackenzie King, the Canadian prime minister, he was one of the more colourful of Scottish emigrants.

Maclean, Sir Harry Aubrey de Vere (1848 – 1920)
Piper, Adviser to the Sultan of Morocco

After seeing service during the Fenian invasion of Canada, in 1877 Maclean left the British army to become army instructor to Sultan Mulai Hussan of Morocco. Spending more than thirty years in this position, Maclean became the Sultan's personal advisor, fought against rebel tribesmen in the backcountry and even visited Tafilet, one of the forbidden cities of the world. Despite court intrigues and kidnap by those opposed to the ruling regime, Maclean also operated as an agent of the British crown.

He was a tall, broad man, cheerful in disposition but well able to take care of himself. Maclean was also musical, playing the bagpipes, guitar, piano and accordion, and in his spare time he was an enthusiastic inventor. Although he received the K.C.M.G from King Edward VII, he is best remembered for his piping, which seems to have been well received at the Moroccan court.

MacLeod, Norman (1784 – 1860)

Pastor, settler

Born at Assynt, MacLeod graduated in divinity but returned home to pastor his own flock. After a disagreement with the parish minister, MacLeod guided his people to a new Promised Land across the Atlantic. He settled them in Pictou, Nova Scotia, and pastored to them, woman, man and child for years of bitter winters and Christianity. Again MacLeod became unsettled and sent on his son to pastures new.

Australia was their next destination, thousands of miles across a sea that was not Red to a land where milk and honey were not abundant. They reached Australia in 1851, with the 71-year-old pastor in front and his flock following with trust and love. They knew of his faults, his theocratic domineering, his paternalism, but also knew his genuine warmth and sincerity so another shipload of Highlanders soon followed, as MacLeod's people willingly put themselves under his control.

After only three years in Australia they were on the sea again, sailing the comparatively short hop to New Zealand, which was like Scotland in many ways, but lacked the class system that so stifled its people. In 1854 they settled at Waipu, their wanderings at last complete, but MacLeod continued to pastor to them, visiting even the most remote of his people at the age of eighty.

Maclure, William (1763 – 1840)
Father of American geology

Born in Ayr, Maclure was privately educated and became a merchant and entrepreneur. He travelled briefly to the United States before settling in London, where he worked for an American firm and indulged in much business travel. As well as Ireland, he spent much time in France, where he was a witness to many events in the Revolution. He also lived in Spain and Mexico. By 1796 Maclure was a wealthy man from his commercial activities and possibly from a family inheritance. Again crossing the Atlantic, he became an American citizen and put down roots in Philadelphia, although his business also took him to Richmond. Extremely successful, he had the money and time to indulge his passion for travelling and geology.

Maclure visited Europe, Russia and North America. While he travelled, he examined the local geology and contacted the leading geologists of the area. Moving to London, he continued to travel before immigrating to the United States in 1800. Maclure wrote about his geological work and was instrumental in founding the Academy of Natural Sciences in Philadelphia, over which he presided from 1817 to his death in 1840. Over the next decades, the Academy became a focal point for visiting scholars as well as a centre for North American exploration. Maclure wrote *Observations on the Geology of the United States.*

Maclure was also interested in educational reform, working toward republican democracy and universal education, in the old Scottish manner. He continued his travels, visiting many nations in Europe, where he spoke to the leading educationalists. One of his most important contacts was Johann Pestalozzi in Switzerland, whose rational education system Maclure particularly admired. Maclure also returned to Scotland to study the educational pioneer work at New Lanark, which he attempted to reproduce at the Utopia settlement of New Harmony, Indiana. Maclure was remembered both for his educational and geological work in the United States.

MacNab, Archibald, 13th Laird of (1777 – 1860)
Laird and promoter of emigration

The 13th Laird of MacNab was brought up near Killin, Perthshire but like many of his peers, he spent more than his lands could raise. He left his ancestral home in 1822 when his creditors became too pressing and travelled to Canada with the intention of making money. As eloquent as he was profligate, he persuaded the Canadian authorities to grant him 81,000 acres alongside the Ottawa River. He intended to settle a great many of his clan on this land.

While the Canadian government believed MacNab to be a government agent allocating free land, he told his emigrant countrymen that he was sole proprietor of the township and ensured that they paid him rent. However, Highland loyalty to their chief was weakening since the Clearances and MacNab's feudal tyranny invoked a stream of complaints. The Canadian government evicted MacNab, who complained that he had been "betrayed by his own serfs"

Retreating to Orkney, he lived with a mistress. When he became a father at the age of eighty, the local population was scandalised and MacNab again fled, this time to France, where he died.

Maconochie, Captain Alexander (1787 – 1860)
Australian penal reformer

Born in Edinburgh, Maconochie was the son of a solicitor. When his father died, the nine-year-old Maconochie was raised by Allan Maconochie who later became Lord Meadowbank. Although he was brought up to enter the law, Maconochie joined the Navy. He served in the Caribbean and the Baltic, and in 1811 was shipwrecked off Holland and for two years was a prisoner of war.

With the defeat of Bonaparte, Maconochie rejoined the navy and commanded the gunboat *Calliope* during the American War, but was laid off at the peace. After thirteen years studying and writing in Edinburgh, Maconochie married in 1822 and six years later moved to London. By 1830 he was the University College of London's first Professor of Geography, then became secretary of the new Royal Geographical Society.

Maconochie seemed destined for an academic life until 1837 when Sir John Franklin asked him to compile a detailed report on the prison system on Van Dieman's Land. At that time Franklin was involved in the Society for the Improvement of Prison Discipline.

As soon as he arrived in Hobart, Tasmania, Maconochie realised that the Australian authorities could manipulate Franklin with some ease, while they disliked his own bluntness. He also thought the penal system "cruel, uncertain prodigal, ineffectual either for reform or example" and was dependent on "extreme severity." Coming from a man who had served in the Royal Navy during the reign of the cat, and who had experienced the hardship of prison life at first hand, these were powerful statements. He also spoke against the use of convicts on chain-gang labour, writing of a "moderation" in both "physical suffering" and "moral pain." He envisaged prison discipline with an emphasis on rewards and a target worth aiming for. Good behaviour was to be rewarded, rather than bad behaviour punished. Convicts would get 'marks' for good behaviour, and after a certain number of marks, they would be free.

After some editing, Franklin submitted Maconochie's report to the government in London, but Maconochie added a shorter unexpunged version. The reports reached London at a time of violent anti-transportation debate. Realising that they were now reviled as virtual slave owners, the people of Hobart vented their spite on Maconochie. Pressed by his colonial peers, Franklin sacked Maconochie, although Lady Franklin, one of the most steadfast women of the nineteenth century, gave him her personal support. His wife was equally staunch.

Unbowed in adversity, Maconochie drew on support from London to continue his push for penal reform. In May 1840 the Colonial Office advised that Maconochie should be sent to Norfolk Island to test his theories. Norfolk Island was populated by over a thousand hardened criminals, victims of one of the harshest penal systems imaginable. Maconochie brought another three hundred freshly transported from the United Kingdom, as well as his wife and children, who must have wondered to what kind of place their father was condemning them. Maconochie thought the "old lags" were a "demonical-looking assemblage" but when he announced his more humane system to these damned souls, they cheered him to the echo. In place of torture, Maconochie had brought hope.

Celebrating the Queen's birthday with rum, food and a measure of freedom for the convicts, Maconochie won their hearts. He brought books and music, but the colonial authorities did not always honour his promises to the punished. He threw down the permanent gallows, built a brace of churches and made space for a synagogue, allocated allotments where fruit, vegetables and even tobacco could be grown.

Norfolk Island, however, was no paradise. Blight ruined the crops, disease decimated the desperate convicts, and colonial critics spoke of anarchy and escapes. When Governor Gipps visited, he found a quiet and orderly island, perfectly disciplined. Even so, those who opposed Maconochie were powerful and he was recalled from Norfolk.

Returning to Britain, Maconochie continued to campaign for penal reform, but a minor crime wave argued against leniency. He wrote a lengthy book on his mark system, governed a Birmingham prison for two frustrating years and retired, to live into his seventies.

Macpherson, Allan (d 1759)
Soldier who chose to be decapitated

James Macpherson was an ordinary Scottish soldier serving with Montgomery's Highlanders in North America. He was in a detachment that was captured by the French and Indians, possibly in Virginia. As the Indians proceeded to torture the prisoners to death, Macpherson devised a strategy to escape this hideous end. Calling the Indians to him, he used an interpreter to tell them he knew the secret of a medicine that could make him invulnerable, and, if his life were spared for a few minutes, he would show them. When the Indians agreed, Macpherson gathered together some plants, rubbed his neck with their juice and, placing his head on a log, invited them to chop it off, saying that their sharpest tomahawk would make no impression. The Indians did so, killing him quickly and saving him from torture. It was said that the Indians were so impressed by his ingenuity that they also spared the lives of the other captives, which is how the story became known.

Macpherson, Gillies (1844 – c1898)
Prospector, Australian explorer
Probably born at the Dalwhinnie Inn in Badenoch, Macpherson was the son of Graham Macpherson and his common law wife Isabell. Macpherson immigrated to Queensland, Australia in 1873, where he immediately started to prospect. After hunting gold in Queensland, Macpherson prospected for tin in Western Australia and gold again around Kimberley near Darwin.

In the late 1880s, Macpherson was again in Western Australia, first at the Southern Cross goldfields, then to the east of Kalgoorlie. Legends insist that on one occasion he nearly died of thirst but his native guide tied him to the last horse and led him to safety. Legend also claims that Macpherson helped Arthur Bayley find the Coolgardie goldfield.

Macpherson also prospected at the Murchison goldfield and deep in the deserts. In 1892, prosperous from his many gold finds, Macpherson married Elizabeth Wisbey. He was 48, full bearded and stocky, Elizabeth was 22 and the daughter of the Mayor of Bunbury. Unfortunately Elizabeth died just over a year later, leaving Macpherson with a young son.

Without a wife, Macpherson returned to prospecting, setting out on an epic trip by camel from the Southern Cross field to Alice Springs. After that feat, Macpherson's movements are obscure, although it is possible that he travelled to Canada for the Klondike strikes and died near Dawson City. McPherson's Pillar in the Gibson Desert was named in his honour.

Macpherson, Sir John (1745 – 1821)
Governor General of India

Born in Skye, Macpherson was the son of a minister. He joined the East India Company as a purser and travelled to Madras, where he used his considerable charm to enter the service of the Nawab of the Carnatic. The Nawab sent him to London, where he acted as agent, but spent too freely. Back in the service of the East India Company, he was dismissed for corruption but talked his way back into favour.

By 1782 Macpherson was a member of the Company's Supreme Council and by sheer seniority, became Governor-general in 1785. He followed Warren Hastings and Lord Cornwallis referred to him as "the most contemptible and contemmed governor that ever pretended to govern." Macpherson was guilty of financial corruption but was still created a baronet and met the Prince Regent.

Macquarie, Lachlan (1761 – 1824)
Father of Australia

Born on the island of Ulva, off Mull, MacQuarie was the son of a tacksman. He joined the Black Watch in 1777, in time to see service in North America during the Revolution. He also fought in India and Egypt, being promoted to command the 73rd Highlanders. In 1809 he voluntarily travelled to the penal colony of New South Wales. He would be the last man to run the colony as a military unit, the longest serving Australian governor and would be remembered, with justification, as the Father of Australia.

As a devout Presbyterian, Macquarie looked at the sordid mess of the colony and resolved to scour it clean. He saw himself as an 'awkward, rusticated Jungle-Wallah' but he was impervious to corruption and too tough to be concerned by the threats of Bligh, his infamous, mutiny-surviving predecessor. He found the colony dominated by the Rum Corps, a group of officers who speculated in land, manipulated the import of grain, fiddled the treasury and controlled an economy that was based on rum. Backed by the 73rd Highlanders, he removed the dishonest hierarchy, reinstated a number of officers and kicked out the drunken judge advocate.

Determined to create a colony out of chaos, Macquarie attempted to reform the image of New South Wales. After two decades in the army, he was no democrat but his despotism was benevolent as he closed three-quarters of Sydney's seedy pubs, raised revenue with a spirit duty and hammered the illicit stills that festered in every conceivable nook and cranny. To reinforce the message, Macquarie ordered that pubs should close during divine service on Sundays, forced bewildered convicts into church and their children into Sunday schools and stopped any trading on the Lord's Day.

The low morals of the colony were next to be addressed. Macquarie would know all about the mass rape that marked the birth of Sydney and the abundance of illegitimate children that swarmed from the Rocks to the outback. His response was to ban cohabitation and clear the lewd from the brothels.

Years in advance of his time, Macquarie believed that their surroundings affected people, so set about altering the built environment of the colony. Where he found houses that were huts, a town "in ruinous decay", public buildings that he likened to pigsties and churches that disgraced the name, he left something like a Georgian New Town. It was his wife, Elizabeth who unearthed a book of town and building plans, from which Macquarie set down guidelines for future building. He planned central Sydney, ordered that Australian streets should be wide and houses as spacious as the land itself. Elizabeth's hand and mind may be seen in his first public building, the hospital with Indian-style veranda and windows that caught the vastness of the landscape. If it was ironical that he should pay for the improvements with a duty on rum, there was more irony in his pick of a government architect.

Francis Greenway was an English convict, and under Macquarie's guidance he produced a string of noble buildings for Australia. The authorities and press in Britain did not approve. "Ornamental architecture", the *Edinburgh Review* called his work, as Macquarie sifted through the newly arrived convicts for skilled tradesmen and builders. He began an honest judiciary, dependable banks with native currency and a post office that would reach the steadily expanding settlements. His roads probed the interior, where his villages sat around a public square with school, church and police station. Possibly more important for the self-respect of Australia, he began to treat the incoming transportees with the first humanity the colony had known.

Meeting each incoming ship, he offered the convicts hope. Once they had served their time, they could settle as free men in a new land and to prove that their crimes had been expunged by their sentence, he promoted an ex-convict to magistrate. His hope was for a class of ex-convicts who would occupy small farms throughout the land. To this end he pardoned the deserving and encouraged self-help. Yet Macquarie was not a spineless sop. When bushrangers threatened to make Tasmania a no-go area for free settlers, he crossed the Bass Strait and left half a score of bodies dangling from suitable trees. "These dreadful examples" he thought, had ended the "Bush-Ranging System."

He could be equally severe with the Aborigines, the original owners of the land. He banned any armed native from the towns, and forbade them to collect in dangerous numbers, but he also introduced them to education and Christianity. Despite all his efforts, Macquarie was not popular with the British government. He had found a prison settlement and left a colony. Although the government allowed him a pension, they offered no other reward, but the people of Australia recognised his worth and his gravestone on Mull recorded him as the Father of Australia.

MacTavish, Simon (1750 – 1804)
Founder of the North West Company

Born in Stratherrick, MacTavish was the son of the John MacTavish, a Garthsbeg tacksman who had served in North America as a lieutenant in the 78th Highlanders. When John MacTavish heard that his daughter and son in law were emigrating, he arranged for the 13 year old Simon MacTavish to accompany them.

At first MacTavish settled in Albany, New York, where he entered the fur trade. In 1771 he petitioned the Governor of New York for 2000 acres of land, and the following year was working from Detroit. By 1773 he was in the Niagara area, but after the American Revolutionary War he joined the exodus that moved north. By the 1780s he was in Montreal, where he became one of the leading businessmen. It was during this period that MacTavish began to trap and trade in the area north and west of the Great Lakes, unlike most of the American traders, who operated to the south and west of the Lakes.

At the age of 43 MacTavish married Marie Marguerite Chaboillez, daughter of an established Quebec based fur family. He established the North West Company, which was manned mainly by Scottish Highlanders, many of whom were related to MacTavish. A very shrewd businessman, MacTavish also travelled to London to speak directly to the Prime Minister, and was vain enough to create his own coat of arms. The French knew him as Le Marquis while the Earl of Selkirk thought him "unequalled in acuteness and reach of thought."

The North West Company based itself at the western edge of Lake Superior, where Thunder Bay now spreads. Later known as Fort William, it was a strongly constructed wooden fort in which the partners and up to 3000 traders and voyageurs met once a year for a roistering few days of celebration. The North West Company that MacTavish created and built up was to be the main rival to the Hudson Bay Company.

Makee, James (c 1810 - 1879)
Whaling master and Hawaiian planter

James Makee was a Scottish whaling master who captained American vessels out of Boston. Sometime around 1843 he was severely injured, either in a bar room brawl in Honolulu or, more charitably, in an accident on board his ship. In either event he settled in Hawaii, in 1856 buying the 20,000-acre Torbert Plantation at Honua'ula in Maui. Makee became a rancher, renamed the property Rose Ranch after his wife Catherine's favourite flower.

Bringing Catherine and their five daughters from Massachusetts, Makee's hospitality soon became legendary on the island, perhaps especially after the ex-seaman introduced grapes for wine into the island. Makee built a large house with a tennis court, a bowling green and billiard room. He planted over 150,000 trees including the Queensland Kauri, which was excellent for ship's masts. He also grew roses, bred horses and sugar and became wealthy. He is remembered by the Hawaiian dance Hula O Makee and by Makee Island near Honolulu.

Marshall, Peter (1902 –1949)
Clergyman

Born in Coatbridge, Marshall was educated at Coatbridge Technical School, studying mechanical engineering. After a very brief spell in the Royal Navy he found work locally but became involved with the YMCA. As his hero was Eric Liddle the Scottish Christian runner, he found himself drawn to the church. However, his lack of formal education counted against him in Scotland, but the United States welcomed him. He arrived at Ellis Island in April 1927.

After various manual jobs, Marshall entered and graduated from Columbia Theological Seminary at Decatur in Georgia. Thereafter he worked as a Pastor in the South for a number of years, where he was known as the 'charming young Scot with the silver tongue.' He married Catherine Wood, an all-American girl with an all-Scottish name, and who was later to write his biography.

In 1937 Marshall was appointed to the New York Avenue Presbyterian Church in Washington DC. Eleven years later he was appointed chaplain to the United States senate, where he was remembered for his concise prayers. As Dr Cranford, pastor of Washington's Calvary Baptist Church commented, 'there was in Peter the rare combination of poet and prophet. His sermons were poetic prose... when he spoke, men listened.' A film of his life, based on his wife's book, later appeared.

Marshall also wrote *Mr Jones, Meet the Master*.

Matheson, James (1796 – 1878)

Opium smuggler and businessman

Born at Lairg, Matheson was the illegitimate son of a gentleman. Rather than disown him, his father honoured his responsibilities by sending him to Edinburgh University, where he studied political economy. As soon as he graduated, Matheson was shipped abroad. He became a merchant in India, and in 1819 the company sent him on a Danish passport to Canton in China. Matheson joined the world of opium smuggling, operating so effectively that after only a few voyages across the Formosa Strait he had a small fortune.

Matheson proved to be an astute businessman and, despite the trade that he engaged in, was a likeable, sophisticated individual with a hard edge that could destroy a rival with charming mercilessness. In 1832 he entered partnership with **William Jardine** from Lochmaben, a combination of Highland and Border that boded ill for any competition. They traded under the Scottish Saltire, and within a few years Jardine Matheson was the most important company in Canton, then in the Orient. In 1833 the company willingly embraced Free Trade, their fast clippers carrying up to 6000 chests of opium annually from India, and each chest making a formidable profit. When the Chinese protested against the illegal opium trade, Jardine Matheson was among the foremost voices in demanding war to open Chinese ports. They got their way.

During the Opium War of 1839 – 1842 Jardine Matheson initiated trade from Hong Kong, using the Danish flag as neutral cover for their smuggling. After the Treaty of Nanking in 1843, the Chinese allowed trade in a number of ports and Jardine Matheson moved into Shanghai. The company was to dominate Eastern trade for decades.

When Matheson turned his attention to Scotland, he purchased the island of Lewis, 'improved' the economy by clearing the population in a move as cynical as any of his Eastern ventures, and renovated Stornoway Castle for his own use. Benjamin Disraeli knew him as 'Mr Macdrug' and claimed that he had "a million in opium in each pocket."

McAdam, John (1827 – 1865)

Analytical chemist and medical practitioner

Born near Glasgow, McAdam was educated at the Andersonian Institute in Glasgow, where he studied chemistry. In 1844 he was appointed as Senior Assistant and proved to have a talent for analytical chemistry. He moved on to Edinburgh University, where he studied under Professor William Gregory, one of the leading chemists of his day. Between 1846 and 1847 McAdam added to his education when he assisted Dr George Wilson at his Brown Square laboratory.

From that date onward, McAdam's life was one of constant appointments and committees. In 1847 he taught chemistry in Glasgow and was elected a Member of the Royal Scottish Society. The following year he became a member of the Glasgow Philosophical Society, while studying medicine at Glasgow University. Thereafter he was appointed Lecturer in Chemistry and Natural Science at the Scotch College in Melbourne, a position he held from 1855 until 1865.

Simultaneously with his lecturing duties, McAdam was a member of the Philosophical Institute of Victoria. He was also involved in the Exploration Committee for the Burke and Wills expedition, when he recommended medical and safety procedures. In 1858 the Victorian government appointed him their analytical chemist, and two years later he became the Health Officer for the City of Melbourne, while sitting on the Legislative Assembly.

It is sometimes difficult to grasp the amount of work that these expatriate Scots assumed, but perhaps that accounted for their early death. McAdam was only 37 when he died, still busy and very respected.

McCallum, David Craig (1815 – 1879)

Engineer, builder, railroad manager

Born in Johnston in Renfrewshire, McCallum was only a child when his family immigrated to Rochester, New York. After an elementary education, he started work as a carpenter, but eventually became an architect and engineer. While he was still a young man he married Mary McCann, with whom he had three sons.

In 1851 McCallum made his name and his fortune when he invented and patented the inflexible arched truss. From that time on, McCallum's invention was included in every timber bridge to be built in the United States. With his fortune assured, McCallum could concentrate on his career, becoming a noted bridge builder as well as becoming involved in railroad administration.

From 1852 McCallum lived in New York and three years later was appointed general superintendent of the Mew York and Erie Railway, a position he held until 1856. The subsequent three years saw the Mc-Callum Bridge Company involved right across the American West as well as in South and Central America.

When the American Civil War began, McCallum's expertise was again in demand. He was appointed Director and Superintendent of the United States Military Railroad. As such he managed the railroads in the occupied Confederate States. There had been a limited use of railways to carry supplies in the Crimean War, and a slightly more extensive use by the French in their 1859 war with Austria, but the American Civil War saw the first wide scale use of rail. McCulloch was a pioneer in railroad use and administration, and his efficiency gained the admiration of everybody. Created a Brigadier General in 1863, McCulloch was promoted to Major General the following year. After the war he became involved in the United States Pacific Railroad.

McCallum, Francis McNeish McNeill (1823 – 1857)
Alias Captain Melville, Bushranger

The enigmatic Captain Melville hovers always on the borders between folklore and fact, so that reality is as elusive as any Australian bushranger. He was born in Scotland, probably in Perthshire, for when he was 13 the Perth authorities arrested him for housebreaking and sentenced him to seven years transportation to Van Diemen's Land. McCallum, now using the name Edward Melville, was not a model prisoner and had his sentence increased for twice trying to escape. He succeeded at the third attempt, and in 1851 ran to Victoria, then busy with the gold rush. Not one to grub hard for gold, Melville became a bushranger.

Melville operated for around a year, so his reputation in Victoria grew. He robbed travellers and became a horse thief, but there is a possibility that some of the stories told in his honour referred to other bushrangers with the same name. Captain Melville became famous in December 1852 when he and a man named William Roberts robbed 18 men at a house belonging to Mr Aitcheson, and then made Mrs Aitcheson feed them before ransacking the property.

With a reward of £100 on his head, Melville was lucky to have survived so long, but it was a prostitute who gave him away to the police when he visited a Geelong brothel and boasted of his identity. Melville escaped, but was captured outside the building. Sentenced to 32 years on board a prison ship, he led a mutiny in 1856, killed a guard and tried to escape by boat. Recaptured, he was sentenced to life in Melbourne jail, where he tried to kill the governor. Known for his violent temper, he was placed under medical observation but still managed to commit suicide.

McClung, Alexander Keith (1811-1855)

Gunman and politician

McClung was one of the most feared men in the early West. Known as the 'Black Knight of the South', his name tells of his Scottish blood, although he was born in Virginia. McClung ran away from home at an early age and after service as a midshipman in the United States Navy, and in the 1st Mississippi Regiment during the war with Mexico. He studied law and set up in a legal practice before earning his reputation as a duellist. He was known as a dark eyed killer who drank, a handsome man liked by women and a gambler, but McClung also fought fair. He was a crack shot with pistol and rifle and made Kansas wild many years before the days of Jesse James or Billy the Kid. McClung was the US Charge d'affaires to Bolivia for a short time and committed suicide in Jackson, Mississippi.

McCosh, James (1811 –1894)

Philosopher, president of Princeton

Born in Carskeoch, Ayrshire, McCosh attended Glasgow University between 1824 and 1829, and then studied at Edinburgh University. He graduated in theology and became a Church of Scotland minister. He worked at Arbroath before moving to Brechin but then left to join the Free Church. From 1852 to 1868 he was Professor of Logic and Metaphysics at Queens College Belfast and in 1866 he toured the United States, lecturing philosophy to packed audiences.

Toward the end of 1868 he elected president of Princeton University. As a minister of religion but also a scientifically minded educationalist, McCosh was torn in the debate over evolution. He was perhaps the first significant Protestant in the United States to merge science and religion, maintaining that the students of Princeton should pay regard to scientific evidence while considering evolution. Nevertheless, McCosh believed that the periodic religious revivals of the time helped keep the students under control.

McCosh was instrumental in making Princeton a non-parochial university that appealed to students from all across the United States. In the 1870s he also embarked on a major building programme. Quick tempered, he was also capable of great kindness, while his wife Isabella acted as nurse to the students for two decades. The University infirmary was named after her.

Among other things, he wrote *Institutions of the Mind* that argued for the common sense school of Scottish philosophy.

McCulloch, Sir James (1819 – 1893)

Australian Prime Minister

Born in Glasgow, McCulloch immigrated to Melbourne to manage a Glasgow based business. In 1854 he became the Wimmera member of the Legislative Council. An astute politician, McCulloch was soon promoted to Minister of Trade and Customs. In 1862 he became Prime Minister for the first time. After resigning over a trade dispute, he was voted in for a further three terms of office. In 1877 he fell from power.

McDougall, Alexander (1732 – 1786)

Banker and American patriot

Born in the island of Islay, McDougall was taken to Fort Edward, New York at the age of six, then to New York City. Although McDougall senior prospered in his new country, Alexander McDougall preferred to go to sea. He returned to Scotland in 1751, visited Islay and married Nancy McDougall, a distant relative. They remained married until her death in 1763, by which time she had given him three children. In 1767 he married again, to Hannah Bostwich, but produced no more children.

McDougall seemed to have inherited some of the daring of his Hebridean ancestors for during the Seven-Year War he commanded a duo of privateers that preyed on French and Spanish shipping. With the peace he became a merchant in New York City. By now more American than British, he supported the Livingstone faction that hoped for moderate resistance to British tax demands, rather than the more extreme Sons of Liberty. However his 1769 pamphlet *To the Betrayed Inhabitants of the City and Colony of New York* saw his reputation soar with the patriots, particularly as it earned him a spell in prison. He was reputedly the first American to be imprisoned for making speeches for independence. When he was released, McDougall became ever more involved in revolutionary politics. As well as organising New York resistance to the Tea Act in 1773, he helped turn back ships carrying tea to the city and in 1774 repeated the Boston Tea Party in New York Harbour.

As a member of the New York Committee of Correspondence, McDougall was a leader of the Revolutionary movement. In July 1774 he was principal speaker at a popular meeting that decided to act against the British Coercive Act and during the next two years he was a member of several New York provincial congresses. McDougall, however, was not just an organiser. Joining the New York Militia, he rose from Colonel in 1776 to Major General in 1777. He took part in the battles of Long Island and White Plains and remained in active service for most of the war.

After the patriots retreated from New York City, McDougall fortified the Hudson Highlands against the British, and then became commander at West Point. With the end of the war, McDougall was elected to the New York Senate and was also the first president of the Bank of New York. He lived long enough to see the United States emerge free of colonialism.

McDougall, Alexander (1845 – 1923)
Built first steamship on the American North West Coast
Born in Islay, McDougall immigrated to Canada in 1854 but a few years later moved south to Chicago. He became a shipbuilder on the Great Lakes, creating many fine vessels. However by 1892 he was working on the West Coast and built the first steamship on America's Pacific Northwest. McDougall was also the founder of Everett Washington Hydro-Electrics.

McGill, James (1744 – 1813)
Canadian philanthropist and entrepreneur
Born in Glasgow, the son of a merchant, McGill was educated at Glasgow University. There seems to be some dispute about the date he emigrated to Canada, but it was perhaps around 1765. Like many Scots he became involved in the northwestern fur trade, but unlike most he made and retained money, which he invested in the North Western Company.

. Settling in Montreal, where he was known for his wealth, McGill was a member of the House of Assembly and Colonel of the First Battalion of the Montreal Militia. McGill died young, but in his will he returned some of his fortune to Canada when he bequeathed land and money to found McGill College. In 1821 this college became McGill University.

McGillivray, Lachlan (1719 – 1799)
Indian trader
McGillivray was born in Dunmaglass in Strathnairn, son of William McGillivray and grandson of the chief of the McGillivrays. At the age

of 16 he accompanied Captain George Dunbar to Darien in the colony of Georgia, where the Highlanders were being used as a buffer to protect the English colonies from the Spanish of Florida. Sailing from Inverness, Lachlan and the other colonists arrived at Tybee Roads in January 1736. The Highlanders wore their traditional plaids, which endeared them to the local Indians, who could easily distinguish them from their English and Lowland compatriots. With the Indian tribal divisions similar to the Highland clans, and a shared interest in hunting and oral tales, the two peoples were not dissimilar.

Lachlan joined the mainly Jacobite colony, many of whose members had been exiled for their part in the 1715 Rising, and learned the language of the local Creek Indians. McGillivray took part in the Spanish War that started in 1739. He may have been at the defeat at Fort Mosa, and if so was one of the few that escaped.

At that time there was a profusion of companies trading with the Indians, the largest being headed by Archibald McGillivray, an exiled Jacobite. Rather than a career as a soldier, McGillivray joined his kinsman Archibald in the Indian trade. In 1741 he acted as interpreter when James Bullock led a diplomatic mission into Creek territory. By 1743 he was trading on his own account, travelling to the Upper Creeks of the Coosa River. McGillivray prospered as an Indian Trader and only the following year he became one of the founders of Brown Rae & Company, who were to dominate the Indian trade in Augusta.

Rather than live in any of the relatively stable colonial towns, McGillivray chose to settle on a plantation near Little Tallassee, which was a mere nine miles from a major French base at Fort Toulouse. The more time he spent with the Creeks, the more influential McGillivray became, until the Georgian authorities asked his advice on many Indian matters.

Around this time, McGillivray married Sehoy Marchant, a Creek woman, daughter of a woman of the Wind Clan and a French military officer. Their son, Alexander McGillivray, was to become chief of the Creek nation and wield enormous power and influence in the southeast. In the meantime Lachlan McGillivray rose higher in the public service, acting as intermediary between the Governor of Georgia and the Creek Nation

In 1755, just before the Seven Years War erupted, McGillivray took his family to Augusta, where his house became the focal point for many Creek visitors. Although he was now prosperous, he was not idle and led Creek and Choctaw war parties against the Cherokees and French during the 1760s Cherokees War. The people of Augusta were grateful for his protection.

Never a man to sit still, in 1762 McGillivray bought 50,000 acres of land on the Ogeechee River and experimented with rice plantations around Savannah. He continued to act as an intermediary between the colonial authorities and the Creek Nation and was present when Georgia's borders with the Creeks were agreed. Nonetheless, dark times were looming as revolutionary fervour rumbled through the colonies. McGillivray was elected to the Assembly in November 1775, but left when the Patriots took control of Georgia in 1776. He returned briefly when the British regained control but thereafter returned to Scotland. He settled again in Dumnaglass, a man who had helped settle the colony of Georgia but whose greatest legacy was probably his son, chief of the Creek nation.

McGregor, John (1808 – 1836)
Piper at the Alamo

Born somewhere in Scotland, John McGregor was living in Nacogdoches, Texas by 1836. He was heavily involved in the Texan war against Mexico, fighting at the siege of Bexar. During the siege of the Alamo he served as a second sergeant, and allegedly engaged in musical duels with Davie Crocket, playing his bagpipes against Crockett's fiddle. According to legend, McGregor's piping won by noise alone. He died in the Alamo on March 6th.

McIntosh, Lachlan (1727 – 1806)
Planter and Officer of the Continental Army

Born in Badenoch, the son of John Mhor McIntosh and Margaret Fraser, McIntosh immigrated to Georgia in 1736. He was one of a number of Highlanders in a party led by his father. They intended to settle at Darien, Georgia to act as a buffer for the more northerly British colonies against the Spanish of Florida. As a Georgia Ranger, McIntosh took part in the unfortunate battle of Fort Mousa, after which he attempted to ship to Scotland to join the 1745 Rising.

After his mixed fortunes during the War of Jenkins' Ear and the War of Spanish Succession, in 1748 McIntosh moved to Charleston, South Carolina, but later returned to Georgia. After a spell as an Indian Trader, he succeeded in establishing one of the most extensive rice plantations in the colony. In 1756 he married Sarah Threadcraft, who was to give him eight children, then for a short time was a member of the Colonial Assembly.

As the colonists' resentment of British policies grew, McIntosh became a Whig. At that time many of the Highlanders, whatever their allegiance to Stuart or Hanovarian in Scotland, tended to the Loyalist cause, but McIntosh had spent most of his life in America. He had little cause to support a Hanovarian monarch and soon became a Patriot leader in the south of Georgia.

In 1776 McIntosh became Colonel of the Georgia battalion of the Continental army, and as such prevented British attempts to snatch supplies from Savannah. He also led raids into Florida, temporarily disrupting the British supply routes. However, a rival Patriot, Button Swinnett, accused him of not doing enough, so McIntosh challenged him to a duel. The pair exchanged pistol shots; McIntosh was wounded but killed Swinnett. When he recovered, McIntosh joined Washington at Valley Forge in 1777, where he commanded a brigade of the Continental Army.

Washington, who believed him "an officer of great worth and merit," sent him westward, where McIntosh built Fort McIntosh and Fort Laurens, both of which secured an American presence in an area claimed by Britain. By 1779 he was again in the south, leading the Georgia and South Carolina Continentals against the British in Savannah. He fought hard, but the British regulars repulsed him, whereupon he was temporarily suspended from command. When the British took Savannah in 1780 they captured McIntosh, but released him in a prisoner exchange the following year.

When the war ended, McIntosh was appointed Commissioner for Loyalist Estates and the state representative at various discussions with the Indians. However, the war had proved disastrous for McIntosh's own estates and he was never to regain the position he once held. Although a patriot and a brave fighter, McIntosh had not gained by American independence.

McKay, James (1808 – c1880)

Blockade-runner, founder of cattle trade with Cuba, possible Union spy

Born at Thurso in Caithness, McKay gained his Master Mariner's certificate before he was 25, but when he tried to marry Matilda Alexander, her mother disapproved and emigrated with the girl. McKay followed, married Matilda anyway and settled in Florida. During the Civil War he took ships through the Union blockade of the Southern ports. McKay was also appointed head of the Fifth Commissary District for the Confederate Army, but in 1861 the State of Florida accused him of treason for selling cattle to Union occupied Key West and Dry Tortugas. When Union vessels arrested him for gunrunning, he is alleged to have taken an oath of loyalty to the North. When he returned to Tampa he was one of the first to fly the Confederate Flag, although some have accused him of delaying shipments of cattle to the Confederate forces. There is a possibility that McKay, and other Florida cattlemen, were looking after their own interests rather than those of the Confederacy.

After the war McKay invested heavily, and successfully, in land and property. True to his seafaring instinct, McKay also dabbled in shipping. Buying two schooners, he was the first American to ship cattle to Cuba.

McKenzie, George Henry (1837 – 1891)

Professional chess player

Born at North Kessock, Easter Ross, McKenzie was interested in chess from an early age. In 1862 he won the London Chess Championship, and immigrated to the United States the following year.

Like many newly arrived immigrants, McKenzie entered the army very soon after arrival. He fought in the 83rd New York Infantry but did not continue his army career. Becoming a professional chess player, McKenzie was virtually undefeated in the New York area and in 1880 he won the American Chess Championships. However, chess was not a lucrative profession and he lived his life in poverty. He died of pneumonia in New York.

McKinlay, John (1819 – 1872)

Australian explorer

Born at Sandbank beside the River Clyde, McKinlay immigrated to Australia in 1836. Working in the outback, he became experienced at tracking and surviving in some of the harshest territory in the country. When the Burke and Wills expedition failed to return in 1861, the authorities asked McKinlay to lead the South Australia Burke Relief Expedition to search for the missing men.

Using camels as well as horses, McKinlay left Adelaide in August that year and travelled to Cooper's Creek, where he learned that only one of the party had survived. From Cooper's Creek McKinlay explored in the direction of Central Mount Sturt (now Central Mount Stuart) and across to the Gulf of Carpentaria. As usual in Australian exploration, the main problem was the heat and lack of water.

The party was trapped by lack of water for weeks, and even when they could move, sunstroke killed the bullocks. When it rained, gluey mud slowed their progress and they had to find refuge on an island against rising floodwaters. It was here that the camels came in particularly useful as they carried their load high above the water. Menaced by dingoes, McKinlay poisoned them with strychnine, as he noted the sudden explosion of bird life. When they reached the Gulf, McKinlay had hoped to board a ship for Melbourne. Unfortunately the ship had already sailed, so McKinlay headed instead for Bowen on the Eastern Queensland coast.

The six hundred mile trip proved arduous, with terrible drought. McKinlay made rawhide boots for the camels as men fell sick and flies plagued them. The journal entries tell a grim story:

"Maitland so ill he can hardly hang on to the horses back...Kirby...is a mere bag of bones...Palmer has been complaining some time and gets little better." Eating their horses and camels, the explorers struggled on, to reach Bowen in August 1862. He had not lost a single man. Six foot four tall and heavily bearded, McKinlay was one of the most successful, if lesser-known Australian explorers. Although he was soft spoken and quiet in demeanour, McKinlay proved a natural leader, for he could be firm when it was required.

In 1865 McKinlay was sent into the Northern Territory to search for a suitable site for a capital city. Although it was unusually wet, he explored the Victoria, Roper and Liverpool Rivers, where he found excellent land for stock raising. There is a picture in the National Library of Australia of naked, nervous looking men wading through a river, pushing a raft as a bevy of crocodiles leered toothily down at them. However, the reached the sea and safety. It was on McKinlay's advice that Port Darwin became the capital of the Northern Territory.

That was McKinlay's last trip of exploration. Instead he became a farmer in South Australia. He died young, his constitution damaged by the hardships he had endured. The people of Gawler, near where he farmed, built a fine monument in his honour.

McLaren, John (1846 – 1943)
Designer of Golden Gate Park

Born in Bannockburn, McLaren trained as a gardener in Edinburgh's Botanic Gardens at a time when Scotland was a world leader in botanical skills. Emigrating to the United States of America in 1872, when he was 26 years old, he became a notable landscape gardener. In 1887, after managing a number of estates around San Francisco Bay, he became San Francisco's parks superintendent, spending the next half century transforming the 1,017 acres of barren sand dunes near the Golden Gate into one of the world's finest urban gardens, as well as one of the largest man made parks in the world. It is bigger than New York's Central Park.

McLaren had to develop a new ecological system to force trees and grass to grow on barren sand dunes, and give the park its present lushness. He followed the initial design of William Hall, a civil engineer, but collected trees and plants from all over the world. He intended to protect the natural beauty, but over time a number of statues and other structures have been added. While under McLaren's guidance in 1894, Golden Gate Park hosted the Midwinter International Exposition, with the Japanese Tea Garden still a reminder. McLaren also helped organise a vast refugee centre after the 1906 San Francisco Earthquake left 200,000 homeless. Never a man to waste an opportunity, he used the children as a cheap labour force in the garden, and he also prevented the Municipal Railway from running through the garden.

Today McLaren is well remembered in the Golden Gate Park, but unknown in Scotland.

Mclean, John (c1797 –1890)
Fur trader and explorer

Born in Argyll around 1797, Mclean worked for the Hudson Bay Company between 1821 and 1845. His first position was in Montreal, but from 1837 to 1842 Mclean commander Fort Ungava in Labrador. After only one year at Ungava, Mclean made the first overland expedition across the Labrador Peninsula, discovering the Great Falls of Labrador en-route.

When he retired from the HBC, Mclean settled in Guelph, where in between working as a clerk for the divisional court, he wrote *Notes of a Twenty Five year Service in the Hudson Bay Territory*. He also found time to marry twice, producing two sons and three daughters, the youngest of which moved to Victoria in British Columbia, where Mclean spent the last years of his life.

McLeay, Alexander (1767- 1848)

Father of Australian Zoology

Born in Wick, where his father was provost of the town, McLeay was middle aged when he sailed to Australia as Colonial Secretary for New South Wales. While not working, McLeay continued and extended his lifelong interest in entomology, but also studied new species of birds. McLeay lived at Elizabeth Bay, where his garden became a focal point for those interested in rare plants. After the cold climate of Caithness, presumably he found Australia more fertile.

McLeay was the first known man to take an interest in Australian insects, thus earning his title of 'father of Australian entomology.'

McLeod, Donald (1779 –1879)

'Patriot' general

Born in Aberdeen, McLeod was educated at the University of Aberdeen. He joined the Royal Navy at the age of 24 and served until 1808, when he joined the army. After surviving the retreat to Corunna, he was posted to Canada, seeing action along the American frontier at Queenstown Heights, Chrysler's Farm and Lundy Lane. With the American War finished, McLeod was shipped to Europe in time to participate in the Battle of Waterloo.

Once the threat of Bonaparte was over, the army dismissed McLeod, who returned to Canada. He opened a classical school and founded a reformist newspaper named the Grenville Gazette.

When the Canadian troubles of 1837 and 1838 began, McLeod assumed the title of 'General commanding the Western Division of the Patriot Army' and made a number of pinprick raids along the borderline with the United States. The Americans promptly arrested him, put him on trial for breaking United States neutrality laws and then set him free. McLeod then settled in Cleveland, Ohio and wrote a *History of the Canadian Insurrection* and other works.

McMillan, Angus (1810 – 1865)

Australian explorer

Born in Glenbrittle in Skye, McMillan immigrated to Australia in 1837. As was not uncommon among Scottish emigrants, McMillan sought out another Scot. Captain Lachlan Macalister, who employed him as am overseer at Camden station in New South Wales. Macalister was another Skyeman, who had overlanded cattle in his time, so knew a lot about thrusting through unsettled countryside.

Macalister also helped fund McMillan's exploration. In 1840, guided by an Aborigine named Jimmy Gibber, McMillan set off for the interior, equipped with a chart made by Matthew Flinders and a compass. "We had not even a tent," he said, as his party traced the River Tambo all the way to Lake Victoria, "but used to camp out." McMillan explored the area between Melbourne and the Murraro Plain, discovering and naming the Mitchell River.

He discovered the area of Victoria now known as Gippsland. McMillan originally christened the land 'Caledonia Australis' but some people in authority believed the name to be too Scottish. McMillan settled at Bushby Park in Victoria and dabbled in politics. He represented South Gippsland in the Legislative Assembly for Australia and was often sought out by other Scots for his sound advice on local matters. McMillan made a great deal of money, but was reputedly extremely callous toward the local tribesmen

McPherson, James Alpin (1842 – 1895)
Bushranger

Born in Invernesshire the eldest of eight children, in 1855 McPherson immigrated to Moreton Bay in Queensland. He attended local schools in Brisbane, learning some French and German before moving onto Brisbane Mechanics School. However, he preferred adventure to study and in 1863 he absconded to work on various stations in the bush. Tiring of that, he attempted to join the bushranging gang of Ben Hall. Riding south to New South Wales, he faced his first disappointment when the police killed Hall and demolished the rest of the group. McPherson went solo instead. His first victim was more of an act of vengeance than a robbery, for he took money from a foreman who had cheated him. His next target was a hotel, which he robbed successfully.

McPherson travelled between New South Wales and Queensland, robbing mail coaches and stealing horses. He adopted a host of aliases, such as John Bruce, Scotia or Kerr, but most people knew him as the Wild Scotchman. He successfully evaded capture by the police, outrunning them on fast horses but never killing anybody. He was thought to have only injured one person in his career, and even that was doubtful. At the time he was operating with some extremely unsavoury characters, who probably fired the shot that injured a hotelkeeper.

More like an 18th century highwayman than a desperate killer, he regularly drank in the Star Hotel in Naningo and hoped to fight a duel with Frederick Pottinger, head of the New South Wales Police. Like so many of his schemes, this one came to nothing, possibly because he had no desire to kill anyone. There were rumours that he even loaded his pistol with blank cartridges.

McPherson did manage to steal Black Eagle, reputedly the fastest racehorse in Queensland, but it escaped.

McPherson was not universally popular, for a bevy of farm labourers captured him and handed him to the police. It was then that his luck turned. While awaiting charges for attacking Henry Pottinger, his alleged victim died in an accident. Those charges were dropped, but there were plenty more. Rather than wait to see the outcome, McPherson twisted free at Mackay and ran into the bush. Again caught, he was sentenced to 25 years for armed robbery and sent to St Helena Penal Settlement in Moreton Bay.

Eight years later, in 1874, McPherson was set free. There were rumours that the attorney general had looked favourably on a man who had once stood up for him against a crowd.

Perhaps the time in jail changed McPherson, possibly he had matured or maybe he had merely worked the wildness from his system. Either way McPherson settled down. Marrying, he worked as a stockman and raised six small Mcphersons. Ironically, the man who lived by the speed of his horse died in a riding accident.

McTammany, John (1845 – 1915)

Inventor

Born near Glasgow, the second son of John McTammany and Agnes McLean, McTammany emigrated with his family in 1862. They settled at Unionstown in Ohio, in the United States of America. Although McTammany dreamed of becoming a concert pianist, a childhood of illness and low income stunted his dreams. He did, however play on an amateur basis, and learned much about the mechanics of musical instruments.

Poverty meant that McTammany had a poor education and started work young. Employed at many of the local factories, he settled longest at a firm that made and repaired agricultural equipment, where he discovered a talent for improving machinery. McTammany's designs improved much of the farm equipment built in Unionstown, including the mechanical reaper.

When the American Civil War broke out, McTammany joined the 115th Ohio Volunteer Infantry. He saw action at Chattanooga, where he was wounded. While he recovered at the military hospital at Nashville in Tennessee, he worked at a local pawnshop, repairing and restoring musical instruments. McTammany combined his musical and mechanical skills to design a mechanical piano.

With the end of the war, McTammany returned to Ohio, where he found work as a piano salesman. He also taught music, while in his little spare time he began a new career as an inventor. He created a pneumatic 'player' but the established piano manufacturers were not interested in a machine that might undercut their profits and McTammany remained undiscovered and poor.

In 1876 he struck out on his own, manufacturing and selling 'organettes'. There was no doubting his inventive or musical skills, but McTammany was no businessman. His marketing techniques were poor so he was soon back in his customary poverty. Others, however, capitalised on his inventions, so McTammany took them to court, won his case and in 1881 was awarded a patent for his pneumatic piano. He also invented a mechanical banjo.

McTammany did not only work with musical instruments. He invented the world's first mechanical voting machine, a tabulating machine and an automatic typewriter, but he never made money. He died in 1915 at a home for old soldiers, but he had helped to bring music to the masses.

Menzies, Archibald (1754 –1824)
Botanist

Born in Weem, Perthshire, Menzies was an early convert to botany. While at home in Castle Menzies, he developed his interest in plants, but gained a degree in medicine at Edinburgh University. He joined the Royal Navy as an assistant surgeon and in 1792 sailed to the Pacific coast of North America with Captain George Vancouver.

While on the coast, Surgeon Menzies reverted to his original interest and studied the local plants. He catalogued over a hundred specimens, few, if any, of which were previously known. Some of his discoveries are now famous, such as the Sikta Spruce and California poppy. It was Menzies who first brought monkey-puzzle trees, Aaucaria araucana to Britain after a 1795 expedition into Chile

Menzies, Paul (c1635 –1694)
Russian diplomat and Lieutenant General

Son of Sir Gilbert Menzies of Pitfoddels, Menzies fought with the Swedish army before transferring to Russian service around 1661. He married a Russian wife and accompanied Boyar Feodor Michaelovich Milotawski on a diplomatic mission to Persia. The Csar must have trusted Menzies, for he sent the Scot as an envoy to Prussia in 1672, and then to Austria to negotiate an anti-Turkish alliance.

On the same extended mission, Menzies also travelled to Rome to persuade Pope Clement X to drum up help for Poland against the Turks. It was said that he also asked the Pope to hold a service to commemorate Saint Margaret of Scotland. On his return to Russia in 1674, Menzies was promoted. At some time in the next few years Menzies acted as tutor to Peter the Great, but in 1689 he was back in the military role, fighting the Crimean Tartars. He returned to Moscow in 1689 and remained there until his death. His wife and children survived him.

Mercer, General Hugh (1725 – 1777)
United States soldier

Hugh Mercer was born in Aberdeen, where he was trained as a doctor at the university. Like many in the northeast, Mercer supported the Jacobite cause and, despite warnings from his Presbyterian father, served as an assistant surgeon at the Battle of Culloden. After the failure of the Rising, Mercer hid from the Hanoverians and in 1747 he boarded a ship at Leith, bound for the American colonies.

Mercer settled in the Allegheny Highlands where his medical skills were useful and the inhabitants were not dissimilar to the mountain people he had known in Scotland. When the Seven Years War began, Mercer became a friend of George Washington, then a militia officer. He joined General Braddock's expedition against the French and Indians and was marching to relieve Fort Shirley when the Indians attacked. Wounded, dismounted and separated from his men, Mercer made his way through a hundred miles of hostile forest to reach safety. When he arrived at Fort Shirley, having survived on berries, freshwater clams and raw rattlesnake, he became an instant hero at a time that the war was going badly.

Out of uniform again, Mercer settled in Fredericksburg, Virginia. He married his sister-in-law Isabella Gordon and worked as a surgeon. Mercer prospered in America. He opened an apothecary's business and bought land, creating roots in his adopted home. Not surprisingly, when the American Revolution began, he became colonel of the Third Virginia Regiment. He was as opposed to Hanoverian rule in America as he had been in Scotland, declaring that he "would cross the mountains and live among the Indians rather than submit to the power of Great Britain."

He led his men to a number of small victories, leading the attack at Washington's famous victory over the Hessians at Trenton. He planned the subsequent night assault at Princeton where the Americans were also successful, but was wounded on the head. He fought on regardless, ignoring the British requests to "surrender, you rebel" and the bayonets that plunged into him.

Mercer died a few days later. Thousands attended his funeral, Congress cared for his wife and family and the Republic erected a splendid monument at Laurel Hill, Philadelphia, but he is hardly known in Scotland.

Middleton, Sir John (1619 –1674)
Soldier, Governor of Tangier

Few Scots of the seventeenth century had a career as varied as that enjoyed by John Middleton. He first came to attention as an ordinary pikeman in Hepburn's Regiment in the Thirty Years War, but by 1639 he was a colonel, joining the many Scots who returned home to fight in the Bishops Wars. By 1645 he was a Lieutenant General and Second in Command of the Covenanting forces at the battle of Philliphaugh where Montrose's Highland and Irish army was defeated.

Middleton's military career continued with a string of defeats, at Preston in 1648, Worcester in 1650 and finally the Drumochter Pass in 1654. After a spell in England, Middleton was eventually appointed as governor of the new colony of Tangier, possibly the first Scotsman to hold a position of authority in Africa. He died in office, reputedly by drunkenly falling down a flight of stairs.

Mitchell, Sir Thomas Livingstone (1792 – 1855)
Surveyor and explorer

Born in Craigend, Stirlingshire, Mitchell was well educated, particularly in science and languages, with a fine artistic hand. He joined the army as a surveyor. He saw service during the later stages of the Peninsular War, surveying some of the battlefields. By 1827 he was a half-pay major, probably contemplating a bleak and useless future. However, in 1828 Sir George Murray, the Scottish Secretary of State for the Colonies who as Quartermaster General had known Mitchell in the Peninsula, appointed him surveyor-general of New South Wales.

Mitchell travelled with his wife and growing family. He was to spend the next two decades surveying Australia. His first impressions were not favourable, with few instruments and fewer staff. Mitchell's first task was a general survey to plan towns and roads with absolute accuracy.

Mitchell made four expeditions into the interior of eastern Australia between 1831 and 1846, during which he determined much of the geography. Each expedition was organised like a military campaign, with nighttime camps ready for defence from any enemy. It was a convict that inspired Mitchell's first trip, when he reported an unknown river in the interior of northern New South Wales. Searching for the river, Mitchell instead he found trouble with a group of hostile natives.

On his second expedition in 1835, Mitchell traced three hundred miles of the Darling River, despite natives who attacked them "with as little remorse as wild beasts seek their prey." On this trip the Scottish botanist Richard Cunningham got lost in the wilds and was killed by natives.

The third expedition was in March 1836, to finish the survey of the Darling River. Reaching the Murrumbidgee River, he traced it to the Murray and next followed that river to its confluence with the Darling. Mitchell had thus led the first expedition into Australia Felix, that part of Australia that was most suitable for European settlement. This area became western Victoria, and Mitchell became Sir Thomas.

Mitchell's fourth expedition was intended to locate a route to the Gulf of Carpentaria, with the idea of improving trade with India. This journey was not a complete success. He left with 31 men, mainly convicts from the iron-gangs of Cockatoo Island. He also had a large supply train, but hostile natives again blocked his path and a river he had hoped to run north proved maddeningly inconsistent.

It was Mitchell who surveyed the goldfields of Bathurst in 1851, leading to the gold rush that virtually reinvented the colony. Mitchell also ensured that the original native names were retained throughout much of Australia, as his accurate surveys opened up much of the interior.

3

A quick-tempered man, Mitchell fought a duel when he was nearly sixty years old, putting a pistol ball through his adversary's hat. Mitchell also had an inventive mind. He devised the boomerang propeller for steamships, which was a forerunner of the reversible turbine. He died in his own home in Sydney in 1855.

Moffat, Robert (1795 – 1883)
Missionary, father-in-law of David Livingstone

Born in poverty at Ormiston, East Lothian, Moffat's first worked as a gardener at various estates in Britain, but in 1815 he became interested in missionary work. After contacting the London Missionary Society, in 1818 he arrived in Great Namaqualand, Southern Africa, spreading Christianity to the native peoples. Returning to Cape Town, he married and again set off to the interior.

Surrounded by wild people, Moffat was also under pressure from the Boers, who disliked the missionaries' championship of the natives' cause. However, in 1826 he settled at Kuruman in Bechuanaland, where he remained until 1870. By sheer hard work, Moffat transformed Kuruman into a vibrant Christian centre, an oasis of civilisation and sanity in the wilds. Not content to sit and wait for converts; Moffat took his ox-wagon north into the lands of the Matabele, an offshoot of the Zulus and one of the most warlike tribes in Africa. Using a personal doctrine of the 'Bible and the plough', Moffat's gardening skills came in handy as he taught horticulture and carpentry as well as scripture, adding elementary hygiene and medicine and the manufacture of ploughs.

When on leave in London in the early 1840s, Moffat met young **David Livingstone,** and talked him into working in Africa. The relationship was not one sided, for Livingstone was instrumental in Moffat's foundation of the first white settlement in Central Africa. His personal friendship with Mzilikazi, the Matabele chief, helped enormously.

Rather than try and force his culture onto the locals, Moffat first translated, and then printed, both the Old and the New Testament into Sechwana. Then he did the same with the Psalms and *Pilgrim's Progress*. Moffat was the first to print anything in Sechwana. He also published *Labours and Scenes in South Africa*. It is perhaps unfair that he should be best remembered for being the father-in-law of David Livingstone.

Morehead, Robert Archibald (c1814 – 1886)
Owner of the largest sheep and cattle station in the world

Born in Edinburgh, Morehead was the son of the Episcopal Dean of Edinburgh. The Scottish Australian Investment Company, an Aberdeenshire company, sent Morehead out to Australia as its manager in the early 1840s. He was a sharp businessman who kept the company in profit for all the 40 years that he remained in charge.

Morehead's work was made more difficult by poor communications that means a six-month gap between instructions being sent from Aberdeen and arriving in Australia. That said, the distance also allowed him scope to use his own initiative. On one notable depression in 1843, he bought a group of buildings on the Sydney waterfront, renamed them the Bon Accord Wharf and Stores after the Aberdeen motto and waited for the prices to rise. When they did, Morehead had made the company a tidy profit.

Through Morehead's management, the Scottish Australian Investment Company became one of the largest in Australia within a few years of its conception. In the 1850s, as gold fever hit the colonies, the profits soared even further. In 1866 Morehead purchased Bowen Downs in Queensland, at that time and for years after the largest cattle and sheep station in the world.

Morrison, Robert (1782 – 1834)
First Protestant missionary to China

Born near Jedburgh in the Scottish Borders, Morrison taught himself theology. In 1807 the London Missionary Society sent him to Canton, where he became the first Protestant missionary in China. Only two years later he began to translate and print the New Testament into

Chinese. He followed this with a translation of the Old Testament and by 1823 he had compiled and published a Chinese Dictionary.

An educationalist as well as a scholar, Morrison also established an Anglo-Chinese College in Malacca. He was only the first of many Scottish missionaries whose work has been largely forgotten, but who helped ease the understanding of Chinese culture and who remained a significant presence in the country until the 1950s.

Mounsey, Dr James (fl 1740)
Russian physician
Born in Lochmaben, Dr Mounsey travelled to Russia and worked in hospitals in both Moscow and St Petersburg. He was later appointed as personal Physician to the Empress Elizabeth. He is also credited as having first brought rhubarb to Britain as a medicine.

Muir, John (1838 – 1914)
Naturalist, father of modern environmentalism
Born in Dunbar, East Lothian, Muir spent his boyhood exploring the wilder parts of his local surroundings. In 1849, partly for religious reasons, the family immigrated to Wisconsin in North America. Muir's first American home was at Fountain Lake, but after a few years they moved to Hickory Hill Farm. Muir's childhood was hard, with an authoritarian father, and a great deal of manual labour. He is rumoured to have dug a 90-foot deep well entirely by hand, but in 1860 he started three years at Wisconsin University.

Muir was blessed with an inventive mind, creating various ingenious devices, but most of the jobs he found were in factories. He moved to Indianapolis but the loss of an eye in an industrial accident in 1867 forced him to take stock of his life. Returning to the nature he had known in Scotland, Muir began to explore the American outdoors. That same year he walked one thousand miles, from Louisville in Kentucky to Florida.

Muir then headed west, wandering and wondering round California, in particular the Yosemite Valley. Working as a shepherd and later in a sawmill, Muir also spent months just walking, later writing about the land from Alaska to Montana to California. In 1880 he married Louie Wanda Strentzel, whose Austrian father had been instrumental in establishing the Californian fruit industry. Muir settled as a successful farmer, while simultaneously campaigning for a national park in California.

In 1890 Congress approved the Yosemite National Park, but there was still opposition to the idea. Muir continued to argue and write for the cause of wildlife conservation. President Roosevelt's support may have been crucial in finally securing the future of Yosemite.

An accomplished writer, Muir wrote *The Mountains of California, Our National Parks, My First Summer in the Sierra* and *The Yosemite*. There is now a John Muir Trust and a John Muir National Park in Scotland, and a worldwide interest in landscape and wildlife conservation. John Muir, the boy from Dunbar, would have been proud to know what he started.

Niven, David, (1910 – 1983)
Soldier and actor

Although born in London, Niven belonged to Kirriemuir in Angus. His original name was James David Graham. In 1927 he entered the Royal Military College at Sandhurst, graduating two years later. When asked to select a regiment, Niven gave his choice as the Argylls, Black Watch and "anything but the Highland Light Infantry." Naturally he was commissioned into the HLI, the famously tough Glasgow Highlanders. Four years later, he left the army. After a number of short-term positions, Niven became an actor at Hollywood, mixing with famous names such as Clark Gable. In 1936 he was an extra in *Mutiny on the Bounty*, but his career took an upturn when Samuel Goldwyn signed him. Niven played the hero in films such as *The Charge of the Light Brigade* and *The Dawn Patrol*, but when the Second World War began he returned to Britain and rejoined the army.

By 1940 Niven was a second lieutenant in the Rifle Brigade and volunteered to join the Phantom 'A' Squadron of the Commandos. This unit would have worked on counter-invasion reconnaissance. Promoted to major, Niven served in Normandy in 1945. Promoted to Lieu-tenant colonel, he was decorated with the American Legion of Merit and when the war ended, Niven returned to acting. For three decades his suave style graced the screen. He perhaps made his biggest impact as Phineas Fogg in *Around the World in 80 Days*, although in *Separate Tables* he won an Academy Award.

His two-volume autobiography, *The Moon's a Balloon* and *Bring on the Empty Horses* perfectly matches the characters that he played so well.

Ogilvie, Major General George (1648- 1710)
Russian and Polish soldier

Son of George Ogilvie, Governor of Spielberg and grandson of Ogilvie of Airlie, Ogilvie seems to have started his career with rapid promotion in the service of the Emperor of Austria. In 1698 he met the Csar, who brought him to Moscow, where he quickly became a Field Marshal.

Ogilvy began a much-needed reorganisation of the Russian army, following the better Prussian principles of drill and discipline. He also took part in the actions at the eventual capture of Narva in 1704 and helped in the negotiations of the Peace of Ivanogrood, where the King of Poland awarded him the Order of the White Eagle.

Leaving Russian service, Ogilvie next fought for the Poles, with who he remained for the remainder of his life. He bought the estate of Sauershau, which was left to his wife, Marie-Anastasia, and his chil-dren.

Oudney, Walter (1792 – 1824)
African explorer

An Edinburgh man, Oudney graduated in medicine and worked as a surgeon with the Royal Navy before starting his own practice in Ed-inburgh. In 1822 Sir John Barrow of the African Association recruited him to lead an expedition to find the source of the Niger.

Small, slender and suffering from tuberculosis, Oudney was not an ideal candidate for the position, but he was courageous beyond his strength and added **Hugh Clapperton** to his party. Almost as soon as it was conceived, the expedition altered shape, with Oudney marked as British vice-consul in the scarcely known but powerful African kingdom of Bornu.

Starting from Tripoli, they crossed the Sahara in ninety hard days and were the first known Europeans to view Lake Chad. On the 16th February 1823 they reached Kukawa, the Bornu capital. It was the first meeting between Europeans and the head of the Bornu state. Unfortunately Oudney was sick by the time they arrived, but still managed to accompany Clapperton in exploring the southern fringes of Lake Chad.

Although he was dying, Oudney started the 400-mile journey to Kano, but died on the 12 January 1824 at Murdur. The Colonial Office gave his mother compensation of £100.

Owen, Robert Dale (1801 – 1877)
Social reformer

Born in Glasgow, Owen was the son of Robert Owen of New Lanark fame. In 1825 father and son travelled to the United States with the intention of creating a Utopian settlement. Owen senior paid £30,000 for an area of Indiana that he named New Harmony. When Owen senior returned to Scotland, Robert Dale Owen ran New Harmony. He became a teacher at the settlement and also edited the *New Harmony Gazette*. He also became friendly with the Dundee reformer **Fanny Wright**.

Moving to New York in 1829, together with Wright, he became editor of *Free Inquirer*, which advocated universal suffrage, the abolition of slavery and socialism. At that time there was a great debate in the United States over slavery, but woman's suffrage and any kind of socialism were not popular subjects. However, Owen proposed even more radical social changes, including altering marriage laws, making divorce easier for women, teaching birth control and introducing universal education.

In 1832 Owen returned to Indiana. He was a member of the Indiana legislature between 1836 and 1838 and entered congress in 1843, where he argued for using government money for public schools. After a spell as *charge d'affaires* in Naples, between 1855 and 1858 he was US ambassador to Italy.

When he returned to the United States, Owen was even more dedicated in his opposition to slavery, and it is possible that his arguments helped persuade Lincoln to free the slaves. As well as a committed emancipationist, Owen was also a spiritualist. His writings include *The Policy of Emancipation* and *The Wrong Slavery.*

Park, Mungo (1771 – 1806)
African Explorer

Born in Foulshiels near Selkirk in 10th September 1771, Park was the seventh child in a family that would grow by a further six. After education at Selkirk Grammar School, at 15 he became an apprentice surgeon to Dr Thomas Anderson, who prompted him to study medicine at Edinburgh University. At the age of 21 Park was appointed assistant surgeon on the East Indiaman *Worcester* as she sailed to Sumatra. Three years later the African Association accepted Park, "a man of no mean talents" as an explorer.

At that time the River Niger was nearly as mysterious as the upper Nile, so that Europeans were unsure in which direction it flowed or where it reached the sea. The African Association instructed Park to collect information "on the rise, the course, and the termination of the Niger, as well as of the various nations that inhabit its borders."

Too self-assured to wait for the 50-man escort that the Association advised, Park travelled to the slaving post at Pisania, run by Dr John Lindlay, another Scotsman. It was inevitable that Park should catch fever, and equally inevitable that he should spend the recuperation time profitably. After learning Mandingo and making contradictory comments on the Slave trade, in December 1795 Park pushed inland. He followed the river for 200 miles, and then crossed overland toward where he hoped the upper Niger would be. Park found the African potentates suspicious and the women sometimes too friendly. Indeed some female dancers "vied with each other in displaying the most voluptuous movements imaginable."

The Moors of the interior were less friendly and Ali, king of Ludamar imprisoned Park for months. Park was threatened with death even as native women offered to inspect him to see if Scotsmen were circumcised. It was the women who eventually secured Park's release, and he travelled into the land of the friendly Bambaras. Alone and impoverished, he reached the Niger at Sego, which he thought "a prospect of civilization and magnificence." It was July 1796.

Park followed the river westward to Bammaka, enduring the curious natives, the heat and the mosquitoes. However fever, the scourge of Europeans in West Africa, and disquiet at the nearness of fanatical Moors stopped his progress. His adventures were not over, for now he was believed to be a Bambara spy. Stripped naked by a band of thieves, Park fell back on his Christian faith for strength and found friendship among the slave traders. Nineteen months after he set out, a slaver named Karfa brought him back to the coast, weak but alive. He was the first European to discern in which direction the Niger flowed, a question that had puzzled geographers for nearly 2000 years. All they had to do was ask the local natives.

Back in Scotland, Park published *Travels in the Interior of Africa* and married Ailie Anderson, the daughter of his erstwhile mentor. He settled in Peebles as a surgeon, but found the life tame and in 1805 he was back in Africa, this time as leader of the first ever exploration expedition with British government backing. He also had his brother-in-law Alexander Anderson and a military escort.

There were 45 people in the company that he led from Pisania on the Gambia River, but fever had killed all but seven by the time he reached the Niger. Most had been criminals who volunteered for service abroad rather than dying on a prison hulk, and their health was broken long before the first mosquito thrust its proboscis into their flesh. Seeking easy plunder, predatory natives haunted the expedition, stealing what they could and stripping the clothes of the dying. Park carried baggage and the sick, drove off thieves and encouraged his men.

Temporarily halting at Sansanding in November 1805, Park ordered his journals and letters to be transported back to the coast, while he and four Europeans set off in a boat down the River Niger. They were weak with fever and travelling through a region where fanatical Moslems hated Christians. While Park was driven by determination, one of the surviving soldiers, Lieutenant Martyn, was a drunken bully. Some accounts claim that they shot their way through Africa, others that they only responded to native attack, but Park did not manage to pass Boussa. There was certainly some kind of fight, perhaps an ambush by hostile natives, and Park was killed. He had travelled around 1500 miles of unknown river and was only 600 miles from the sea.

There is a tragic postscript to Park's death. One of his sons refused to believe that his father had died and thought him a captive in Africa. He set off on a rescue mission, only to die of fever in the forest.

Paterson, William (1658 – 1719)
Financier and founder of Bank of England

Paterson was born in the farm of Skipnayre in Tinwald, Dumfriesshire. After trading around the Caribbean, Paterson returned to London, where he made himself a fortune. In 1691 he became a prime mover in the creation of the Bank of England, which was founded three years later. Initially, Paterson was one of the bank's directors, but held the post for only a year before departing for Edinburgh. The Bank of England, he thought, was too limited for his plans.

It was in Edinburgh that Paterson expounded a scheme that he may have been considering since his Caribbean days. He became involved in the Company of Scotland that would trade to Africa and the East as well as to the Americas. The idea may have been sound, but opposition from the Honourable East India Company, backed by the English government, disposed of his English and European investors. Instead Paterson concentrated on an alternative idea of a Scottish colony in

Darien in Central America. It was to be the 'door of the seas, the key of the universe' that would act as an entrepot between Asia and Europe.

With a reported fifty per cent of all Scotland's capital backing the scheme, Paterson embarked on the first colonising fleet. "Trade will beget trade," he said, "and money will beget money." However, the colony failed due to inexperience, a bad climate, fever and Spanish opposition. The Scots, however, did make friends with the native people, and succeeded in defeating the Spanish at the battle of Toubacanti before eventually succumbing to superior force. King William of Orange refused to help his Scottish subjects. Paterson returned to Scotland in December 1699.

After initial opposition to the Union and friendship with Andrew Fletcher of Saltoun, Paterson eventually supported the union of the Scottish and English parliaments. He was again residing in London and helped draw up the fiscal side of the 1707 union. He also became the MP for Dumfries and helped Walpole create the Sinking Fund, consolidated the national debt and cheerfully pocketed £18000 to compensate for his personal losses in the Darien Scheme, or perhaps as a bribe for his pro-union stance. To those thousands of Scots who lost their lives and savings in Central America, he would not be a hero. In Scotland, if he is remembered at all, it is for his part in the Darien scheme. Possibly it would be better to remember him as the founder of the Bank of England and the originator of paper banking.

Philip, James (Scotty) (1858 – 1911)
Preserver of the Bison

Born at Auchness near Dallas, Moray, James Philip grew up with the notion of immigrating to the romantic American frontier. When he was 15, Philip sailed from Scotland to the United States and travelled to Kansas, where he found life hard and the work menial. Looking for excitement, Philip moved west, to Cheyenne, Wyoming, near to the gold mining area of the Black Hills. Although the American government had promised the land to the indigenous peoples, miners still managed to encroach. After working on a ranch, Philip joined the miners, only for the United States Army to eject him. Working for a time as a government teamster in Fort Laramie, he moved again, became a cowboy, bought a team of mules and built up his own cattle herd.

Marrying Sarah Laribee in 1879, Philip began ranching and freight hauling at Clay Creek, moving in 1881 to Grindstone Creek. He established a Post Office that later moved again. As his wife was part Native American, Philip could ranch in Indian Territory, where he built up a large herd. It was around this time that Philip decided to preserve the American buffalo, which were on the verge of extinction from over hunting. He bought five buffalo calves from a man named Pete Dupree, bred them and pastured the growing herd near the Missouri River.

Philip's buffalo herd grew to a thousand animals, then the largest in the world, and was used to stock state parks all around America. Philip was respected throughout the country and when he died in 1911 a special train had to carry the mourners. It was said that the buffalo also came down from the hills to watch the funeral of the Scotsman who had saved them from extinction.

Phyfe, Duncan (1768 – 1854)
The 'American Chippendale'

Born on the shores of Loch Fannich, Ross and Cromarty, Phyfe immigrated to Albany, New York in 1783. Becoming a cabinetmaker, he prospered so moved to the larger centre of New York City. By 1795 he had his own cabinetmaking business, and eventually became the best known cabinetmaker in New York.

Phyfe was among the earliest cabinetmakers to use mahogany wood in his work. In an age of change, he earned the sobriquet 'the last of the great Georgians' and the 'American Chippendale.' He was especially noted for his chairs, tables and sofas.

Pinkerton, Allan (1819 – 1884)
Founder of the world's best-known private detective agency

The son of a police sergeant, Allan Pinkerton was born on August 25 in Glasgow. In his early life he was indentured as a cooper, then becoming heavily involved with the Chartist movement. He took part in both the Glasgow spinner's strike and the bloodier affair at Monmouth in 1839, when dragoons killed twenty of the Chartists. Pinkerton, in common with the other Chartists, fled and, in his own words, "skulked home to Scotland by all the back ways of the countryside."

He returned to coopering, but on hearing that the police were searching for Chartists, he hastily married his fiancée, Joan Carfrae, and in the 8th April 1842 shipped for North America. Their ship ran aground off Sable Island, and when they eventually reached the mainland a group of Indians robbed Joan of her wedding ring. At first she refused to give it up, but Pinkerton persuaded her that discretion was better than a hatchet in the head. After travelling from Canada to Detroit and Chicago, the couple settled at Dundee, Illinois.

Pinkerton had intended opening a cooperage, but while searching for suitable timber he unearthed a gang of counterfeiters. When he brought them to justice, the townspeople offered him the post of sheriff. He accepted, and soon moved on to become sheriff of first Kane, then Cook County in Chicago. Pinkerton, small built, burly and dour, was aggressive enough to cope. In 1850 he made another giant stride onward with the position of Special Mail Agent for the United States Post Office. Pinkerton was successful in reducing the number of robberies on the mail, and in 1851 he struck out on his own with the Pinkerton National Detective Agency. His initial task was to free Chicago rail yards from thieves but he expanded to perform any required detective work.

Pinkerton called his employees 'operatives' and trained them in his own theories of detection. He wrote the *General Principles of Detection* and employed Kate Warne, the first female detective in America. He also created a Rogues Gallery of known criminals. Pinkerton's men have also been depicted as among the pioneers of surveillance. One account has them sitting inside barrels, listening to the conversations of criminals. The idea is interesting, as Pinkerton was an ex-cooper, and perhaps Robert Louis Stevenson adopted the procedure for *Treasure Island*. Around this time the famous motto of Pinkerton's became known. 'We Never Sleep.'

Despite his growing fame as an upholder of the law, there was another side to Allan Pinkerton. Perhaps because of his early career with the repressed workers of Scotland, he had sympathy with the black slaves. He was an active member of the Underground Railroad that whisked escaped slaves from the South to freedom in British Canada. After John Brown's Missouri escapade in December 1858, Pinkerton met eleven freed slaves in Chicago, ensured they had adequate funds and a railway car and escorted them to the sanctuary of the Union Flag.

As an abolitionist, it was a natural progression for Pinkerton to offer the resources of his agency to Abraham Lincoln when the American Civil War started in 1861. He had mixed success in the next five years, for while his overestimates of Confederate strength possibly led to Union losses in 1862; he also unearthed a plot to assassinate the president. Unfortunately he could not repeat the feat when Lincoln was murdered a few years later. However, Pinkerton's activities in sending agents into the South laid the foundations for the Federal Secret Service.

With the end of the war, Pinkerton's operations expanded westward. Employed by the Adams Express Company, Pinkerton caught the Frank Reno gang, America's first great train robbers. His men became famous for their hard riding pursuits of outlaws, but life had not been kind to Pinkerton. When he suffered a severe stroke in 1869, the doctors said that he must resign himself to life in a wheelchair. Instead he fought back to fitness, only for the Great Fire of Chicago to destroy the agency building and its' Rogues Gallery. To prevent the situation worsening, Pinkerton ordered that posters be printed, threatening looters with death.

The following year, 1872, the Pinkerton agency came against the James Gang. At this time the west was winning its legendary sobriquet of 'wild' as outlaw gangs and range wars kept the land unsettled. Jesse and Frank James, with Bob Younger, were amongst the worst of the bad men. In 1871 they robbed a bank in Corydon, Iowa of $6000, following up a year later with a $10,000 haul on a Kansas City fairground. While irresponsible sections of the United States Press lauded the gang's daring, the more realistic banks called for Pinkerton.

Something of a personal war now ensued, with Jesse James asking "Where is Mr Pinkerton?" as he robbed a train at Gad's Hill, and subsequently killed three operatives in a shootout. The Agency responded by throwing a bomb through the window of a cabin where the James gang was reputed to be hiding. Unfortunately the only occupants were James mother, who lost an arm, and his nine-year-old nephew, who was killed. It was said that Jesse James hunted for Pinkerton in Chicago to gain revenge, while the press sided with the outlaws. The two men never came face to face. Bob Ford, one of James' followers, shot the outlaw in the back.

As his agency continued to flourish, Pinkerton declined. Perhaps his last great achievement was against the Molly Maguires. Initially the Molly Maguires had intended to preserve the Irish identity and keep rent-collectors under control. By 1875 they were a violent gang of thugs that controlled the Pennsylvanian coalfields by fear and force, ensuring that only Irishmen obtained positions of authority and intimidating miners of other nationalities. After a strike in 1875, Pinkerton sent an operative to infiltrate the organisation and his evidence broke the Maguires.

Allan Pinkerton died in 1884, apparently of gangrene after he bit his tongue, but his sons continued the agency. In 1988 CPP Security Services of Los Angeles bought the company over, but such was the fame of Pinkerton's that CPP changed its name to Pinkerton's. Not a bad legacy for a Chartist cooper from Glasgow.

Pitcairn, Robert (1747 –1770)
First man to sight Pitcairn Island

Born in Burntisland, Robert Pitcairn was the son of John, who was prominent in the action at Bunker Bill. He joined the Royal Navy when young. As a midshipman on board the sloop *Swallow* in 1767, Pitcairn was the first man to sight the island now known as Pitcairn. In time

Pitcairn Island became the refuge for the *Bounty* mutineers, then the first British colony in the Pacific.

Unfortunately, Pitcairn did not have a long career. In 1770 he was serving on board *Aurora* when she sailed into a cyclone off Mauritius and was lost with all hands.

Porteous, Robert (c1605 – 1661)
Prussian merchant

Possibly from the Dalkeith area, Porteous immigrated to Poland around 1622. He seems to have been apprenticed to a John Laurenstein, and was fined 50 florins for assault. A Protestant when he arrived in Krosno, he was converted to Roman Catholicism in 1627, the same year that he married Anne Mamrowitz, who was eleven years older than him and a widow. Perhaps there is a connection between his conversion and his marriage. The marriage produced at least four children, of whom three died.

Porteous became a successful trader, with links from Scotland to Lithuania, Silesia, Prussia and deep into the Austrian Empire. At one time he was one of the major suppliers of Hungarian wines throughout the region. However, he was sometimes unpopular because of his high profit margins, selling wine at four times the price he bought it. Porteous became extremely rich and lent money to the town of Krosno.

Nevertheless, Porteous was renowned for his honesty. Once he reported finding a cask full of money inside a cargo of wine, and when unable to locate an owner, he handed the money to the Church. He also gave much of his wealth to churches, hospitals and for civic improvement. He restored the nave and vaults of the parish church, as well as providing new bells, a font, paintings and vestments. When he died, he was buried in a personal vault. His will provided great gifts for the church and town of Krosno.

Porter, Edwin S. (1869 – 1941)
Influential film director

Scottish born, Porter was a seaman when he immigrated to the United States. He became an apprentice at Thomas Edison's New Jersey workshops, and then moved into film editing. It was Porter who created many of the skills of dramatic editing, whereby scenes were shot at different times and then joined together to form a single sequence. This technique was first used in 1903 during the first- ever American documentary, *The Life of an American Fireman*. Porter directed *The Great Train Robbery* that same year, a film that created a standard length for the industry. It also involved the first close-up film photography and was something of a pioneer in the Western genre. By now Porter was recognised as one of the most important people in the film world. He continued to create films, and by the time of his last, *The Eternal City* in 1915, had helped set the foundations for the United States Film Industry.

Quincy, Robert de (fl 1190)
Crusader
Robert de Quincy was a Scotto-Norman nobleman from the south east of the country. His ancestors came from Cuinchy, near Bethune in Flanders, but de Quincy came into some of his possessions when he married Orabile, the daughter of Ness, who owned lands near Tranent in East Lothian. He was a man of high position, having held the office of royal justiciar. In common with a number of Scottish knights, de Quincy took the Cross for the Third Crusade, meeting with King William in Perth in 1189.

De Quincy would have crossed France by land before joining the army of Richard of England at Marseilles. After playing a part in the siege of Acre, de Quincy was chosen as ambassador to Tyre for the English king. Richard also selected him to lead a force of 100 knights and 50 sergeants to help defend Antioch. De Quincy remained in Outremer until at least late in 1192, returning safely to Scotland.

Rae, Dr John (1813 – 1893)
Arctic and Canadian Explorer

Born at the Hall of Clestrain near Stromness in Orkney, John Rae spent much of his childhood in an 18-foot yawl, learned to shoot before he was strong enough to hold a musket and as his writings say "delighted in being out in the worst of weather." Rae studied medicine at Edinburgh. In 1833 he became a doctor for the Hudson Bay Company.

After a spell as resident surgeon at Moose Factory, James Bay, Rae made two exploring expeditions in 1846 and 1847. In these trips he surveyed nearly 800 miles of Arctic coastline and, with his fellow Orcadians, over wintered in the north, living in a stone hut and hunting deer for food. He had nearly completed the survey of the Arctic coastline of North America, discovering Rae Strait in the process.

In 1848 Rae accompanied Sir John Richardson in a search for the missing explorer Franklin, covering another five hundred miles of coast, mostly on foot. When he returned the Royal Geographical Society awarded him a Gold Medal. Not surprisingly, his contemporaries considered Rae to be "one of the best snow-shoe walkers in the business." Unlike most explorers of the period, Rae preferred to live in the manner of the Inuit.

Five years later he was back in the wilds, heading an expedition to King William's Land, where some Inuit informed him of the probable death of Franklin, which gained him a £10,000 Admiralty award. Unfortunately he also brought news that Franklin's men may have descended to cannibalism. In 1860 Rae was again busy, surveying a telegraph line to the United States by way of the Faeroe Islands and Iceland. He also visited Greenland and surveyed for a telegraph line across the Rockies from Winnipeg.

Ramsay, Andrew Michael (1686 – 1743)
French writer

Born in Ayr, Ramsay was the son of a baker. He joined the army as a youth, fighting in Marlborough's wars in the Low Countries. In 1710 he became a convert to Catholicism and from 1724 to 1725 was Bonnie Prince Charlie's teacher in Rome. His writings include *Vie de Fenelon* and *Les Voyages de Cyrus*.

Ramsay, James (d.1593)
Academic
Ramsay was first educated at St Andrews, where he graduated with a BA in 1571 and an MA the following year. He was also one of the first students to attend the new university of Leiden, matriculating in the Facility of Law in 1588. However, he was immediately appointed as a lecturer on Aristotle's Logic, later being accepted as an 'Extraordinary professor of logic'. He thus became the first Scottish teacher of philosophy at Leiden. In 1593 the university granted Ramsay the degree *doctor iuris honoris causa*, while also appointing him sub-regent of the college. However, he died later that same year.

Ramsay, Sir James (c1589 -1639)
Mercenary
Born around 1589, James Ramsay was university educated and in 1603 travelled to London with King James VI. For the next few years Ramsay lived as a courtier. In 1630 he sailed to Sweden and joined the Duke of Hamilton as a soldier of Gustavus Adolphus.

Ramsay was undoubtedly a brave soldier, for there are many anecdotes that mention him. For instance, he crossed a river by boat to capture the defended town of Marienberg. On another occasion he led 200 Scottish soldiers to capture Oppenheim, after which Gustavus commented "My brave Scots, why, you have been too quick for me." Ramsay commanded a section of the first line reserve at the battle of Breitenfeld, but a wound during the storming of Marienberg kept him out of action for a year.

When the battle of Nordlinger stopped the Swedish advance, the Duke of Weimar, commanding the Swedish army appointed Ramsay as governor of the fortress town of Hanau on the River Main near Frankfurt in October 1634. Ramsay prepared himself for a siege, but rather than sitting tight, launched a series of raids that rocked the Austrians. The Austrians tightened their grip and Hanau began to suffer. First the money ran out, and then food ran short and then the inevitable disease. Ramsay refused to surrender. He tried to prolong the siege by pretended negotiations but eventually the Austrians realised that there would be no surrender and stopped negotiating. When the Austrians attacked, Ramsay repulsed them as the relief came.

Relief, however, was not the end of Ramsay's war. With his garrison enlarged, he became a thistle in the foot of the Imperial forces. He organised offensive patrols and issued Ramsay Passports, without which merchants could not trade in the market of Frankfurt. He sent vessels to relieve the beleaguered garrisons of Ehrbreitstein and Hermanstein. When the former town fell, General Von Werth advanced on Hanau with a large army. Ramsay knew that his weakened garrison could not hold out so negotiated an honourable withdrawal. However, the Austrian Major Winter attacked during the talks.

Ramsay was wounded, captured and questioned but refused to betray any military secrets, saying that "it was against the rule of the service and the fidelity of an officer to give the enemy any information of his sovereign's military plans." First his secretary was killed, and then the Austrians threw Ramsay into a dungeon, still wounded and in chains, and fed him bread and water until he died. For years afterward, Ramsay's name was a byword for bravery in Germany.

Ramsay, James Andrew Broun, Marquis of Dalhousie (1812 – 1860)

Governor General of India

Known as the 'Greatest of Indian proconsuls,' Ramsay was born at Dalhousie Castle in Midlothian. After a boyhood in Canada, where his father was Governor General, he was educated at Harrow and Christ Church College, Oxford. After some time abroad he married the daughter of the Marquis of Tweeddale. In 1832 he became Lord Dalhousie. Ramsay was extremely interested in politics, standing unsuccessfully as the Conservative candidate for Edinburgh in 1835. Two years later he became MP for Haddingtonshire, now East Lothian. When his father died the following year, Ramsay entered the House of Lords as the Earl of Dalhousie. He became Vice President of the Board of Trade in 1841 and President four years later. After sturdy work with the developing railway system, where he proposed that the state should control such a novel means of transport, in 1847 Dalhousie was appointed the youngest ever governor-general of India. He was thirty-five years old.

His first report from India indicated that the country was quiet, but Dalhousie was to become the most energetic and perhaps the most controversial of all governor-generals. During his term of office, Dalhousie expanded British India.

The Sikhs were first. Already defeated in a previous war, they murdered two British envoys at Multan and attacked British India. Dalhousie despatched an army under the Irishman Sir Hugh Gough, who won stunning victories. Dalhousie enfolded Duleep Singh, the young Maharaja in the 'protective custody' of the British crown, sent the Koh-I-noor diamond to Queen Victoria and formally annexed the Punjab. It is heartening to know that Duleep Singh, known as the Black Prince, was popular in his new home in Perthshire.

Burma was next. When the Burmese maltreated British merchants at Rangoon, Dalhousie sent a brace of punitive expeditions and annexed Pegu province. It was Dalhousie's 'doctrine of lapse' that aroused the ire of many Indians. He stated that if the ruler of an Indian state died without leaving an heir, that state would be annexed to British rule, despite the Hindu custom of allowing adopted rulers to succeed. Dalhousie also grabbed lands from the Nizam of Hyderabad and acted against perceived misrule in native states when he annexed the important territory of Oudh.

As important for the future of the country, Dalhousie embarked on a colossal modernisation scheme. He planned an extensive railway network to join the various states and territories together. He opened 4000 miles of telegraph wire so that one end of the country could communicate with the other in hours rather than weeks. He made 2000 miles of roads and bridges and opened the Ganges Canal and, possibly more importantly, he opened many miles of irrigation canals.

On the social level, Dalhousie acted against suttee, the burning of widows along with their husbands, and thuggee, a particularly nasty religion of murder that reputedly killed thousands of Indians each year. He also stamped firmly on such cheerful institutions as female infanticide and the slave trade. A moderniser above all else, Dalhousie reorganised the Legislative Council, improved training for the Civil Service, and opened its ranks to any British born subject of any colour or creed. He improved Indian trade, modernised agriculture, mining and the post. On top of all this, he planned western style education and the creation of three Indian universities.

By the time Dalhousie was finished, India had communications that rivalled anywhere in Europe and exceeded most. He had restored the old Mughal Grand trunk Road from Peshawar to Calcutta, instigated a programme of industrialisation and cultivated forestry and tea, while ensuring that the ports and harbours were free for trade.

In 1848 Dalhousie became a Knight of the Thistle. The following year he was raised to a marquis. However, the sheer hard work of the position took its toll. Sick and old before his time, Dalhousie left India in 1856, to see the Indian Mutiny tear much of his work apart. He died in 1860.

His time in India had done much to improve and modernise the land, but had also sown the seeds for future trouble. He had a tendency to ignore advice, while Napier, the military commander in chief, believed he was "as vain as a pretty woman."

Reid, Sir George Houston (1845 – 1918)
Prime Minister of Australia

Born in Johnstone, Renfrewshire, Reid immigrated to Australia with his parents when he was just seven years old. At the age of thirteen he moved from Melbourne to Sydney. After a decent education, he obtained a position was with the colonial treasury.

Returning to university, Reid studied law and practised as a barrister, then was appointed secretary to the attorney general of New South Wales. His political career properly began in 1880 when he joined the Legislative Assembly of New South Wales. By 1891 he led the New South Wales opposition, and took the position as premier of that state from 1894 to 1899.

With the federation of Australia in 1901, Reid continued to represent his original constituency, but also led the opposition in the House of Representatives. In 1904 he became Prime Minister of Australia, but only lasted one year. Withdrawing from political life in 1908, the following year he was appointed the first high commissioner of Australia to London. He held that position for eight years, before entering the House of Commons as member for Hanover Square.

Reid, Hugo (1810 – 1852)
Californian settler and businessman

Born in Cardross, near Dumbarton, Reid was the son of a shopkeeper. He studied at Cambridge, but left for the New World when his fiancée jilted him. After a few years in Mexico, he moved up the coast to California, where he settled.

In 1834 he became a businessman in the tiny settlement of Los Angeles as a general merchant. Three years later he married Dona Victoria, a Californian Indian. Their relationship lasted, despite the jeers of his European friends, and Victoria's father gave Reid two of his farms. Growing vines and raising cattle, Reid prospered and built a house in the San Gabriel Valley. He also had a boat, with which he traded along the coast and as far as Hawaii.

Reid was not the only Scot in California, for he befriended James McKinlay who presented the younger Reids with a kilt apiece. When the Mexican-American War started, Reid's property was confiscated so he tried his hand at gold mining, then, in partnership with McKinlay opened a small business in Monterey. The business was not a success, so Reid was left with only a fraction of his previous holdings. However, he retained some of his influence, if not his wealth.

Reid wrote extensively on the native peoples of California, arguing for justice and better treatment than they had hitherto enjoyed. After the United States annexed California, Reid served on the Boundary Commission, worked on framing State Laws that gave more rights for women and Indians, and modernised the education system.

Seen as a founding father of California, Reid died in Los Angeles.

Reid, John (1840 – 1916)
Established first golf club in the United States
Born in Dunfermline, John Reid immigrated to New York when he was twenty-six and brought his love of golf with him. It is said that he taught golf to his friends at a field near his Yonkers home, and established the first golf club in the United States. The club he founded became the St Andrews Golf Club of Winchester County, New York.

Reid, William (1822 – 1888)
Founder of the famous Reid's Hotel, Madeira
Born into a Scottish farming family and living in Kilmarnock, William Reid was only 14 when a doctor advised him to leave Scotland for a warmer climate. In 1836 he worked his passage to Lisbon and then to Madeira, arriving with £5 that his father had given him. At first working in a bakery, Reid saved his pay and by the time he was 25 he was the owner of a wine exporting company.

Having landed in Madeira for his health, Reid soon realised the potential of tourism on the island, a fact with which many doctors in Great Britain agreed. In an era before mass travel, Reid and his partner, William Wilkinson, opened a company to lease the island's large quintas –private houses – to visitors from Britain throughout the winter months. One visitor was the Marchioness Camden, with whom Reid fell in love and married in 1847. The Reids soon moved into the hotel business, acquiring the Quinta das Fontes, which they renamed the Royal Edinburgh Hotel. Alfred, second son of Queen Victoria gave permission for this name, for Reid knew him well enough to call him Auld Reekie.

Only 14 years after his arrival, Reid owned a chain of small, but good quality hotels on Madeira, but his dream was to build a luxury hotel. He picked the ideal spot on top of a cliff on Funchal Bay, persuaded the owner to sell and set to work. Commissioning George Somers Clarke, who had already designed the famous Shepherd's Hotel in Cairo, Reid began the building in 1887. Set in ten lush acres, Reid's Hotel was a masterpiece of luxury, but unfortunately William Reid died the following year, three years before it was completed. In November 1891 his two sons announced the formal opening. Reid's became one of world's most prestigious hotels.

Renny, General Patrick (fl 1812)
Russian general

Born in Montrose, Rennie came from a family that had a long connection with Russia and the Baltic through trade. However, Renny chose to join the Russian army, rose to general and was an *aide de camp* to the Csar when Bonaparte invaded in 1812.

With the war won, Renny returned to Britain. He was in the crowd when the Csar embarked on a state visit to Britain, and may not have been surprised when the Csar recognised him, halted the solemn procession and embraced him in public

Richardson, Sir John (1787 – 1865)
Arctic explorer and naturalist

Born in Dumfries, Richardson was a surgeon in the Royal Navy between 1807 and 1855, during which time he saw active service in North American and European waters. When the French and American wars ended, Richardson became a vastly experienced Arctic explorer. He served in Parry and Franklin's expedition of 1819 to 1822, where he travelled to the Great Slave Lake and helped accurately survey 550 miles of the Canadian coast. Between 1825 and 1827 he was back in the north, probing the unknown coast between the Mackenzie and Coppermine Rivers and travelling some 2000 miles in only ten weeks. In 1848, working with the Orcadian John Rae he also helped search for Franklin when that explorer became lost in the north.

His writing was perhaps as important as his exploration work. He wrote *Fauna Boreali-Americana* and *Ichthyology of the Voyage of HMS Erebus and Terror.*

Robertson, Archibald (1765 –1835)
Artist

Born at Monymusk, Robertson studied art first in Edinburgh, then at the Royal College in London, before immigrating to the United States in 1791. Working with his brother Alexander, he founded the Columbia Academy of Painting in New York City the following year. When his style and skill became known, Robertson was closely associated with the American Academy of Fine Art.

A writer as well as an artist, Robertson wrote *Elements of Graphic Art*. However, he is better remembered for his fine portraits and his watercolour views of the growing city of New York.

Robertson, Christina (1796 –1854)
High priced Russian Artist

Born as Christina Saunders at Kinghorn in Fife, Robertson moved to Marylebone in London to work as a miniaturist painter. Working with her uncle, the artist George Saunders, she soon established herself as a high quality artist. In 1822 she married James Robertson, another artist, and mothered a clutch of children, although in those days of high infant mortality only four survived childhood. Robertson was the first woman to be accepted as an honorary member of the Royal Scottish Academy in 1829, when she was already seen as a fashionable artist who exhibited in the most important London galleries. She made her reputation painting the gentry and aristocracy of Britain, including such people as William Adam, the lord Chief Commissioner for the Jury Court of Scotland, the Marchioness of Lothian and the duke and Duchess of Buccleuch.

Around 1835 Robertson began to travel abroad, first visiting Paris then, in 1839 St Petersburg, where she became a member of the Imperial Academy of Arts in St Petersburg, and painted the elite of society. She returned to London in 1841, but was back in St Petersburg a few years later.

Robertson was one of the most favoured painters in Russia, painting every member of the Imperial family from Csar Nicholas I downward. She was also famous for the extremely high prices that she charged, which possibly acted as a stimulus rather than a deterrent to the Russian aristocracy. It was in St Petersburg that she died, still painting, in 1854, the year that the British and Russians waged war in the Crimea.

Rogerson, Dr John (d 1823)
Russian physician and court confidant

Born in Dumfriesshire, Rogerson left Scotland for Russia in 1766, accepting an appointment as the Imperial Physician. With such a position, Rogerson was privy to even the most intimate details of the court. He knew the truth of the too frequent sudden deaths, including that of the Empress.

Rogerson seems to have used his position to advantage, accepting bribes when they were offered. It was said that the doctor received so much in bribes that he bought the lands of Wamphray in Dumfriesshire for himself, and erected the splendid mansion of Dumcrieff, where he retired when he left Russian service.

Ronaldson, James (1769 – 1841)
Caster of the first ever American dollar sign

Born in Edinburgh, James Ronaldson immigrated to the United States, where he met fellow Scot **Archibald Binny**. In 1796 they founded a type foundry and the same year cast the first ever American dollar sign. The firm of Binny and Robertson was the first successful American typecast firm that ended reliance on European printing.

Ross, Sir James Clark (1800 – 1862)
Polar explorer

Ross was at sea from the age of twelve, serving with his uncle, the explorer **John Ross** in surveys of the White Sea. When he was just eighteen years old, James Ross accompanied his uncle again on an attempt to find the Northwest Passage. After sailing with Parry on four Arctic expeditions, he was with John Ross between 1829 and 1833. It was on this expedition that James Ross, travelling by sledge, located the magnetic North Pole.

On his return, Ross carried out a magnetic survey of the United Kingdom. Between 1839 and 1843 he was in Antarctic waters. Sailing on *Erebus* and *Terror,* he discovered and took possession of Victoria Land in Antarctica. In this most memorable Antarctic voyage, he also discovered a volcano he named Mount Erebus. Wintering in the Falkland Islands, he probed further south than any other seaman, finding pack ice and penguins. His account of the journey was published in *Voyage of Discovery.*

In 1848 he made his last trip as an explorer. As Captain of *Enterprise,* he helped search for the missing Franklin expedition. One of the most endurable of 19th century polar explorers, the Ross Sea, Ross Island and Ross's Gull commemorate his exploits.

Ross, Sir John (1777 – 1856)
Arctic Explorer
Born at Inch manse in Wigtownshire, Ross was the fourth son of the parish minister. At the age of ten he entered the Royal Navy. After three years he transferred to the merchant service, but returned to the Senior Service, slowly climbing from Midshipman to Commander during the Napoleonic War but when the wars ended in 1815 there was little employment for even experienced naval officers.

However, the Admiralty sent Ross to probe for a route to the Pacific by way of Baffin Bay. Ross took two vessels, the chartered whaler *Isabella* and the smaller brig *Alexander* commanded by Lieutenant Parry. Ross met Inuit who had never met a European man, and even a tribe who had never met another Inuit and who believed that Ross's ships were living creatures. Ice and fog barred Ross's passage through Smith Sound, so he pushed hopefully into Alderman Jones Sound. At first things seemed favourable, but they could not push through. Ross tried Lancaster Sound next, but on 30 August 1818, he thought he saw land ahead. Although others in the ship denied their existence, Ross was convinced that a vast mountain range blocked their route and again turned back.

There was no range and Ross was blamed for the expedition's failure to find the North West Passage. It was 1829 before Ross was back in the Arctic, in an expedition financed by the gin distiller Felix Booth.

This time he sailed in *Victory*, an auxiliary powered sailing ship with stores to last three years. He invested £3000 of his own money, picked his nephew, the experienced **James Clark Ross** to accompany him and steered for Prince Regent Inlet. *Victory* proved a slow sailer and it was July before they reached Greenland. Ross must have hidden his feelings as they eased through Lancaster Sound with no sign of a mountain range. Nevertheless, the voyage was not trouble free as the compass failed and the engine proved underpowered.

When the weather deteriorated James Clark Ross explored in a sledge and located a safe haven. They discovered and named the peninsula of Boothia and moored for the winter. James Clark Ross explored their surroundings on a sledge, finding no passage free but locating the western sea. It was September 1830 before the ice released its grip, but the relief was temporary as *Victory* sailed only three miles before the next winter freeze began.

There was another Arctic winter to endure, and then in June 1831 James Ross located the Magnetic North Pole, claiming it in the name of King William. It was a major discovery, but they seemed no closer to discovering the North West Passage. After yet another winter in the ice, John Ross decided to abandon *Victory*, take to the boats and search for the whaling fleet.

The journey was difficult, and when ice damaged the boats the explorers were condemned to yet another winter in the ice. Not until late in the summer of 1833 did they set off again, probably with little hope. They reached Baffin Bay, where a whaler rescued them.

With his honour restored by his near miraculous survival, Ross returned to Britain. He sailed north again at the age of 73, searching for the missing explorer John Franklin. As with his earlier expeditions, he failed in the search, but there was no doubting his resolution or courage.

Sandeman, George (1765 – 1841)
Founder of a port dynasty

Born in Perth, George Sandeman became the founder of one of the world's best-known wine companies. With a £300 loan from his father, Sandeman left Perth for London, where in 1790 he began his business in Tom's Coffee House in Birchin Lane, importing port from Portugal and selling it in London. His Sandeman 1790 became the world's first vintage port. Not satisfied from trading from London, Sandeman made frequent trips to Spain and Portugal, despite the obvious dangers of the ongoing Napoleonic War in the peninsula. Indeed, Sandeman exploited the war by having dinner with the Duke of Wellington and selling two pipes (around 1400 bottles) of the 1797 vintage to General Calvert.

Very successful, Sandeman made a fortune, employed scores and passed on a thriving company to his descendants.

St Clair, Henry (1345 – 1400)

Navigator, possible discoverer of North America

More of a mystery man than even most Scots, Henry St Clair had already made the pilgrimage to the Holy Land before his exploits in the North Atlantic. Known as 'Henry the Holy', he was Lord of Orkney and Shetland at a time when both island groups were owned by Norway. According to legend, St Clair was also a member of the Knights Templar, who asked him to make a reconnaissance across the Atlantic to find new lands for them to settle. With an Italian, Antonio Zeno, he crossed the ocean and landed in Prince Edward Island, Nova Scotia and Massachusetts, ninety years before Columbus. Interestingly, the Micmac peoples of Nova Scotia have folk tales of such a visit, while Roslin Chapel in Midlothian boasts carvings of North American Maize. The St Clair family owned Roslin, which was built decades before Columbus. History, however, has its doubts.

Saunders, William (1822 – 1900)

Landscaper

Born in St Andrews, Fife, Saunders was forty when he immigrated to the United States. He became one of the finest landscape artists in the country, laying out several of the most impressive estates. He is probably best remembered for the vibrant garden and park system of Washington DC, but also designed The Fairmount and Hunting Parks in Philadelphia and the National Cemetery at Gettysburg.

Not content with using what was readily available, Saunders also introduced previously unavailable species into the United States. He brought the Australian eucalyptus trees into California, as well as the more practical Satsuma orange from Japan. Satsuma oranges became popular in the California fruit industry.

Scott, James George (1851 – 1935)
Asian Explorer

Born in Dairsie, Fife, Scott lost his father while young. His mother took her family to Stuttgart, Wurtemberg, to give them a wider education. After schooling in Stuttgart, Scott was sent to King's College School, London, then to university at Edinburgh and Oxford.

By 1875 Scott was in Malaya, working for the *London Evening Standard*. In this position he accompanied a punitive expedition to Perak. Shortly after, he taught at St John's College, Rangoon, where he rose to acting Headmaster by 1880 and was said to have introduced football into Burma. At the same time, Scott continued to work for a variety of newspapers and in 1882 he wrote *The Burman: his life and notions*. Despite public demand for an eastern expansion of India, Scott wrote against annexation of Burma. Scott also explored Kachin and Shan villages, but in 1882 he travelled to London to study law.

By 1884 he was back in Burma, reporting on the French expansion into Tonking and in January 1886 he lectured about Tonking at the Royal Geographical Society. Having passed his law qualification, Scott worked with the Burma Commission while they discussed annexation. Back in Burma, he controlled the Meitkila District, struggling against guerrilla forces. Anxious that the French would move into Upper Burma, Scott led an expedition into the Shan States in 1887. As Acting Political Officer, he explored the eastern frontiers of Burma and was the first European to travel the road to Kengtung. He also visited the state of Kenghung and the Wa states, populated by headhunters that acknowledged neither British nor Chinese law.

Created a Companion of the Order of the Indian Empire for his endeavours, Scott became acting British Minister in Bangkok in 1893. Scott was the British Commissioner for the Burma-China Boundary Commission between 1998 and 1900, but his Scott Line was not a success. However, his multi-volume *Gazetteer of Upper Burma and the Shan States* that appeared at the same time was a remarkable achievement. In 1902 Scott was promoted to Superintendent of the Shan States, but that was the end of his explorations. Married twice more, he eventually retired to a peaceful, but not prosperous, life in Britain.

Scott, Michael (Possibly c 1214 – c 1290)
Scholar, astrologer and supposed necromancer
Believed to have been a son of the Laird of Balwearie in Fife, Scott may have been born there, although some authorities state Durham as his birthplace. His birth date is equally unclear, as is the year of his death, for he is variously supposed to have lived in the twelfth or thirteenth centuries. However, it is possible that Scott studied at Oxford, Paris and Padua before becoming tutor and astrologer to Frederick II at Palermo. At that time Frederick was known as *Stupor Mundi* or the 'Amazement of the World'. He is reputed to have studied astronomy, chemistry and Arabic in Oxford, theology and mathematics at Paris and magic at Padua, which place was famed for the subject.

Settling at Toledo in what is now Spain; Arabic and Jewish scholars taught him physics, arithmetic and various sciences. Having learned the language, he translated Arabic versions of Aristotle's works, which was used by Dante, and the writings of Averroe. He returned to Frederick's court at Palermo, where the king had gathered the best available scholars from Christendom, Islam and the Jewish world, but he turned down the archbishopric of Cashel in Ireland. The Pope mentioned Scott to the Archbishop of Canterbury, and he held benefices in both Scotland and England. Scott became Astrologer Royal, wrote on alchemy and the occult and was reputed to have second sight

Around this time he wrote his *Quaestio curiosa de natura solis et lu-nae*, a treatise on astrology, but his contemporaries preferred to believe him a magician. His reputation was Europe wide, but in Scotland he was known as the 'wondrous wizard.' He was said to have magically transported food from royal courts to Scotland, but this legend may only be an example of the simplicity of Scottish food when compared to the Moorish dishes brought home by Scott.

Scott returned to Scotland and may have died around 1290. He is said to be buried in Melrose Abbey, along with a 'mighty book' of magic that contained many spells.

Scotus, John Erigena (c815 – 877)
Churchman

John Scotus seems to have been born on the coast of Ayrshire, although Ulster also lays claim on him. He was certainly church educated and was possibly in the Roman Catholic monastery of Bangor, then one of Western Europe's great Christian centres. When John was young, a Viking raid slaughtered many of the monks, so John would have fled with the survivors.

When John was thirty-five, Charles the Bald, King of France invited him to head his Court School. As well as his native Gaelic, John knew Latin, Greek and French. Charles the Bald commissioned John to translate the texts of the Pseudo-Dionysus. John was one of the outstanding scholars of the Dark Ages, a combination of thinker, philosopher and theologian. It was his independence of thought that made him stand head and stubborn shoulders above his contemporaries.

John taught that reason was the best method of finding truth, with the Church the greatest truth of all. He believed in pantheism; the unity of God, nature and the universe, while, far in advance of his time, he stated that religion was only one part of humanity's progress toward his ultimate destiny. Even more inflammatory for the time was John's statement that the very Christian ceremony of the Lord's Supper was symbolic, and there was no Holy Blood or Body consumed.

John's argument was beyond the theology of the day, and has never been properly resolved. Certainly Charles the Bald was confused.

John also supported Hincmar, Archbishop of Reims with his dispute over predestination. According to tradition, John became Abbot of Malmesbury, but his students stabbed him to death with their quills 'for trying to make them think.' Many students today would sympathise with their actions.

Perhaps John's greatest contribution to Christian thought was his *The Divisions of Nature*, which argued that God was the beginning and end of everything. However it did not always find favour with the Pope.

Scotus, John Duns (c1265 – 1308)
Scholar

Probably born at Duns in Berwickshire, John was educated at the local Fransiscan school, became a Fransiscan and was ordained as a priest in St Andrews Church, Northampton in 1291. After studying at Oxford, possibly at Balliol College, where he also lectured on the Scriptures he continued his education with four years in Paris. From there he may have spent time in Cambridge and then at Cologne. As he studied, he taught and wrote.

He mainly wrote on Biblical themes, but also commented on Aristotle and Peter Lombard. Although he did not complete many of his works, his contemporaries collected and edited them. Not all the editing was kind. Scholars believe that his major works were *Opus Pariense* (the Parisian Lectures), *Opus Oxiense* (Oxford Lectures), *Tractatus de Primo Principio* and *Quaestiones Quodlibetales*.

John's philosophy ran counter to many of the main teachings of the period. A natural sceptic, he wrote against both Aquinas and Aristotle and advocated the importance of the individual, stressing individual will in the ongoing discussion over universals. Will, memory and intellect, he believed, were inseparable from the soul, with will dominating over the intellect. He put practical Faith as the foundation of Christian philosophy. John also taught that any philosophy could progress only by close scrutiny of conflicting theories. A philosopher of note, he contended that matter was not passive, but held a unique nature separate from its form. Far in advance of his time, he argued that all matter could be reduced to an ultimate entity, a theory that quite radically sustained the exploration for the Philosopher's Stone. As he was a Fransiscan, the Dominicans naturally opposed his views.

The Franciscan order followed the teachings of John, terming him *Doctor Subtilis*, the Subtle Doctor in respect for his refined and penetrating learning as he criticised Thomism. However his teachings were scorned during the Renaissance, when Scottists were termed Dunses, from which the word dunce derives. They were seen as obstinate and conservative. The wheel of belief, however, continues to turn and his beliefs have since been reconsidered in a better light. In 1965 a large number of religious men collected in Duns to pay their respects to John's memory. As they entered the small Border town they would see, proudly displayed, the motto, 'Duns dings a.' Those that understood might have been better able to comprehend the stubborn individuality of John's philosophy. He remains as possibly the most controversial free thinker of his time.

Scroggie, Ebeneezer (died 1836)

The original Ebenezer Scrooge

Not much is exceptional about Ebeneezer Scroggie, except that Dickens misrepresented him in a scandalous manner. Born in Kirkcaldy, Scroggie led a successful and blameless life. He was the first merchant to be contracted to supply whisky to the Royal Navy at Leith, a corn dealer and a Baillie of Edinburgh. Cheerful and popular, he was dandified in his dress and so popular with the ladies that his amorous exploits were the subject of gossip.

The association began when Dickens was in Edinburgh in the early 1840s. He was walking through the Canongate Kirkyard when he came across Scroggie's gravestone, which said that Scroggie had been a 'meal man.' Misreading the words as 'mean man', Dickens presumed that Scroggie had been tight-fisted even by Scottish standards and, three years later, introduced Scroggie as Scrooge, the anti-hero of *A Christmas Carol*.

Seget, Thomas (c1570 –1628)
Academic

Seget was one of the earliest graduates of Edinburgh University, receiving his MA in 1588, and then travelled to Leiden to continue his studies. He was back in Scotland in 1592, becoming employed as a tutor in the household of Robert Seton of Seton. When Seget delivered a funeral oration in Latin, the Haddington presbytery ordered him to make public confession of this sin.

From that time on Seget travelled Europe, writing a fascinating account in his *Album amicorum*. Seget became a humanist, meeting and corresponding with some of the best brains of his day, including Galileo Galilei. He worked as administrator of the library of J V Pinelli, spent some time in jail, worked with John Kepler and studied in Altdorf before returning to Leiden.

Sheppard, Kate (1848 – 1924)
New Zealand women's Rights activist

Born in Islay, Kate Sheppard immigrated to New Zealand when she was young. She became a journalist, writing many forthright articles, and was a vibrant supporter of women's rights. Her speeches and writing were amongst the most effective in pushing forward the feminist cause, so that in 1893 New Zealand became the first country in the Empire to recognise female suffrage. The United Kingdom had to wait another quarter century for women to achieve the vote.

However, Sheppard continued to campaign to better women's conditions. She created women's groups all over the country to seek real equality. Her pressure was so successful that when she died, she was within months of seeing the first female MP elected to the New Zealand parliament. Although she has been all but forgotten in Scotland, New Zealand commemorated her on the ten-dollar bill.

Simpson, George (1792 – 1860)

Controlled Hudson Bay Company

Born in Wester Ross, a great grandson of Duncan Forbes of Culloden, Simpson was born illegitimate to a family with no money. His
grandfather, minister of Avoch, brought him up, and when he was old
enough Simpson began work for his uncle, a London sugar broker. He
joined the Hudson Bay Company when he was young and soon rose
to Governor-in chief. In 1821, when he was only 25 years old, he ruled
the Company.

At that time the Hudson Bay Company controlled a huge area of
land, including Oregon and the west of Canada as well as the Canadian
Arctic, but also had trading posts as far south as California and as
far north as Alaska. As the Company existed to trade in furs, it had
no interest in settlement. Although Simpson's headquarters were at
Lachline near Montreal, he often travelled around his lands in a large
canoe with Indians, Voyageurs or Orcadians as paddlers. Simpson sat
in the stern, wearing a tailed coat and top hat and with his personal
piper always present.

Unlike others of his generation, Simpson did not try to educate or
Christianise the indigenous peoples, believing that 'an enlightened Indian is good for nothing.' Probably happy to be left in peace, the native
peoples responded by bringing their furs to his posts in return for trade
goods. There were also about 12000 people with European blood, Scots
or French, in Simpson's territory, and he also allowed them to live as
they pleased, so long as they did not interfere with Company's trade.
He permitted the Highland settlement at the Red River as it grew food
that the Company could use.

Simpson, however, always attempted to expand the Company
boundaries. To remove the threat of the rival North West Company,
he amalgamated the companies and borrowed their style while removing many of their employees. He improved the trading routes that
stretched across the rivers and lakes of Canada to York Factory on
Hudson Bay. He inaugurated commercial fishing on many of Canada's
lakes, started agriculture along the Mackenzie River valley and ex-

changed the traditional birch bark canoes for the clumsier York Boats that could contain a far larger load of furs.

With his internal improvements complete, Simpson looked to extend the frontiers of the Company. Simpson initiated the explorations of **John Ross** and **John Rae**, but he also headed west. In 1824 he spent 84 days in travelling toward the Columbia River, which he claimed for Britain on the basis that his fur traders had opened it up before any American had set foot in the area. Realising that the United States was his chief rival, he undercut their traders and outmanoeuvred their managers, while always appearing genial.

Few were fooled by his occasional smile. People knew him as 'soul of ice,' 'the little Emperor' or 'Emperor of the Plains,' but he could be a loyal friend and companion. Small in stature, stocky, with fair hair, Simpson made a point of swimming every day, despite the weather. He had accepted Canadian life with gusto, trekking like a voyageur, braving ice and snow, exploring new territory and eating with his men. He was always erect and had the ability to overawe even the toughest subordinate.

Simpson left North America to travel overland to St Petersburg, where he met the Csar like one emperor to another. While Simpson leased the Alaskan panhandle for the Company, he agreed to feed the Russian posts in the area and curb American incursions in the Northern Pacific. Simpson expanded the Company posts as far south as San Francisco. He had an interest in the Pacific, visiting Honolulu to establish posts on the island while repelling other companies and even sending a Chinook-Scot, Ranald Macdonald to Japan five years before the celebrated American mission of Commodore Perry. Macdonald seemed to relish the appointment, for he learned Japanese so well that he was soon teaching it to other Europeans.

On a personal level Simpson was unconventional. Victorian morality had not yet begun to bite deep, so there were fewer concerns about mixed marriages. However, his clutch of illegitimate children would not have been welcomed in a traditional Scottish household. Nonetheless, in 1830 he married his18 year old cousin Frances Simpson, to whom he remained loyal, the rest of their married life. Frances added a further three daughters and two sons to Simpson's total of children.

Unfortunately, Simpson was not to see his expansionist dreams realised. After the Mexican War, the Unites States annexed California and New Mexico. Simpson withdrew his trading post from San Francisco. Almost at the same time, Britain and the United States agreed to extend their 49th Parallel frontier to the Pacific, thus cutting off much of the Oregon territory that Simpson's men had explored and exploited. Simpson saw his Empire shrink. Nevertheless, by sending **James Douglas** west, he secured Vancouver Island for the Company, and British Columbia became part of his hunting territory.

Simpson died in 1860, the last and possibly the greatest of all the Hudson Bay magnates. In his place came the march of the British Empire.

Skene, Alexander Johnston Charles (1837 – 1900)
Gynaecologist and Professor of Medicine

Born at Fyvie, Aberdeenshire, once Skene had completed his education at Kings College, Aberdeen, he immigrated to Canada. He studied further at Toronto and then Michigan and obtained his M.D. at Long Island College Hospital Medical School in Brooklyn in 1867.

After a year as Assistant Surgeon with the University Volunteer Corps in South Carolina, Skene worked as a gynaecologist then, in 1872, was appointed Professor of Gynaecology at Long Island Hospital. Between 1884 and 1886 he returned to South Carolina, later becoming Dean of the Faculty at Long Island. From 1893 to 1900 he was president of the school, while also acting as consulting physician to several other medical schools. Simultaneously, Skene hoped to build and run his own private sanatorium in Brooklyn: Skene's Hospital for self-supporting women.

Skene was one of the most influential gynaecologists of his day, but did not just practice his art. In 1880 he discovered the Paravrethral glands, also known as Skene's glands, and he also created improved instruments for his work. One of the most widely used was the hemostatic forceps. Skene was president of King's County Medical Society between 1874 and 1875 and a founding member of the American Gynaecological Society and the International Congress of Gynaecologists and Obstetricians in Geneva.

Not content with his busy life, Skene also wrote medical journals and even a novel, but perhaps ironically, he and his wife Annette Van der Weyer did not have any children.

Skinner, James (1778 –1841)
Commander of Skinner's Horse

With a Scottish father named Hercules Skinner and a Rajput mother, his contemporaries termed Skinner an Anglo-Indian, but none would doubt his military ability. He was apprenticed to a printer, but ran away and joined the Mahratta army at fifteen years old. In 1803 he swapped his allegiance to Britain and was soon promoted for his bravery. At one point he was dismissed from the army due to his mixed race, but General Lake recognised his ability and invited him to form Skinner's Horse.

Originally a troop of riders who had deserted from the Mahratta army, Skinner's Horse became one of the most famous regiments of the Indian Army. The title was later transferred to the Ist Bengal Cavalry, which became known as the 'Yellow Boys.' Skinner took part in a dozen campaigns and rose to become lieutenant colonel, although Horse Guards did not recognise the rank until 1827. As was customary at the time, Skinner combined soldiering with looting and when he eventually retired he bought a town house in Delhi, a small estate nearby and a number of wives.

Like so many eminent Scottish soldiers, Skinner was also a man of words and he wrote books in Persian. He also used some of his plunder to found a temple, the Church of St James and a mosque. The Church of St James was erected within the Kashmir Gate "in fulfilment of a vow made while lying wounded on the field of battle... in testimony of his sincere faith in the truth of the Christian religion." He was said to have criticised the interior designer, mentioning that his initials were JHS, not I H S.

When he died, he was buried with great style, as befitted a noble Scottish warrior.

Slessor, Mary (1848 – 1915)
Missionary

The second of eight children, Mary Slessor was born in Aberdeen but moved to Dundee with her family as a child. She had a hard upbringing as her drunken father beat her, and she witnessed the early death of four of her siblings. At the age of eleven Slessor began work in a Dundee mill, while also taking evening classes. On Sundays, Slessor worked as a Sunday school teacher. Her Christianity was practical and genuine for she also worked with destitute children.

The death of **David Livingston** in 1874 caused a surge of interest in missionary work and the United Presbyterian Church's Foreign Missionary Board accepted Slessor as a teacher. At the age of 28, Slessor was sent to Calabar on the West Coast of Africa. The mission was a haven of peace and Christianity, but was surrounded by forests that contained cannibals, slavers and tribes that practised human sacrifice.

Based at the village of Old Town on the Calabar River, Slessor became renowned for her common sense Christianity. Experienced in hardship, Slessor cropped her hair, donned trousers and worked at physical and spiritual tasks with equal relish as she eventually headed the Old Town mission. It was said that when she found some women being raped, she drove away the rapists with her umbrella.

She was also the first white woman to enter Chief Okon's village, deep in the interior. The natives rushed to see her, fingering her white skin to see if it was just painted on. Some believed that she was a spirit, but soon they were calling her 'Ma.'

Slessor did not forget her family in Dundee. She returned briefly to Scotland in 1879 and moved her elderly mother and her four surviving sisters away from the unhealthy town centre to Downfield, which was then a village beyond the city. She returned in 1883, this time accompanied by an African child whom she had rescued from human sacrifice. Slessor saw the child settled in Dundee and, despite the malaria that racked her body, she sailed again for Africa.

Perhaps it was her knowledge of the unhealthy working conditions in the Dundee mills that made Slessor as hygiene conscious as she was. Although eminently practical, she had high moral standards that she passed on to the people at the mission.

Okyong was her next destination. Slessor became an Administrator, judging the people and administering impartial justice as she taught Christianity and cared for the weakest members of society. On one occasion she saved intended victims of human sacrifice by standing guard over them for days.

Slessor married David Adeyemi Adeyemo, bearing two of his children. Slessor was known as the 'White Queen of Okoyong' as she administered for all the people within a 2000 square mile area. However, hard work took its toll in arthritis that gradually crippled her. Slessor died in January 1915. She had an impressive funeral, with thousands gathered, police and government officials paying their respect. She was buried at Mission Hill, Calabar, the place where she had spent most of her life.

Smith, Douglas Alexander, Ist Baron Strathcona (1820 – 1914)
Businessman and politician

Born near Forres in Moray, Smith immigrated to Canada in 1838 and became a clerk in the Hudson's Bay Company. He found the life in Labrador tough, but persevered until he was a practised fur trapper. He was also the first to plant vegetables and potatoes on the bleak shores of Labrador. Within twelve years he had risen to become chief trader and factor on Hudson Bay.

In 1869 Louis Riel led the Metis in revolt against the incorporation of the North West Territories into Canada. It was Donald Smith, then resident Governor of Montreal, who travelled by sleigh across the snow to Fort Garry to uncover the source of the rising. He suggested to the Government that the Hudson Bay officers could help 'restore and maintain order' in the Northwest. Smith used a minimum of force, so there was little resentment when the British and Canadians quelled the trouble. He was equally adept at arranging compensation for the traders who lost some of their source of income.

Chief executive of the Company in 1868, Smith and his partners bought a controlling interest and rose to Chief Commissioner, then Director and finally in 1889, Governor. A far seeing man, Smith bought a failing railway company and created the St Paul, Minneapolis and Manitoba Railway. In 1880 he was also a major promoter of the Canadian Pacific Railway. Smith banged home the final spike of the railway at Craigellachie in British Columbia, high in the Rocky Mountains.

In character Smith may not have been immediately loveable, but he had driven deep roots into Canada. His wife came from native stock in Rupert's Land, his wealth from Company shares. His education was due mainly to long hours of reading in the grim dark of the North. With as little charm and as much raw drive as a bull moose, Smith understood his adopted country and used it well.

In 1896 he became High Commissioner for Canada in London, and was ennobled the following year as Lord Strathcona and Mount Royal However, Smith was not only a businessman and a politician. As a philanthropist, he gave impressive funds to Scottish and Canadian Universities, opened up Canadian rivers to steam ships and was a notable member of the Pacific Cable Board that linked Canada to Australia and Britain.

When the Boer War started, Smith raised the superb Strathcona's Horse from the western prairies of Canada and he lived to see the successful termination of that conflict as Canada grew in stature and confidence. Also unusually, but very much in character, he ensured that his peerage, by special dispensation, descended to his daughter.

Smith Peter (1829 – c1891)
Founder of Dundee, Natal
Born in Angus, Smith was brought up at Holemill Farm, Kirkbuddo. He immigrated to South Africa, settling on a farm that he named

Dundee. He lived on the farm until 1882. However, the area was close to the theatre of the Zulu War of 1879, and Fort Jones was built near Dundee to house soldiers withdrawn from Zululand after the defeat at Isandlwana.

By the time the soldiers re-launched their invasion, Fort Jones had become a focal point for merchants, missionaries and hunters. Along with his son, son in law Dugald McPhail, who was reputed to have escaped from Isandlwana and a man named Charles Wilson, Smith announced the birth of the town of Dundee. By 1889 Smith had placed the Dundee Coal Company on the Stock Exchange in London, and the town became prosperous, with the first theatre north of Durban, quality residences and the 'meeting place of the seven roads' to the north.

Spence, Catherine (1825 –1910)
Australian writer and feminist

Born near Melrose in the Scottish Borders, Spence was the daughter of a lawyer and banker. She immigrated to Australia with her parents when she was fourteen years old. Her father had lost money on the wheat exchanges and hoped to recoup his losses in South Australia. Settling in Adelaide, Spence had twin ambitions: to be a teacher and writer. Working with a governess, Spence achieved the second of her ambitions in 1854 when she had *Clare Morrison; a tale of South Australia During the Gold Fever* published. Spence was the first women to write a novel about Australian life. She wrote another five novels.

From 1878 Spence became a literary critic and courted controversy in 1880 when she presented *Handfasters* to the *Sydney Mail.* The newspaper commented her story was "calculated to loosen the marriage ties" and was "too socialist."

A dedicated social reformer, in 1872 Spence was a prime mover in the Boarding Act Society, which found foster homes for destitute, orphaned and wayward children. Four years later she became an active member of the Children's Council of South Australia as well as a member of the Destitute Board.

Although Spence never taught in schools, she was an educator as she toured Britain and the United States giving lectures on social problems of poverty. Spence proposed proportional representation for voting and was the prime mover in the Effective Voting League in South Australia, arguing for proportional representation and after 1891 for female suffrage. She also became vice president of the Woman's Suffrage League of South Australia. As if that was not enough, Spence was also Australia's first ever female candidate in the federal convention of 1897.

Although Spence had been brought up a Presbyterian, she decided, after much thought, to join the Unitarian Christian Church. At first she contented herself with writing sermons, but eventually gave sermons to the congregation.

It is no wonder that Australia has fond memories of Catherine Spence, and when she died they knew her as the 'Grand old woman of Australia.'

Spotswood, Alexander (1676 – 1746)
Governor of Virginia and entrepreneur
Spotswood's father was the personal physician to the **Sir John Middleton**, and when the Earl became governor of the colony of Tangier, Spotswood's parents sailed there so Spotswood was born in a colonial environment. He became an ensign in the Earl of Bath's Regiment of Foot in 1693 and rose to captain in 1704. He was wounded at the battle of Blenheim, but recovered in time to be captured at the equally bloody battle of Oudenarde.

In 1710 George Hamilton, Earl of Orkney was the Governor of Virginia, but rather than concentrate on the position, he appointed Spotswood as Lieutenant Governor, with the agreement that Spotswood should perform the governor's tasks and receive half the emoluments. In essence Spotswood became governor, earning around £1200 a year.

Spotswood was not always a popular governor, for he seems to have been honest, and supported strong rule from Britain. However he was hard working and energetic. He campaigned for Royal Naval patrols at the mouth of the Chesapeake to keep down the French and Spanish privateers and protect coastal trade. Unfortunately the Navy would also stop the local Virginians from smuggling. At a time when the colonies were anything but united, Spotswood's acrimonious relationships with neighbouring North Carolina did not prevent him from offering help during the Tuscarora War of 1711 to 1713.

With the European wars continuing, Spotswood built defences along the Chesapeake ready to repel a French attack that never occurred. He also created the gridiron plan for Williamsburg and gave the colony firm government. In 1716 he led a party of 63 men westward from the then boundary of his colony to the Shenandoah River, which he made the new boundary. At a time when most colonials and virtually all the British could barely see beyond the crest of the Appalachians, Spotswood expressed his opinion that the colony should stretch all the way to the Mississippi. He was the first colonial official to vocalise the 'manifest destiny' that became part of the American psyche in the following century.

Spotswood also saw that it was necessary to remove any lawless elements, and he worked hard to eradicate the pirates who terrorised this coast. He pestered the British government to send over the Royal Navy to "the Bahamas to dislodge the Pyrates." Among the worst of the pirates was Captain Teach, popularly known as Blackbeard, who played havoc with colonial shipping from the Caribbean northward. Already in receipt of a pardon from Governor Eden of North Carolina, Blackbeard based himself in that colony while he plundered at will. Governor Eden also officiated at Blackbeard's fourteenth marriage, to a girl of around sixteen, despite the fact that at least a dozen of his previous wives were still alive. It was one of Blackbeard's less endearing customs to lend his wife to others of his crew, another to fire pistols at the legs of his gambling partners if he was losing. There was little romance in this pirate of the Caribbean.

When the merchants of North Carolina asked Spotswood to help catch Teach, he agreed. In November 1718 he offered a reward for the death of "Edward Teach, commonly called Captain Teach, or Black-beard" and sent out Lieutenant Maynard in the royal ship *Pearl.* Maynard was successful, returning with Blackbeard's head hanging from his bowsprit. However relieved the merchants, there was a furore when the governor of North Carolina complained that Spotswood had sent an armed force into his waters to capture the pirate.

During his tenure of office, Spotswood had accumulated some 85,000 acres of land, albeit by dubious means. He returned to Britain, confirmed his claims and married Anne Brague, with whom he had four children. When he sailed back to Virginia around 1730 he exploited the raw materials on his lands. His blast furnace was the largest in the Americas and revealed the industrial potential that the colonies could possess. Overall Spotswood showed more vision for the colonies than most governors, attempted to quell the natural lawlessness of a frontier community and sowed the seeds of the American Industrial Revolution.

St Clair, Arthur (1736 – 1818)
First Governor the American North West Territories

Born in Thurso, St Clair immigrated to the American colonies when he was twenty-two and settled in Boston. He married in 1764 and relocated to Bedford in Pennsylvania. During the run up to the American War of Independence, St Clair became a Patriot and when the war started he sided with the revolutionaries. He was an aide of Washington during the Battle of Brandywine and in 1787, after independence, St Clair was President of the Continental Congress.

Between 1788 and 1802 he was the first Governor of the North West Territories, which today make up the states of Ohio, Indiana, Michigan, Illinois, Wisconsin and part of Minnesota. It was during this period that St Clair led an American army against an Indian insurrection led by Little Turtle and Tecumseh. At the battle of the Wabash River, St Clair was totally defeated.

St Clair was also one of the founders of the Pittsburgh iron industry, yet despite his power and influence he liked the simple life and spent the last period of his life in a log cabin on Chestnut Ridge.

Steel, William (1809 – c 1880)
Organiser of the Underground Railroad
William Steel was born in Biggar in 1809. In 1817 he immigrated to the United States with his parents, with the family settling first in Virginia, then in Ohio. In 1830 Steel began to work the Underground Railroad, running slaves from the South to freedom in the North. He was one of the leaders of the Railroad in Ohio State. Steel was so successful that the Virginia slave owners offered a reward of $5000 for his head, and, being Scottish, Steel offered to collect the money in person.

Working as a merchant, Steel made a great deal of money, but over-reached himself and lost it all in 1844. As a Liberal Party candidate, Steel helped defeat the pro-slavery Henry Clay.

Stewart, John (c1381 – 1424)
Constable of France
In the middle Ages many Scotsmen fought for France. One was John Stewart was the son of the Duke of Albany and nephew of Alexander Stewart, Earl of Buchan and Wolf of Badenoch. In 1408 he became Chamberlain of Scotland. In 1418 the French, under English attack, sent to Scotland for aid. Scotland sent an expeditionary force, funded by France and commanded by John Stewart, the Earl of Buchan.

The Scots landed at La Rochelle in the autumn of 1419. John Stewart defeated the English at the Battle of Bauge on 22 March 1421 and was made constable of France. Speaking of this battle, the Pope remarked that the Scots acted as an antidote to the English. He was killed, together with much of his army, at the battle of Verneuil in August 1424.

Stewart Lockhart, James Haldane (1858 - 1937)
Colonial official
Born in Argyllshire, Stewart Lockhart was educated in Edinburgh. In 1878 he became a cadet in Hong Kong. Working for his obligatory

year at the Colonial Office, he learned Chinese and in 1879 arrived in Hong Kong. Almost at once Stewart Lockhart became a dedicated Orientalist, collecting Chinese art and studying the culture of the people.

An excellent administrator and linguist, Stewart Lockhart and the Chinese enjoyed a mutual liking. He became Colonial Secretary and Registrar General to Hong Kong at a time when foreign powers were beginning to nibble at China. As the Japanese, Russians and Germans all grabbed chunks of Chinese territory, Britain enlarged her lands around Hong Kong by leasing the New Territories. It was Stewart Lockhart who marked out the boundaries in 1898. He was also appointed as the first civil commissioner of Weihaiwei, another new British acquisition in the area.

More of a scholar than a man of commerce, Stewart Lockhart did not fully develop the economy of Weihaiwei, despite his enthusiasm. He retired from colonial service in 1921, but continued his interest in Chinese art until his death. Lockhart Road in Hong Kong remembers him.

Stirling, Sir James (1791 –1865)
First Governor of Western Australia

Born in Lanarkshire, the fifth son of Andrew Stirling of Drumpellier, Stirling joined the Royal Navy when he was fourteen years old. After service in the West Indies, he was present at the Battle of Cape Finisterre in 1805, at actions off the River Plate in 1807 and commanded HMS *Brazen* in 1812, operating against the Americans from the mouth of the Mississippi to Hudson Bay and completed some valuable survey work.

In 1824 Stirling was sent to establish a settlement in Raffles Bay in the north coast of Queensland at Torres Strait. It was while he explored the coast to the west that Stirling observed that a colony on the western coast of Australia might be useful. Two years later he was ordered to take settlers to that area.

Arriving in the spring of 1829, Stirling planned the cities of Perth and Freemantle, and established settlements that expanded to 1300 souls within four months. For ten years Stirling remained as governor, steering the infant colony safely through the inevitable teething troubles. It says much for his governorship that Perth was untainted by some of the less savoury aspects of early colonial history. Stirling Gardens still retains his name.

When rumours of another French War reached Australia, Stirling demanded to return to active service. Back at sea, he rose to be Admiral and Commander in Chief of the China and East Indies station, but did not fight again. It is Perth, Western Australia that remains his memorial, and who could want for a better?

Stout, Sir Robert (1844 – 1930)
Prime Minister of New Zealand

Born in Lerwick in Shetland, the son of a merchant and eldest of six children, Stout was educated at Lerwick Academy and appointed a student teacher at the age of thirteen. In 1860 he qualified as a surveyor. With his father a Free Church Elder, Stout grew up believing that "theological disputation was part of life." Debating the Bible sharpened the oral skills that would come so handy later in his career.

In 1864 Stout immigrated to Dunedin, New Zealand, being employed as a maths teacher in Dunedin Grammar School and helped found the Otago Schoolmasters Association, which became a branch of the New Zealand Educational Institute. By the end of 1867 Stout had embarked on a legal career, becoming a solicitor in 1871. A few years later he was the senior partner in Stout, Mondy and Sim, by which time he had also obtained a first class university degree in Moral Science and Political Economy.

From 1873 he was lecturing in Law at Otago University, but he also became interested in philosophy, adapting his views on individuals advancement within the state. A member of the Otago Provincial Council from 1872, Stout was Provincial Solicitor between 1874 and 1876, by which time he was also in the House of Representatives. Attorney General in 1878 and 1879, Stout still had time and energy to work as the Minister for Lands and Immigration.

 Stout's marriage to Anna Logan in 1876 produced six children. With his wife a sincere believer in temperance, Stout also became active in that field, while Anna worked hard for women's suffrage as well as for legal and workplace equality. Stout's political career began to take shape as he argued for secular schools and higher education. However between 1879 and 1884 he left politics to concentrate on law, while continuing to pursue his philosophical thoughts.

After 1884 Stout was back in politics, arguing strongly for freedom of speech and free thought, and then introduced a Police Offences Bill to increase freedom on Sundays. Between 1884 and 1887 Stout was Prime Minister of New Zealand, as well as Attorney General and Minister of Education. In this very busy period Stout's government gave more rights to women, developed secondary education, hospitals welfare, and the civil service.

Voted out in 1887, Stout fought for social issues, including better employment conditions for Dunedin seamstresses. He also argued for licensing control and was instrumental for pushing through the 1893 Electoral Bill that gave women the vote. However, Stout was never again to be Prime Minister. Moving to Wellington, he was Chief Justice between 1899 and 1926 and worked for Maori rights and a wider university system, helping found Victoria University College. He also became an active member of the Unitarian Church in Wellington. A rationalist and believer in free thought; Stout was one of the most philosophical of New Zealand's politicians.

Stuart, John MacDouall (1815 – 1866)
Australian Explorer
Born at Dysart in Fife, Stuart attended the Scottish Naval and Military Academy in Edinburgh, but was considered to small and sickly to join the army. Instead he immigrated to South Australia in 1839, where he found work in the Survey Department.

He accompanied the English explorer Captain Sturt as a draughtsman on the expedition of 1844 to 1845. They spent seventeen months working in the unknown, from the fringes of the deserts to the lands of hostile tribesmen. Sometimes the heat was so strong that it evaporated the ink on the nib of the pen and the expedition was besieged by lack of water.

In 1858 Stuart explored the area around Lake Eyre and Lake Torrens, returning the following year. With all this experience, it was natural that Stuart should try for the £10,000 prize available for the first man to cross Australia from south to north.

Beginning at Adelaide on the 2nd March 1860, Stuart passed his old stomping ground of Lake Eyre. He marched onward, through the Macdonnell Ranges and on the 22nd April 1860 he camped a couple of miles from a prominent hill that he named Central Mount Sturt, after his ex-leader. To claim ownership, Stuart planted a large Union Flag. Three cheers echoed over the silent vastness of Australia. Still determined, he pushed on, despite the debilitating scurvy, the heat and the constant threat of hostile tribes. At last, 1500 miles from Adelaide, confronted by hostile tribesmen and with Stuart hardly able to see, the party turned back.

He tried again the following year, with the identical result. Heat, thirst and hostile country guarded Australia's secrets. However, Stuart, despite being too weak for the army, had a character of solid oak. Leaving Adelaide in October 1861, he tried for the third time. He termed his party the Great Northern Exploring Expedition, and gave careful orders for its conduct and organisation. By March 1862 Stuart was in the arid centre and still trekking, step by agonising step across Australia. His water bags leaked and the sheer scale of the country daunted the new men in the party.

There was always heat, always lack of water, but now Australia varied the torments with which she afflicted the explorers. There were ugly marshes, alive with biting ants and whining mosquitoes. There were sand flies and there was scurvy. But eventually Stuart noticed that the countryside was changing. At length, sick, nearly blind, exhausted but elated, Stuart reached the Indian Ocean.

The return was a nightmare of thirst and sickness. Vomiting blood, Stuart was unable to walk, so his men constructed a stretcher and carried him, suspended between four horses, for seven hundred agonising miles. "What a miserable life mine is now," he wrote, "the nights are too long and the days are too long."

They reached Adelaide on the 17th December 1862, over a year since they left, but Stuart had not lost a single man. Adelaide exploded with jubilation and announced a public holiday.

Already a Royal Geographical Society Gold Medal holder, Stuart became the leaseholder of 1000 square miles of Australia. However, his exertions had weakened him so he could not farm. He travelled to London and handed over his writings to a publisher, but died lonely and blind in 1866. His legacy in Australia was the Overland Telegraph that followed his route, and, fittingly, Central Mount Sturt was renamed Central Mount Stuart.

Sutherland, Donald (1839 – 1919)
New Zealand explorer

Born in Wick, Caithness, Sutherland was a seaman from his early teens, arriving at Auckland, New Zealand, in 1862. Joining the Armed Constabulary, he returned to his old career as a sailor on a government steam ship during the Maori Wars and also took part in the gold rush at the Thames Field at Westland in the South Island, and in 1880, prospected for gold at Milford Sound.

As well as prospecting and soldiering, Sutherland also tried his hand at sealing, but it is as an explorer that he is best remembered. He explored the west side of South Island, the spectacular Fjord Country, and the New Zealand Alps. He was the first European to see Lake Ada and the tall Sutherland Falls, at 580 metres once believed to be the highest in the world, but now known to be the fifth highest.

Sutherland later settled down with Elizabeth McKenzie. By now he was known as the Hermit of Milford Sound, but he and Elizabeth gave splendid hospitality from their boarding house until Sutherland's death in 1919.

Swan, James (1754 – 1830)
A Son of Liberty and failed financier

Born in Fife, James Swan immigrated to the American colonies when still young. He settled in Boston, Massachusetts, where he found work as a clerk in a counting house. As an impressionable sixteen-year-old he joined the Sons of Liberty and took part in the Boston Tea Party, but he proved his revolutionary fervour was no youthful idealism when he carried his musket to Bunker Hill. The British regulars shot him twice, but he survived both wounds.

Swan continued the fight, rising to become a major and ending the war as a lieutenant colonel. He married a woman with money and repaid the British for his wounds by snapping up confiscated loyalist estates in Virginia, Kentucky and Pennsylvania. On a roll, in 1786 he bought a small archipelago off Maine, but then over-reached himself when he dabbled in French affairs.

After his war experience Swan had become friendly with Lafayette, who helped him buy into military contracts as well as managing the United States war debt. When the French removed their monarchy, Swan was created an Agent of the French Republic, and continued to dabble in high finance. However clever his schemes appeared, he only managed to dig himself deeper into debt. His attempt to cancel the United States debt failed and Swan was committed to a debtor's prison, where he died.

Swinton, John (1829 – 1901)
Journalist and human rights activist
Born in East Lothian, Swinton immigrated to Canada in 1843. After an apprenticeship, Swinton became a journeyman printer with the *Montreal Witness*. In 1849 he moved to New York City, where he worked on the *New York Times*, making his name as a labour journalist. After a short spell in a seminary, Swinton returned to the printing trade, and then became a prominent writer in the Free Soil movement in Kansas, managing an anti-slavery newspaper *Lawrence Republican*.

Moving to South Carolina, Swinton found work as a compositor in the state printing office, but also held secret underground meetings to educate escaped slaves. By 1857 this extremely mobile man was back in New York, reading law and medicine. He found work with the *New York Times*, which he edited between 1860 and 1870. After that he became a freelance journalist, writing about increased rights for the working man and speaking at demonstrations in aid of the unemployed.

Married in 1877, Swinton fathered four children, and in 1880 met Karl Marx in London. A few years later he began publication of *John Swinton's Paper*, which spoke strongly in favour of better working conditions for women and children. "When we speak of the rights of man," he once said, "those of women are implied every time." However, Swinton also became a Nativist in the 1890s, opposed to immigration and particularly against importing Chinese workers. A candidate for the progressive Labour Party, *Harpers Weekly* remembered him as a "stalwart, bitter champion of the labourer."

Syme, David (1827 – 1908)
Australian newspaper editor
Born in North Berwick, East Lothian, David Syme considered entering the ministry, but decided that the gold fields held more appeal, and probably better financial rewards. Syme found a rich strike and was beginning to dream of wealth when a claim jumper grabbed his land. Disillusioned, he decided to move into the newspaper business. He bought a half share in the Melbourne *Age*, which was owned by his brother. When his brother died in 1860, Syme took complete control.

Syme spent forty-nine years editing the *Age*, using the paper to promote his radical liberal ideals. Syme wanted land reforms, with small farmers replacing the huge landowners. He wanted improved working conditions and protection for indigenous industry as well as compulsory secular education. Some saw him as being influential in the eventual introduction of protection.

Possibly his early religious bent lent strength to his philanthropic ideas, for Syme also campaigned for manhood suffrage. Because of high newspaper sales, Syme had a great deal of clout in local politics.

Governor Sir George Brown was only one of the important politicians who consulted him.

Although a publisher rather than a writer, Syme did produce *The Soul: A Study and an Argument*, which was a work of philosophy. He was a thinker and a manipulator but still refrained from taking a personal part in any colonial committee. He did however, help finance exploring expeditions and academia. It is a measure of his power that his contemporaries termed him King David.

Thompson, Peter (1854 – 1928)
Fought at Little Big Horn
Born in Markinch, Fife, Thomson immigrated to the United States in 1865. At the age of 21 he enlisted in the army, serving in the 7th Cavalry under the famous General Custer. In 1876 he took part in the Battle of the Little Big Horn, where he was wounded while fighting alongside Major Reno. Despite his wound, Thompson left the lines, braving the hostile Sioux, to obtain water for the other casualties, for which action he was presented with the Medal of Honor. When Thompson wrote an account of the battle, he mentioned witnessing the beginning of the end of Custer, so may have been the last white man alive to see Custer. Other veterans of the battle disputed his claims, but Thompson defended himself vigorously. Leaving the army in 1880, Thompson became a miner and homesteader, with a wife and family.

Thomson, Joseph (1858 – 1894)
African explorer
Born at Penpont, near Thornhill in Dumfriesshire, Thomson studied geology at Edinburgh University. In 1878 he became the geologist on the Royal Geographical Society's expedition to East Central Africa. When the expedition set off from Dar-es Salaam it was 150 strong, and headed southwest into the interior. Not long after, Alexander Keith Johnston, the leader of the expedition died and Thomson took over. He was just 21 years old.

The expedition was intended to explore the area around Lake Nyasa and Lake Tanganyika. Johnson became the first known European to reach Lake Nyasa from the north and continued to Lake Tanganyika. At a time when explorers could blast their way through Africa, Thomson's men did not have a single skirmish. Rather than confrontation, Thomson walked around any possible enemy. Even more impressively, he lost only one man from fever. He gave details of this journey in his book *To the Central African Lakes and Back.*

When the Sultan of Zanzibar hoped to modernise his kingdom, he sent Thomson to find coal in the Rovuma River valley. The expedition was not a success. In 1882 the Royal Geographical Society sent him to carve out a route from the coast to Lake Victoria by way of Kilimamjaro. In what was perhaps his greatest achievement, Thomson crossed the Nijiri Desert, passed through the lands of the fearsome Masai warriors and also negotiated the Great Rift Valley. On this journey he discovered Lake Baringo and Mount Elgon, while his note taking was always meticulous.

Thomson was not yet finished with Africa, for in 1885 the British National African Company sent him to explore Sokoto in what is now northwest Nigeria. Five years later, Thomson probed into the Upper Congo, where his carriers mutinied due to fear of cannibals. To complete his exploration of the continent's wild places, he also journeyed to the Moroccan Atlas Mountains. He died aged only thirty-six, a remarkable traveller.

Thomson sought to define his own travels. "I am doomed to be a wanderer," he said, and denied that he was an empire builder, a scientist or a missionary. "I merely want to return to Africa to continue my wanderings." Perhaps these words make him the one of the most honest of all the explorers.

Thomson, Robert Brown (1923 - 2010)
Baseball player

One of the very few Scots to make it big in American baseball, Bobby Thomson was born in Glasgow but immigrated to New York at two years old. His first love was football; playing for Curtis High School in New York, but when he was seen or eight his father took him to his first baseball game. Not until later did Thomson take to the sport, but made his name in baseball's hall of fame. After a few seasons for minor clubs, Thomson was called up for service in the wartime United States Air Corps.

His most famous exploit came on the 3rd October 1951 when he hit a game-winning, ninth-inning three-run homer off the Brooklyn Dodgers pitcher Ralph Branca. His hit helped the New York Giants win the National League. This hit was known as the "Shot Heard Round the World." Thomson also played in the Chicago Cubs and with the Boston Redsox.

Veitch, Captain Samuel (c 1670 – 1733)
Soldier, colonist, governor of Nova Scotia

The son of a noted Covenanter, Samuel Veitch or Vetch (his own spelling) joined the Cameronians as a young man, being present at the battle of Dunkeld when the Jacobite clans were repulsed. He also fought at the battle of Steinkirk, where he was wounded.

Veitch was heavily involved with the Company of Scotland, being chosen as a Councillor for the proposed colony at Darien. He shared the hardships of that unhappy colony with his fellows, where he was thought of as one of the more honest councillors. He was sent to the English colonies to find help for the starving sick men, but was turned away. Only in New York, where the governor was Scots, did he find any help. Veitch remained in New York, marrying his cousin, Margaret Livingstone, daughter of the governor. He began work as a merchant, aware that many of the Darien colonists now despised him as a runaway and traitor. Veitch found New York congenial; he became wealthy and rose to be a Colonel in the Militia. There were rumours that Veitch became involved in smuggling, or that he sold goods belonging to the Company of Scotland for his own profit. Veitch became an expert in trading between Massachusetts and France, despite the state of war that existed between the two places

In 1708 Veitch suggested that Britain should annex the then French colony of Canada. He proposed the 1710 expedition that captured

Nova Scotia, and he was present when Port Royal surrendered to the British. He later became governor of the colony, but political enemies spoiled his career. Taking ship to Britain, Veitch died, deep in debt, in the King's Bench Prison.

Vreeland, Diane (1906 – 1989)
The Empress of Fashion

Born in Paris to a Scottish stockbroker father and an American mother, Diane Dalziel had a distinguished family. Her mother was a socialite and her cousin was Pauline de Rothschild, a noted style icon. Around 1914 the family immigrated to the United States and in 1924 Diane Dalziel married Thomas Vreeland, a New York banker.

Moving from New York to London, Diane Vreeland ran a lingerie business, with Wallis Simpson as one of her clients, moved to Paris in 1935 but in 1937 her husband was transferred back to New York, where Vreeland spent the rest of her life. Vreeland was a society diva, whose words and style influenced generations of up market women. It was said that she created the chic look. Style was everything, and her witty sayings, such as "The best thing about London is Paris" became famous. From 1937 Vreeland worked as fashion editor for Harper's Magazine. Vreeland cut a distinctive figure, with rouged cheekbones, extravagant eyelashes and a penchant for red lacquer, but a desire for elegant clothing trimmed with exotic accessories such as unusual jewellery and splendid footwear. As Andy Warhol said of her "She makes the smallest detail important."

Although some of her advice may have been a little extravagant, for instance suggesting that one's old ermine robe should be made into a bathrobe, or washing one's child's hair in Champaign, Vreeland offered an alternative to the rigid doctrines of taste. Style mattered more than conformity. Becoming fashion director, then editor of *Harper's*, Vreeland moved to *Vogue* in 1963, where she said "Never fear being vulgar, just boring." There was certainly nothing boring about her apartment on Park Avenue, with its red lacquer walls and red sofa with cushions and gilded mirrors.

Between 1973 and 1989, Vreeland was a consultant to the Costume Institute at the Metropolitan Museum, where he helped organise some amazing exhibitions. She died in 1989, leaving a host of memories and sayings, with perhaps her best "Without emotion there is no beauty" worthy of an epitaph.

Waterston, Jane Elizabeth (1843 – 1932)
First recorded woman doctor in Africa

Born in Inverness, Waterston was the daughter of a bank manager. She was privately educated before attending Inverness Royal Academy. In 1865, at the age of 22, Waterston approached the Free Church Foreign Mission Committee, asking to work overseas, and in 1867 she was posted to Lovedale in the Cape Province, South Africa. She remained there until 1873, working as a teacher and simultaneously learning the local Xhosa language.

Waterston soon became known for her support for the disadvantaged and for a strong belief in the rights of women. She also became ambitious for a medical qualification so she could pursue a career as a medical missionary. Accordingly, Waterston travelled to London in 1874 to study under Sophia Jex-Blake, and eventually was entered on to the medical register of the Dublin College of Physicians.

By late 1879 Waterston was working in the Central African Mission at Livingstonia, the first female doctor in Central Africa. After only a few months she was back at Lovendale, then in some of the most deprived areas of Cape Town, where she founded a free dispensary for woman and children. Still ambitious, Waterston returned to Britain to obtain a qualification as a Licentiate of the Royal College of Surgeons. Sailing back to Africa, Waterston dedicated the rest of her life to the most vulnerable people, including lepers and convicts. As well as being Africa's first known civilian woman doctor, she was believed to be the oldest practising female doctor in the whole of the British Empire.

Watling, Thomas (fl 1762)
Convict artist

Born in Dumfries, Watling worked as an artist before he was convicted of forging Bank of Scotland one-guinea notes. Knowing that forgery was an almost inevitable death sentence, Watling, while protesting his innocence, volunteered to save his life by accepting transportation rather than stand trial. A perhaps-lenient judiciary awarded him fourteen years in Australia.

After fifteen months awaiting a transportation vessel, Watling was sent to New South Wales. He arrived in 1792 and was appointed servant of John White, the Surgeon General. As the first trained artist in Australia, Watling's paintings and drawings of the next few years provide an invaluable record of colonial life in pre-photograph days. He shows tattooed Aborigines, previously unknown birds and animals, birds and flowers as well as the birth of a new country. He made at least 123 drawings that have been preserved in the British Museum.

One of the most talented of early Australians, Watling also wrote *Letters from an Exile at Botany Bay to his Aunt in Dumfries*. **John Hunter**, the new Governor from 1795, pardoned Watling, who sailed to India with his son. He worked as a miniature painter in Calcutta for three years then returned to Dumfries.

In 1806, either incredibly stupid or incredibly unlucky, he was again charged with forging a Scottish banknote, but this time the court passed a not proven verdict. Watling is known to have contracted some form of cancer, for he wrote to John Hunter for financial help, but that is the last heard of him.

Weddell, James (1787 – 1834)
Antarctic Explorer

Weddell's birthplace is disputed. Although he was to claim he was born in Massachusetts in the United States, at the time of his birth his parents were in Ostend. His father was from Dalserf in Lanarkshire, his mother was from London and when he was around eight years old, Waddell joined the Royal Navy.

When he found his first ship ruled by unrelenting discipline, Waddell left the navy to work in North Sea colliers. He rebelled against the arbitrary violence on one of his ships and was placed in irons. In 1810 he rejoined the Navy, to take part in both the Napoleonic and American Wars. As Master of the brig *Hope* in 1813, Weddell helped capture *True Blooded Yankee*, a privateer.

Weddell was expert at his job. One of his commanders, Captain Duff, reported he was "particularly fond of Navigation, and in taking of the distance in lunar observation" he was "unusually accurate." Leaving the Navy in 1818, Weddell first commanded *Carlotta*, then met James Strachan, of Strachan & Gavin of Leith. Given command of the 160-ton sealing brig *Jane*, Weddell sailed for the Antarctic. As he hunted for seals around the South Orkney and South Shetland Islands, he also surveyed and mapped the coasts. Weddell was more of an explorer than a sealer. In 1794 the master of the Spanish vessel *Altruda* claimed to have positioned the Aurora Islands, a group that had been located in various places in the far south.

Obsessively accurate, Weddell made his headquarters at Staten Island, south of Cape Horn and steered for the last reported position of the islands. After an exhaustive search "without observing the least appearance of land," Weddell concluded "that the discoverers must have been misled by appearances." He had cleared up one of the many mysteries of the sea and, by meticulous map-making, had made navigation in that area safer. While he was in the South Orkney Islands, Weddell also named and surveyed James Island, performing the same task for the Boyd Strait in the South Shetlands.

In 1820 he visited the Falkland Islands at the same time as a frigate from the United Provinces of South America dropped anchor and Captain Jewitt claimed the group. It may have been significant that the Provinces did not remain united. After collecting his quota of seals, Weddell sailed for Britain.

In September 1822 he again headed south in *Jane,* together with the 65 ton cuter *Beaufoy* commanded by Matthew Brisbane. Coping with a bad leak in *Jane,* Weddell encountered a Portuguese slaver. Although his crew demanded that he free the slaves, Weddell refused, knowing that he could not take the law into his own hands.

South again, to see water spouts off Penguin Island, to perform further survey work in the South Orkney Islands, to name Noble Peak after an Edinburgh companion of Weddell. He continued to push south into a sea that seemed free of ice with no sign of land. Weddell was sailing into an immense unknown bight in the Antarctic continent. However, the crew grumbled that they were sealers, not explorers. Aware that his men were within their rights, Weddell soothed their complaints with extra rum and rations, and continued south.

At a time when Antarctica had not yet been discovered, Weddell theorised if he could keep sailing he might reach the South Pole. On February 20 1823, Weddell hit 74 degrees, 15 minutes south; the furthest south that any vessel would sail in those seas until 1907. Calling for more grog, Weddell had his crew toast their achievement and headed for the sealing grounds. He named the sea after King George. Seventy-seven years later the name would be changed to the Weddell Sea.

The voyage continued with stormy seas off the South Shetlands and the sighting of a mermaid at Hall Island. After that trip, Weddell rested for a while at his Edinburgh home, but soon returned to sea. He became a blockade-runner to Buenos Aires, survived shipwreck but died young. He is remembered by the Weddell Sea and the Weddell Seal, but few people in Scotland have heard of him.

Wedderburn, Joseph Henry Maclagan (1882 –1948)
Mathematician

Born at Forfar, Angus, Wedderburn graduated in mathematics from Edinburgh University in 1903. After spells at Leipzig, Berlin and Chicago, he lectured in Edinburgh University from 1905 until 1909. Moving to Princeton in 1909, he came back to fight for Britain during the First World War. When the war ended Wedderburn again crossed the Atlantic to Princeton, where he worked until 1945. He was an expert on algebra, with two fundamental theorems named after him.

Williamson, Peter (1730 – 1799)
'Indian Peter'

Born at Hirnley Farm, Aboyne, Aberdeenshire, Williamson was visiting his aunt in Aberdeen when he was kidnapped. Shipped to the American colonies, he was sold to a Philadelphia owner as a seven-year indentured servant, Williamson survived that experience, obtained his freedom, married and settled down in Pennsylvania.

In 1754, Cherokee Indians captured Williamson and kept him as a slave. He escaped and enlisted in the army, either for revenge or because he was becoming used to slavery. It was the turn of the French to capture him, but he was released in a prisoner exchange. Returning to Scotland, Williamson attempted legal action against the magistrates of Aberdeen for his initial kidnapping. When the action failed, Williamson was forced out of Aberdeen and moved to Edinburgh. He again pursued legal action, won £100 and opened a Coffee Room in Parliament House. In later life he was instrumental in creating the Edinburgh Penny Post and was the inspiration for the film *A Man Called Horse.*

Wilson, Alexander (1766 – 1813)
'The father of American ornithology'

Born in Paisley and educated locally, Wilson became a weaver at the age of 13. He also made money as a chapman, peddling goods from door to door, while writing poetry about weaving and nature. His *Poems* was published in 1790, and proved so popular that some people mistook them for the work of Burns. Two years later he followed with *Watty and Meg*. However this literary career rebounded when a Paisley mill owner and magistrate accused him of writing a libellous poem. At a time when Britain was terrified that the French Revolution might spread across the Channel, the court decided that seditious poems were too dangerous to allow and sentenced him to 18 months in jail.

When Wilson emerged in 1794 he immigrated to the United States, where he taught in schools throughout rural New Jersey and Philadelphia. On the advice of a naturalist neighbour, he decided on a change of career and became a full time naturalist. He travelled the length and breadth of America collecting and drawing the birds of America. He also returned to his poetry, writing *The Foresters: A Poem* about his inaugural collecting trip to Niagara Falls.

In 1806 the publishers of *Rees's Cyclopedia* employed him as assistant editor and allowed him to create *American Ornithology,* a seven volume illustrated guide to the native bird life. Although there were few subscribers to the first volume, Wilson persevered, requesting people to subscribe as he had once chapped goods from door to door. As well as this monumental work, two birds, Wilson's phalarope and Wilson's Storm Petrel were named in his honour.

The extremely long hours he worked undermined his health and Wilson died of dysentery. There is a statue in Paisley to his memory.

Wilson, Sir Daniel (1816 – 1892)
Popularised the term 'pre history'
Born in Edinburgh, Wilson was educated at Edinburgh University and shortly afterward wrote articles for *Chambers Journal.* Even as a young man antiquities intrigued him. Although he wrote a history of Oliver Cromwell, most of his early work was on Scotland. He became secretary to the Scottish Society of Antiquaries, but in 1853 was appointed professor of History and English Literature at the University College at Toronto.

At that time the College was not yet constructed, so Wilson helped design the buildings. He also vigorously defended the 'provincial universities' against denominational attacks, arguing always that places of learning should not lean toward any particular theology.

In 1880 Wilson was appointed president of University College. He became renowned for his research work in Ethnography and for his interpretations of Darwin's controversial theories. Wilson argued that Darwin's findings certainly extended the geological time-line and perhaps also proved evolution, but did not prove the theory of natural selection. Wilson also stressed that humanity and animals were intrinsically separate.

Knighted in 1888, it is a sad fact Wilson is arguably probably best remembered not for his scholarship, which was flawless, but for popularising the term prehistory to refer to the pre-literate past. He was, however, one of the founders and also the first president of the Royal Society of Canada in 1885. Two years later he became the first president of the University of Toronto.

Wilson's writings include *Edinburgh in the Olden Times* and *The Lost Atlantis.*

Wilson, James (1742 – 1798)
Signatory of American Declaration of Independence

Born at the farm of Carskerdo, near Leven in Fife, Wilson was university educated and immigrated to the United States when he was twenty-three. Settling in Philadelphia, he taught at the College of Philadelphia, where he became interested in the patriotic cause. It was Wilson who circulated pamphlets arguing that the American colonies were subject not to the British parliament, but to the Crown.

Wilson signed the American Declaration of Independence and helped draw up the Constitution. He was instrumental in strengthening the independence of the executive but supporting popular elections. Wilson was also Associate Justice of the United States Supreme Court between 1789 and 1798, as well as the first Professor of Law at Pennsylvania University.

Wilson, Jean (1910 –1977)
Speed skater

Born in Glasgow, Wilson started speed skating when she was fifteen years old. She immigrated to Canada with her family and by 1931 was so proficient at speed skating that she could challenge Lila Brook, the then champion. The following year she hammered home her skill when she became the North American Speed Skating champion.

Selected to represent Canada at the Lake Placid Winter Olympics in 1933, Wilson set a new world speed record in her first heat. Unfortunately she fell while in a gold medal position. Wilson's life ended tragically young when she died aged only 23.

Winton, Alexander (1860 - 1932)

Born in Grangemouth, Alexander Winton worked in the Clyde shipyards before immigrating to the United States sometime between 1878 and 1880. After improving steam engines for ships and building bicycles, in 1897 he founded the Winton Motor Carriage Company, building 'horseless carriages.' He built the first motorcar in Cleveland and one of the earliest in America; it is claimed that Winton's was the first American company to sell a motorcar. Winton established a world record in 1900 when he travelled fifty miles in less than one hour eighteen minutes; the following year he handed Henry Ford his steering wheel assembly, as he believed that Ford's version was dangerous. He later defeated a Mercedes in a race where he achieved seventy miles an hour. In 1903 Horatio Nelson Jackson drove a Winton car across the continental United States, taking eight weeks from San Francisco to New York.

Winton sold his diesel engine business to General Motors. Known as the 'trigger-tempered Scot', Winton lived in some style, but stopped making motorcars in 1924, when the new assembly line system replaced his personal, hand made vehicles.

Witherspoon, John (1723 – 1794)

Signatory of American Declaration of Independence

Born in Gifford, East Lothian, Witherspoon was educated at Haddington Grammar School and Edinburgh University. After graduating in theology, he became the minister of Beith, then Paisley. He must have been an interesting preacher, for he received invitations to minister at Dublin, Dundee and Rotterdam, where was a long standing Scottish Kirk.

In 1768 he immigrated to North America, where he became president of the College of New Jersey, now Princeton University. He held that position from 1768 until 1794. Among his students was James Madison, whose future writings were to reveal much of Witherspoon's political, social and Calvinist influences.

A representative of New Jersey to the Continental Congress between 1776 and 1782, Witherspoon was instrumental in creating the American Declaration of Independence, which he was the only clergyman to sign.

Witherspoon's published works include *Ecclesiastic Characteristics, Serious Enquiry into the Nature and Effects of the Stage, Justification* and *Regeneration.*

Witherspoon died at home on his farm, having eased the birth pangs of what was to mature into the greatest nation on Earth.

Wood, Lieutenant John (c1810 – 1871)
Seaman who explored Central Asia

Born in Perthshire, John Wood joined the navy of the East India Company as a young man. In 1835 he commanded the first steam-powered vessel on the lower Indus in a mission that was supposedly intended to open the river for trade. The following year he was surveying the Kabul River when he was commanded to examine the Kohistan passes of the Hindu Kush. Nearly as soon as he left, he was called back and ordered to accompany Percival Lord to Kunduz in landlocked Central Asia. Lord was a doctor of medicine and Mohammed Beg in Kunduz was seeking help with eye trouble.

Alexander Burnes believed that the River Oxus, the major waterway in the region, was navigable, and if so, then the British should be there first. Wood was ordered to discover exactly how navigable the Oxus was. Wood, however, bore the name of a great Scottish admiral and had his own agenda. "The great object of my thoughts," he wrote, "had for some time past been the discovery of the sources of the Oxus." But first they had to cross the Hindu Kush. The mountain barrier repelled their first attempt, but at the beginning of December they arrived at Kunduz.

Wood was a straightforward sailor, full of hard work, unswerving determination and practicality. He sought permission from Murad Beg to ascend the Oxus, made rough preparations for the mid winter trip and set off. With no fuss, virtually no equipment and only seven men

Wood travelled in Uzbek clothes but never disguised that he was a British seaman.

Travelling on horseback, they reached the town of Jerm within a week. The countryside had been ruined by war and was now desolate with snow, but Wood was happy to be moving. He enjoyed the hospitality of the villagers. However he was less happy when blizzards trapped them for weeks, although he took the opportunity to learn the Badakashi language, treated the people as friends and adapted easily to their culture. It was the end of January before Wood left Jerm, climbing up the 10,000 foot high passes of the Pamir range. At Ishkashim he looked over the Oxus valley, seeing only snow and ice and crossed the river on a bridge of snow.

Heading upriver, Wood passed through the Wakhan Valley, to find that the river divided at Qala Panja. He chose the northern branch, dismissed his mutinous Uzbeg and Afghan escort and recruited the warlike Kirghiz for the final stage to the supposed source of the Oxus. As conditions worsened, his companions drifted away, but Wood pushed on until "the afternoon of the 19th February 1838, we stood…upon the Bam-I-Duniah or Roof of the World." In front of him was a frozen lake, the Sir-I-kol, "from whose western end issued the infant river of the Oxus."

With his quest complete, Wood turned back. Leaving the Indian Navy, he came home to Scotland, where he quietly received the Patron's Gold Medal of the Royal Geographical Society. Only a month later he immigrated to New Zealand with his family, but returned to Britain. He later commanded a small fleet of steam vessels on the Indus.

Wright, Frances or Fanny (1795 – 1852)
Social reformer
Fanny Wright was born in Dundee on the 6th September 1795. Her father was a skilled worker and a radical. Although he died when Wright was very young, his ideas remained with his daughter, for Wright's career was a constant struggle against accepted practices and

oppression. She used the fortune that she had inherited from her father to follow her dreams.

As a teenager Wright wrote the philosophical romance *A Few Days in Athens,* which was received with critical acclaim. When she reached 21, Wright moved to Glasgow, to live with her great uncle, James Mylne, a lecturer at Glasgow University. After only two years in Glasgow, Wright sailed to the United States along with her sister. Settling in New York she saw *Altorf,* a political play that she had written, performed on Broadway.

She returned to Scotland and wrote *Views of Society and Manners in America,* which so impressed the Marquis of Lafayette, a French reformer who professed admiration of the United States, that he invited Wright to Paris. The two became friends and when Lafayette immigrated to America in 1824, Wright followed.

Wright next published her *Plan for the Gradual Abolition of Slavery in the United States, Without Danger of Loss to the Citizens of the South* in 1825. Her idea was to allow slaves to earn enough money to buy their liberty, which would prevent any financial loss to the slave owners. Wright bought nine slaves and a 2000-acre plantation at Nashoba in Tennessee, where she attempted a model plantation based on her ideas.

After a physical breakdown, bad harvests and deteriorating relations between blacks and whites, the plantation idea failed. Instead, in 1826 Wright joined Robert Owen's Utopian community at New Harmony. She at once formed an attachment to the Scots born reformer Robert Dale Owen. In turn Owen admired Wright, who he termed "tall, commanding" and "slender and graceful." He also thought her face "delicately chiselled."

Returning to Nashoba, Wright swapped her idea for a slave haven for a Utopian settlement on the Owen model. She also began to experiment with women's place in society. Her novel ideas gave Nashoba the reputation of sexual licence but where women and men had complete equality. Wright planned to replace marriage with "unconstrained and unrestrained" sexual intercourse. She also wanted many more rights for those women who did marry. Travelling across the United States, Wright became the first public speaker in America as she announced her ideas to the nation. As well as universal suffrage, she also lectured against slavery. Her ideas were not popular among many Americans, men or women and on one occasion a bevy of female Quakers ensured that the male hecklers did not physically attack her.

Wright also wrote on education, marriage, women's rights and sex. She said that equality between women and men would help women become mature while civilising men. In 1838 Wright set aside her principles to marry the Frenchman Guillaime D'Arusmont, whom she had met in New Harmony. Perhaps it was not surprising that their marriage did not last, but Wright did gain a daughter. Still writing and lecturing, she moved to Cincinnati, where she died in 1852.

Wright was one of America's first female public speakers, one of the first women to speak and write against slavery, an early social reformer and speaker for woman's rights, it is no wonder that she has a special place in the hearts of America.

Wylie, James (1768 – 1854)
Russian surgeon

Born in Kincardine, Wylie may have been educated at Edinburgh University, but it is possible that he left without completing his degree. There are also tales of sheep rustling that may have contributed to Wylie's decision to emigrate to Russia. Scotsmen frequently made their home in the land of the Csars, but few rose so quickly and gathered honours from so many nations.

From 1790 Wylie was surgeon to the Sletski Regiment. He attracted the Csar's notice when he performed the first tracheotomy in Russia, saving the life of a favourite courtier. After that, Wylie was created Imperial Physician. However, when Csar Paul was murdered in 1801, Wylie announced that he had died of apoplexy. He became a renowned surgeon, but perhaps won his greatest fame during the Napoleonic invasion of 1812. At the battle of Borodino, Wylie was said to have performed 200 operations in person and insisted that other ranks as well as officers were to receive treatment. Bonaparte awarded him with the Legion d'Honeur for saving the lives of innumerable French soldiers.

Known as Yakov Vassilievich Villiye in Russia, Wylie was a pioneer of field surgery and his reputation ensured a string of wealthy clients. He was also awarded honours from Britain, Austria, Prussia and Bavaria. More importantly, he began a programme to train Russian doctors and left his personal fortune to found a hospital in St Petersburg. There is still a hospital with his name in that city, and a small plaque in his hometown in Scotland.

Wyllie, Robert Crichton (1798 – 1865)
Hawaiian Minister of Foreign Affairs

Born at Hazelbank, Ayrshire, Wyllie travelled to Mexico, where he became a Master Mason at a Lodge in Mazatlan. Around 1845 he arrived in Hawaii, where he became Minister of Foreign Affairs, a position he held for nearly twenty years. Wyllie was successful in this position, for most developed nations recognised Hawaii as an independent kingdom. A keen dancer, Wyllie clashed with both British and American missionaries, who attempted to ban the practice. Instead, Wyllie ensured that dancing was integral to palace protocol. It became common practice for missionaries to leave the palace before the dancing began.

In the early 1860s, Wyllie imported a sugar mill from Scotland for his estate on the Hanalei River. Among his guests was Lady Franklin, widow of the Arctic explorer.

When he died in 1865, the Hawaiian Gazette said that "there went a true friend of our King and His People."

L'envoi

There are more; hundreds of thousands of Scots left their homeland to settle in every corner of the world. Most became submerged in the anonymous mass of humanity but others made their mark for good or ill on the world. It is unlikely that their story will ever be fully told, but this small book is an inadequate tribute to them.

Yet wherever they roam and wherever they live, Scotland remains the place of their blood. Hopefully they will visit. May they never be a stranger in their own land.

Select Bibliography

Adams, Ian and Sommerville, Meredith; *Cargoes of Despair and Hope*, (Edinburgh, 1993)

Australian Dictionary of Biography (Melbourne 1969)

Bruce, William S., *Polar Exploration* (London, 1905?)

Bruce, Sir Michael, *Tramp Royal* (London, 1953)

Bryce, George, *The Scotsman in Canada, Vol II. Western Canada*, (London, 1911)

Bumstead, J. F., *The Scots in Canada*, (Ottawa 1982)

Cage, R. A. (editor); *The Scots Abroad 1750 – 1914* (London 1985)

Calder, Jenni, *Scots in Canada* (Edinburgh, 2003)

Calder, Jenni, *Scots in the USA* (Edinburgh, 2005)

Campbell, Wilfred, *The Scotsman in Canada Vol 1 Eastern Canada*, (London 1912)

De Gramont, Sanche, *The Strong Brown God: The Story of the River Niger* (London 1975)

Dictionary of New Zealand Biography, Wellington 1990

Dillon, Myles and Chadwick, Nora, *The Celtic Realms* (London 1973)

Fergusson, Bruce & Pope, William, *Glimpses into Nova Scotia History* (Windsor, Nova Scotia, 1974)

Fischer, Thomas A., *The Scots in Eastern and Western Prussia* (Edinburgh 1903)

Fischer, Thomas A; *The Scots in Sweden* (Edinburgh 1907)

Fischer, Thomas A; *The Scots in Germany* (Edinburgh 1902)

Fry, Michael, *The Scottish Empire*, (East Lothian & Edinburgh, 2001)

Gage, Delia (Ed), *Dictionary of Woman Artists* (London, 1997)

Garraty, John A & Carnes, Mark C. *American National Biography* (Oxford and New York, 1990)

Glendinning, Miles, MacInnes, Ranald & MacKechnie, Aonghus, *A History of Scottish Architecture*, (Edinburgh, 1996)

Grimble, Ian, *Clans and Chiefs* (London, 1980)

Halpern, Frances (Editor) *Dictionary of Canadian Biography* (Toronto 1972)

Harper, Marjory, *Adventurers and Exiles: The Great Scottish Exodus*, (London 2003)

Hewitson, Jim *Far off in Sunlit Places: Stories of the Scots in Australia and New Zealand* (Edinburgh 1998)

Hughes, Robert, *The Fatal Shore* (London 1967)

Hunter, James, *A Dance Called America* (Edinburgh, 1995)

Johnson, Captain Charles, *A General History of the Robberies & Murders of the Most Notorious Pirates* (London 1998)

Johnson, Gerald W., *The First Captain: the story of John Paul Jones* (New York, 1947)

Keay, John, *The Honourable East India Company: A History of the English East India Company* (London, 1993)

Keay, John, *When Men and Mountains Meet: The Explorers of the Western Himalayas 1820 – 1875* (London 1977)

King, Victor, (Ed), *Explorers of South-East Asia: Six Lives* (Oxford 1995)

Kostof, Spiro, *The City Shaped: Urban Patterns and Meanings Through History*, (London, 1991)

Leiper, Susan, *Precious Cargo: Scots and the China Trade*, (Edinburgh 1997)

Leslie, David, *Among the Zulus and Ama Tongas* (London, 1875)

Lynch, Michael, *The Oxford Companion to Scottish History* (Oxford 2001)

Macquarrie, Alan, *Scotland and the Crusades 1096 – 1560* (John Donald, Edinburgh, 1997)

Magnusson, Magnus (Ed), *Chambers Biographical Dictionary* (Edinburgh, 1990)

Macgregor, Forbes, *Famous Scots: The Pride of a Small Nation* (Edinburgh 1984)

Moorehead, Alan, *The Blue Nile*, (London, 1962)

Moorhead, Alan, *The White Nile* (London, 1962)

Morris, James, *Heavens Command: An Imperial Progress* (Harmondsworth 1973)

Morris, James, *Pax Britannica: The Climax of an Empire* (Harmondsworth 1968)

Morwood, William, *Traveller in a Vanished Landscape: The Life and Times of David Douglas* (Newton Abbot 1974)

Murdoch, Steve & Mackillop, A (Ends) *Fighting for Identity: Scottish Military Experience c 1650 – 1900* (Leiden 2002)

Park, Mungo, *Mission to the Interior of Africa* (London, 1816)

Reese, Peter, *The Scottish Commander: Scotland's Greatest Military Leaders from Wallace to World War II* (Edinburgh, 1999)

Simpson, Grant (editor) *Scotland and the Low Countries 1124 –1994* (Aberdeen and East Lothian 1996)

Smailes, Helen, *Scottish Empire: Scots in Pursuit of Hope and Glory* (Edinburgh, 1981)

Stephen, Sir Leslie & Lee, Sir Sidney, (Editors) *Dictionary of National Biography* (Oxford 1970)

Steuart, A. Francis, *Scottish Influences in Russian History* (Glasgow, 1913)

Szasz, Ferenc Morton, *Scots in the North American West 1790 – 1917* (Norman, Oklahoma, 2000)

That Land of Exiles: Scots in Australia (Edinburgh, 1988)

The Newgate Calendar, (Ware, 1997)

Tranter, Nigel, *Portrait of the Border Country* (London, 1972)

Walter, Richard (Compiler), *Anson, George, A Voyage round the World in the Years MDCCXL, I, II, III, IV,* (London, 1760)

Wellman, Paul, *The Trampling Herd: The Story of the Cattle Range in America* (London, n.d.)

Who Was Who in America (Chicago 1967)
Williams, Harry, *Quest Beyond the Sahara* (London, 1965)

About the Author

Born and raised in Edinburgh, the sternly-romantic capital of Scotland, I grew up with a father and other male relatives imbued with the military, a Jacobite grandmother who collected books and ran her own business and a grandfather from the mystical, legend-crammed island of Arran. With such varied geographical and emotional influences, it was natural that I should write.

Edinburgh's Old Town is crammed with stories and legends, ghosts and murders. I spent a great deal of my childhood when I should have been at school walking the dark roads and exploring the hidden alleyways. In Arran I wandered the shrouded hills where druids, heroes, smugglers and the spirits of ancient warriors abound, mixed with great herds of deer and the rising call of eagles through the mist.

Work followed with many jobs that took me to an intimate knowledge of the Border hill farms as a postman to time in the financial sector, retail, travel and other occupations that are best forgotten. In between I met my wife; I saw her and was captivated immediately, asked her out and was smitten; engaged within five weeks we married the following year and that was the best decision of my life, bar none. Children followed and are now grown.

At 40 I re-entered education, dragging the family to Dundee, where we knew nobody and lacked even a place to stay, but we thrived in that gloriously accepting city. I had a few published books and a number of articles under my belt. Now I learned how to do things the proper way as the University of Dundee took me under their friendly wing for four of the best years I have ever experienced. I emerged with an honours degree in history, returned to the Post in the streets of Dundee, found a job as a historical researcher and then as a college lecturer, and I wrote. Always I wrote.

The words flowed from experience and from reading, from life and from the people I met; the intellectuals and the students, the quiet-eyed farmers with the outlaw names from the Border hills and the hard-handed fishermen from the iron-bound coast of Angus and Fife, the wary scheme-dwelling youths of the peripheries of Edinburgh and the tolerant, very human women of Dundee.

Cathy, my wife, followed me to university and carved herself a Master's degree; she obtained a position in Moray and we moved north, but only with one third of our offspring: the other two had grown up and moved on with their own lives. For a year or so I worked as the researcher in the Dundee Whaling History project while simultaneously studying for my history Masters and commuting home at weekends, which was fun. I wrote 'Sink of Atrocity' and 'The Darkest Walk' at the same time, which was interesting.

When that research job ended I began lecturing in Inverness College, with a host of youngsters and not-so-youngsters from all across the north of Scotland and much further afield. And I wrote; true historical crime, historical crime fiction and a dip into fantasy, with whaling history to keep the research skills alive. Our last child graduated with honours at St Andrews University and left home: I decided to try self-employment as a writer and joined the team at Creativia ... the future lies ahead.

Printed in Great Britain
by Amazon